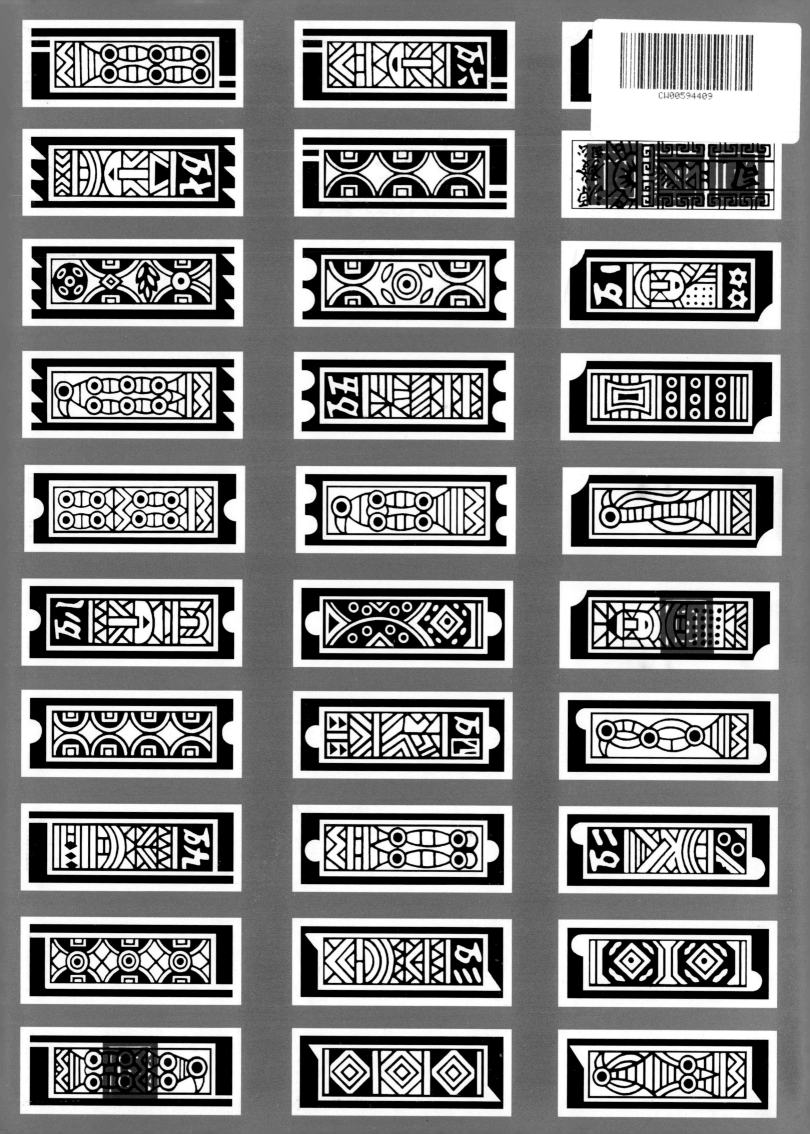

Cuzinhia Cristang

A MALACCA-PORTUGUESE

COOKBOOK

'Fugang cheruzu!
Barriga te-formi.
Ki nona te-kuzih?
Eo kayreh komi.'

'Teng arroz branco
teng pesce fretu,
cari ambiler
sambal pipineo.
Beng santa ne mezah nos tudu
beng kumi juntado.'

'Such delicious smells are
coming from your kitchen!
It whets my appetite.
What's cooking, lady?
I'm starving for a bite.'

'There's white rice
and fried fish,
ambiler curry and
cucumber relish.
Let's all sit at the table
and feast together.'

A typical conversation between a
visitor from the neighbourhood and
the lady of a Cristang household

Cuzinhia Cristang

A MALACCA-PORTUGUESE

COOKBOOK

Celine J. Marbeck

Edited by Winston Ee and Malini Dias

TROPICAL PRESS SDN. BHD.

56-1 & 2, Jalan Maarof

59100 Kuala Lumpur

Malaysia

e-mail: feedback@tpress.po.my

A Tropical Press Book

First published 1998

Perpustakaan Negara Malaysia
Cataloguing-in-Publication Data

Marbeck, Celine J.
    Cuzinhia Cristang: A Malacca-Portuguese Cookbook /
    Celine J. Marbeck.
    Includes index
    ISBN 967-73-0073-3
    1. Cookery, Portuguese. 2. Cookery, Malaysian.
    3. Cookery—Malacca. 4. Portuguese—Melaka—History.
    I. Title. II. Title: A Malacca-Portuguese Cookbook.
    641.592690595118

Sponsored in part by

Designed by Montgomery Lam
Dishes photographed and styled by Hansa Visuals

Printed by
Art Printing Works Sdn. Bhd.
29, Jalan Riong
59100 Kuala Lumpur
Malaysia

Dedicated to
my mother, Elsie Lydia Goonting, on the occasion of her ninetieth birthday in 1995;
my son Julian and his wife, Marianne, on the occasion of their marriage in 1991;
my son Ju Ming, for attaining his law degree in 1994; and
my first grandchild, Tanya-Simone Ding, who was born in 1994.

Contents

left The Malacca Bridge before World War II. This bridge was the site of many battles before it was rebuilt to this design by a renowned Malacca Chinese in the early 1900s.

foreword

A Cristang cookbook? I am tremendously impressed and delighted that Celine Marbeck has prevailed in her endeavour to publish her family's recipes in a book that offers a rare glimpse of Malacca-Portuguese culture and cuisine. I am told that this is the first time anyone has written a cookbook on Cristang cuisine or provided an account of Cristang culture. Having experienced the warm hospitality of the Cristang firsthand, I am glad that such an effort has been made to preserve and promote this little-known culture. (It is a wonderful thing you have done, Celine!)

It is also heartening to note that the publisher, Tropical Press, has spared no effort in making this book unique, colourful and, may I add, appetizing. I would like to express my personal congratulations to Celine and Tropical Press for an exceptional piece of work. I am confident that this book will interest not only those who wish to learn about Malacca's Cristang community, but also members of the community who would like to rediscover their historic past. Of course, for the Cristang who long to reproduce the authentic Malacca-Portuguese food of their childhood, *Cuzinhia Cristang* is an invaluable resource. And for those who have never savoured Cristang cuisine, this book is the perfect introduction to its delights.

Cuzinhia Cristang is more than a cookbook, however. It is a contribution to the story of Malacca. That this town is the history book of Malaysia becomes obvious to anyone who spends time here. Ancient Malay legends abound among the populace and evidence of an intriguing past beckons everywhere one looks. Ruins of the once-mighty A Famosa recall the city's Portuguese heritage, and the famous deep-red Dutch Stadthuys building, not to mention the British-style banks and pillar post boxes, reflect the different phases of the city's past, which is an integral part of Malaysia's history. By bringing the story of the Cristang to the fore, this book adds valuable detail to an already fascinating tale of cultural confluence and synthesis.

My best wishes for the success of *Cuzinhia Cristang: A Malacca-Portuguese cookbook*, and kudos to all who have made this book possible.

Datuk Eugenio Campos
DMSM, JSM
Portuguese Consul to Malaysia

preface

*M*emories are the albums that hold yesterday's treasures. Among my memorabilia is a collection of gastronomic experiences—a culinary legacy culled from my ancestors—that has been preserved in a yellowed, dog-eared exercise book that I possess, not because I excelled in the culinary arts but because I pursued a hobby of collecting and recording recipes.

It has always been my family's habit to sit at the dinner table long after the meal is over and reminisce about dishes or treats that were family favourites in the good old days, dishes that—for lame reasons—we no longer cook. I was fond of these dishes myself and would jot down their recipes on pieces of paper, while those around me described them.

In time my jottings grew into a sizeable collection and my sister Joan suggested that I publish them in a book. The book was to record the culinary aspect of our heritage and create a legacy for future generations of Cristang. It was an interesting idea, but I was neither a writer nor an accomplished cook and the thought of writing a book weighed heavily on my mind. I felt overawed. Furthermore, it has never been in the Cristang tradition to pass recipes on to people outside the family, and I was not sure how my family would respond to the notion of making public our proudly guarded recipes. And so, I dismissed the idea.

But that was not to be the end of it. For some time I had felt that Cristang cuisine deserved more attention than it had been getting. It is commonly being referred to as 'Portuguese food' and no one has attempted to define it or give it the identity that it has earned through five centuries of evolution. Gradually, my dissatisfaction with the situation overcame my apprehensions about the book, and I began to consider the possibility of writing it in earnest.

With mixed feelings I broached the subject to my friends and relatives and, to my surprise, everyone was for it. They even encouraged me by pledging support and reassurance and, above all, expressed their willingness to share their own family recipes. They unanimously agreed that it was time to publish a record of the culinary heritage of the Cristang. Armed with the enthusiasm of my family and friends and egged on by the moral obligation I felt towards the task, I finally summoned up the courage to begin.

From my files I chose the recipes that I considered culturally interesting or important. I discussed their origins and authenticity with family and friends and, on their good advice, decided on the selection that is included in this book. Since one of my intentions for this book is to provide a basic understanding of Cristang culture beyond its cuisine, I was obliged to research the history and traditions of my people. It was also necessary to study the ingredients and cooking techniques they used. I found myself enrolled in cooking classes and hovering over friends and relatives, who were gracious enough to allow me to watch them cook.

With their help I was able to work out a system of converting the empirical measures in the recipes—used for stating quantities of ingredients—into standard units. After months of looking and learning followed by a considerable amount of experimentation, I was able to cook all the dishes in this book. Satisfied with the results at last, I began the most difficult task of all: putting my thoughts down on paper.

Writing does not come easy to one who has not been schooled in the art, but with the help of a personal computer (a present from my husband) I was in a better position to execute the daunting task. I envisaged a cookbook with whimsical headings, supplemented with the history of the Cristang people, descriptions of festivals, cultural anecdotes and interesting vignettes about various dishes.

I have written this book to ensure that the Cristang will be able to present their children and grandchildren with a culinary legacy that many are beginning to forget. It is my hope that the Cristang who read this book will be motivated to write on other aspects of their heritage and, in doing so, give meaning to the words of the fifteenth century Portuguese traveller Joao de Barros: 'Time may destroy material things but the culture and traditions of a community will live on.'

above A wood carving—possibly the figurehead of a Portuguese carrack—of the Virgin Mary and the Child, which was found in a fishing net in the 1970s. It was given to the late Rev. Father Pintado of Malacca.

acknowledgements

I have many people to thank for this book. I feel it is particularly appropriate to begin by acknowledging my gratitude to my mother. It was she who said, 'If something is worth doing, it's worth doing with flair.' These words were my guiding light throughout the writing of this book.

Sincere thanks to my aunt May Reincastle who cooked countless delicious meals for my family and who believes that the art of delicately spicing dishes is a skill that lies in the hand that stirs the pot.

Special thanks to Padre M.J. Pintado, who lent me reference books and permitted me access to his library whenever I needed to check historical facts. To his sister, Lurdes Aurora Pintado, I say *muito obgrigada* for lending me the figurehead from a fifteenth century Portuguese ship to be photographed for this book. Other friends I'd like to thank for allowing their antiques and family heirlooms to be photographed are Don and Angela Beins and Tina Ong's grandmother and aunt.

My appreciation and sincere thanks to everyone who helped in preparing and cooking the dishes described in this book, especially my eldest sister, Teresa, and my housekeeper, Mary Tan Nya Kim, whose help and efficiency during cooking sessions were invaluable. To Tony de Rozario and my sister Christie, who typed the manuscript: thank you very much for your efficient and organized word processing.

My thanks to Prof. Pierre Guisan of Brazil, Ruth Foreman and Doris Irons for their encouragement, and to my friends and relatives in Perth, Australia, who shared recipes and anecdotes: Joan and Charles Reincastle, Barbara and Tony Hendricks, Bob and Anne Hendricks, Bev and Kenneth Lazaroo, Simone Lazaroo and Aunty Elsie Nunis. To my sister Minnie and her husband, Bill, in Cork, Ireland, thanks for keeping in touch about this book's progress. I am also grateful to my friends in Malaysia for their valuable assistance: Francis and Molly Khoo, Jasmine and Lim Guan Chin, Ruth Sivapragasam, Gerry Rozario, and Nani Brosi.

Also thanks to my brother Terrance and his family for their enthusiasm and support for this project. I thank my cousins Hedy and Rene Rodrigues, and Teresa and Griffin Hendroff, who were equally as supportive. I would like to say a big thank you to my sons, Julian and Ming, my nephews David and Martin and my sister Joan for offering advice on many details and for the many hours spent proofreading, criticizing (and laughing at!) my literary efforts. To my nieces Veronica, Anne, Bernie, Clarice, Helen, Margie and Yvette: thanks for lending me the books and antique cake moulds. Also, thank you to nieces Elaine-Jean and Anne Marie Cheong for their encouraging concern. My thanks to my husband for his supportive reassurance during the years that I was writing this book.

I would like to thank Shekar and Peng of Hansa Visuals for their creative genius and photography, which have presented my cooking with such delicious flair, and MAGGI for their generous sponsorship, which has made this book possible.

the Cristang language

The Cristang language exists as a little-known cultural reminder of Portuguese dominance in Malacca for over one hundred and thirty years.

In the past Portuguese priests in Malacca, when attempting to write Cristang, used a Portuguese-style orthography with which they were familiar. Apart from these attempts at writing Cristang, no serious efforts were made to establish a written form of the language. As a result, it never developed beyond the need for oral communication. Despite this handicap, the language has survived because the Cristang people spoke it daily—at home and with friends. They even recited their prayers in Cristang.

Over the centuries the language experienced rapid transformation by incorporating words from the other ethnic groups in the area. Slowly but surely, this eclecticism began to distinguish Cristang from its mother tongue, namely, the Portuguese language spoken in Portugal.

The spelling system for the Cristang words used in this book is my own adaptation of the linguistic sounds known to me. No particular phonetic system has been adopted, as Cristang is made up of words from languages such as Malay, Chinese, Indian, English, Dutch and even Arabic.

The pronunciation guide for the recipes in this book follows the English pronunciation system.

pronunciation guide

Botah Fogu	bought-ta foe-goo
Ambiler kachang	um-bee-le car-chung
Cari Belanda	curry Burr-lun-da
Cari keluak	curry curl-wha
Cari papair cung siput chupaku	curry par-pie-year kung see-put chew-par-coo
Cari pimentu	curry pea-men-te
Cari seccu	curry sac-coo
Debal	day-ble (as in 'table')
Feng	fing
Lardeh	lar-day
Mohlyu	mole-you
Singgang cocu	sing-gung co-coo
Singgang mangger	sing-gung mung-ger
Vindaloo	vin-der-loo

Diabu Caladu	dee-are-boo car-la-do
Sambal belachan	sum-bhall ber-la-chan
Sambal belimbing	sum-bhall be-lim-bing
Sambal cambrung tambrinhyu	sum-bhall come-brung tum-brin-you
Sambal bokras	sum-bhall bo-crus
Sambal capitang	sum-bhall car-pea-tongue
Sambal chilli bedri	sum-bhall chill-lee bay-dree
Sambal chilli taucho	sum-bhall chill-lee tao-cho
Sambal chincaluk	Sum-bhall chin-cha-look
Sambal gerago seccu	sum-bhall ge-ra-go sac-coo
Sambal jantong	sum-bhall jun-tong
Sambal nenas cung pipeneo	sum-bhall nar-nus kung pi-pin-you
Sambal Tante Juliana	sum-bhall ton-ter Juliana
Sambal mangger azedu	sum-bhall mung-ger a-zay-do
Rabaser	ra-ba-sir
Pusah Besu	poo-sa bay-sue
Caldu bayam	cull-do by-yum
Caldu bola pesce	cull-do boar-le pay-si
Caldu boloh mai	cull-do bo-ler my
Caldu pescador	cull-do pes-cur-doe
Caldu galinhia	cull-do gar-lyn-near
Caldu taucho	cull-do tao-cho
Caldu laler-laler	cull-do la-le la-le
Caldu tauhu cung pesce seccu	cull-do ta-hoo kung pay-si sac-coo
Stiu carbra	stew car-bre
Teem	team
Furiada Bedri	foo-ree-ah-der bad-dree ('der' as in 'under')
Achar chilli	are-char chilly
Batata caldu leite cocu	bar-tar-te cull-do lay-tee co-coo
Bendi pas'agu	ben-dee pe-sa-goo
Bredu chapchye	bray-do chup-chai
Bredu chilli mustardu	bray-do chilly mousse-ta-do
Bredu kachang cung baca	bray-do car-chung kung bar-ke
Cebola enchimintu	sar-bo-le in-chee-mint-too
Coubes gulung	co-bis goo-loong
Epuk-epuk sayor	a-poke-a-poke sa-your (*a* as in letter 'a')
Foler cebola cung taukwa	for-le sar-bo-le kung tao-qua
Marergozu fretu	mar-er-go-zoo fre-too
Mohlyu gingibri doce cung taukwa	mole-you gin-jee-bree door-si kung tao-qua
Pongtey	pong-tay
Salade dumingu	salad du-min-goo
Soy limang	soy lee-mung

Dali Cung Mung	dha-lee kung mung
Arroz Gordu	ah-rose gore-do
Arroz Macau	ah-rose macau
Arroz Manteiga	ah-rose mun-tare-gur
Canje parpa	cun-gee par-per
Lampries 'landeh	larm-pris lun-day
Laksa Malaca	luck-sa ma-la-ke
Mi annu	me are-noo
Mezza De Noiba	meh-zer de noy-bur
Ardi bafa cung tempra	ah-dee bah-fah kung tem-pra
Baca pimenta fretu	buh-ke pi-man-te free-too
Figdu tempradu	fig-do tamp-pra-do
Galinhia assa ne saspan	gar-lyn-near are-sa nee sas-pun
Galinhia fretu	gar-lyn-near free-too
Galinhia pai	gar-lyn-near pie
Galinhia stiu	gar-lyn-near stew
Lingu baca bafa	ling-goo bah-ke bah-fa
Ros befe casamintu	rose beef ca-ze-mint-too
Satei goreng	sa-tay go-ring
Semur	sir-more
Comir Noibu	coo-me noy-boo
Cambrang cung cana	come-brung kung cun-ner
Carengguezu cung chilli taucho	car-reng-gay-zoo kung chilly tao-cho
Chicarru soy limang	chee-char-roo soy li-mung
Chorka tambrinhyu	cho-ker tum-brin-you
Chuan-chuan	chew-un–chew-an
Gerago pikkadel	ge-ra-go pea-cur-dell
Doppar	dop-per ('dop' rhymes with 'drop')
Karing-karing fretu	car-ring–car-ring free-too
Obu trubo	o-boo true-bo
Pesce assa	pay-see are-sa
Pesce binagre	pay-see bee-na-gree
Pesce fretu	pay-see free-too
Pesce tambrinhyu	pay-see tum-brin-you
Pesce kertouk	pay-see cur-toh
Tante Maria-se achar pesce seccu	ton-ter maria-sir are-char pay-see sac-coo
Matah Bontade	mar-tar bon-tar-de
Aberjaw	are-burr-jaw
Baca assam	ba-cur are-sum
Baca Soy	ba-cur soy
Carne picada	car-nee pea-car-de

Cerebo fretu — se-re-bo free-too
Mama-se frikkerdel — mama-sir free-cur-dell
Pacheree — pa-cher-ree
Seybah — say-ba
Vinhu de arlu — vee-noo de are-loo

Boca Doce — bor-cur door-see
Abor-abor — are-bow-are-bow ('bow' as in 'bow-tie')
Agar-agar — are-ga-are-ga
Baje — bar-jay
Bibingka de nyami bengaler — bi-bing-cur de nee-are-mee bing-gar-ler
Blueda — blue-de
Bolu cocu — bow-loo co-coo
Canje cha-cher — cun-gee char-chur
Canje mungoo — cun-gee mung-goo
Doce de obu — door-see de o-boo
Dodol sabang — doe-dole sa-bung
Kuih tat — coo-weigh tart
Pang susis — pung sue-see
Putugal — poo-too-gull
Sersagung — sir-sa-gong
Sugee kek — sue-gee cake

Lantah Saode — lon-ta sa-oh-dee ('lon' as in 'London')
Agu gingibri — a-goo gin-gee-bree
Agu sucre rosa — a-goo sue-cree row-za
Brande laranga — bran-dee la-run-jer
Char fruta mistura — char frue-te mis-too-ra
Codial floris sapatu — cordial flow-ris sa-par-too
Gibette — gee-bet
Lembransa brancu — lamb-bran-sir bran-coo
Letite obu bateh — lay-tee o-boo ba-tay
Nona rostu bremeilu — nor-nar rose-too bre-may-loo
('nar' rhymes with 'car'; 'bre' rhymes with 'err')
Soldadu chocolat — sol-da-do chocolate
Tentasung doce — ten-ter-sung door-see ('ter' rhymes with 'stir')

Ungua Historia Cristang

THE CRISTANG SAGA

Five centuries of history

In Ujung Pasir, three kilometres from the heart of Malacca town, on a tiny stretch of coast along the Straits of Malacca, lies a small seaside village of about two thousand people. Founded as recently as 1933, its unassuming exterior belies its importance as one of Malaysia's most popular tourist attractions. There are no physical reminders of a glorious past, no sense of lost-in-timeness about the place. The fishing boats and the shrined statues are quaint rather than antique; youths hawking the delights of the settlement's restaurants and curio shops are strictly late twentieth century in both dress and manners.

But tourism is good business here: visitors come by the thousands to enjoy the distinctively flamboyant performances of music and dance, to witness religious processions and to sample the local cuisine. If the cultural shows are packaged and marketed to accommodate the schedule of the busy globe-trotter, if the cuisine seems of doubtful authenticity, all this is but the façade.

The significance of this village—known as the Portuguese Settlement— is that it is home to a unique ethnic group, fervent in their religious observances and in the celebrations that accompany them. Bound together by ancestry and religion, they are the heirs to a remarkable heritage, to a brief period of European occupation characterized by rapacity, determination and not a little panache.

They call themselves Jenti Cristang (Christian People) or simply Cristang and are descendants of sixteenth century Portuguese navigators and explorers whose luminaries included Bartolomeu Dias, Vasco da Gama and Afonso de Albuquerque. Braving the perils of uncharted waters in search of wealth and glory, these men and others like them mapped out sea routes from Lisbon to Africa and eventually Asia.

They set up outposts on the continents and multiplied the possessions of Portugal with the aim of monopolizing the spice trade. Malacca, then the largest and most successful trading port in Asia, seemed the perfect target for this purpose: 'If we take this trade of Malacca ... Cairo and Mecca are entirely ruined and to Venice will no spiceries be conveyed except that which her merchants go and buy in Portugal.'—Afonso de Albuquerque, Viceroy of India, 1509*.

left Malacca's history began in 1382 with the arrival of the Sumatran prince Parameswara, who had come to the Malay Peninsula to escape from his enemies. Legend has it that the prince was out hunting one day and decided to stop for a rest under a tall tree near a river. A commotion broke out not long after the men had paused. One of the dogs in the hunting party had cornered a mousedeer. It was an uneven match, and the consensus was that the mousedeer was doomed. But, to the amazement of all, the small creature suddenly lashed its hind legs at the dog and kicked it into the water. Then, just as quickly as it had defended itself, the mousedeer disappeared into a nearby thicket. Parameswara was impressed by the animal's courage. He concluded that the event he had witnessed was a good omen and was convinced that he had found the perfect site to establish a new kingdom. He asked for the name of the tree under which he had been resting and was told that it was a Malacca tree. And that, some say, was how Malacca got its name.

* Source: P.P.K.T. Joseph. 'Why was Malacca chosen as the site for a kingdom and how it became an emporium soon?' *The Illustrated Historical Guide to Malacca.* The Rotary Club of Malacca. 1973.

The adventure begins

The first Portuguese mission to land in Malacca arrived from Goa, India in 1509. Under the command of Diego Lopez de Sequeira, they attempted to seek permission from the sultan to establish a trading post. The friendly reception that greeted the foreigners quickly gave way to intrigue and violence. At the instigation and with the support of Indian Muslim traders who were attempting to safeguard their interests, the *bendahara* (chief minister) of Malacca plotted to capture the Portuguese fleet. Warned of the impending attack Sequeira fled the city, leaving two ships burning in the harbour and nineteen men prisoners of the sultan.

Outrage and humiliation only served to strengthen the resolve of the Portuguese, who were not to be easily dismissed. They set sail from Goa again, this time under the leadership of Afonso de Albuquerque who was determined to seize Malacca and avenge the disgrace suffered by his countrymen. Eighteen cannon-fitted carracks carrying approximately one thousand men dropped anchor off the coast of Malacca in 1511. After a week-long battle, on August 24, Albuquerque captured the city and forced the sultan and his men to retreat into the interior.

Victorious at last, the Portuguese, or Franks, as they were called by the local people, set about the business of colonization to tap the enormous potential of their new possession. Albuquerque built an imposing fortress overlooking the Straits of Malacca. He called it A Famosa (The Famous) and placed his administrative machinery there. Resembling a medieval Portuguese city, complete with town hall, offices and homes, the fortress proved impregnable to enemies for a hundred and thirty years. During that period, the Portuguese reaped a rich bounty of tolls imposed on vessels that passed through the Straits, a vital sea lane which they patrolled with armed ships.

Although the Portuguese ruled Malacca, they were greatly outnumbered by the other ethnic groups, whose sentiments ranged from friendly to hostile; in fact there were fewer than three hundred European Portuguese in Malacca at any one time. Clearly there existed a security risk. To remedy the situation and create more collaborators and supporters, the Portuguese established a policy of racial integration that sanctioned marriage between themselves and the local people. Albuquerque not only encouraged his own men to marry indigenous women, but he also brought women from Portugal to be given in marriage to the men of Malacca. Known as 'Orphans of the Queen', these women included commoners and members of the nobility. Interracial marriage suited the missionary objectives of the Portuguese: as a precondition of the union, the local bride or groom-to-be had to convert to Catholicism. Like the European Portuguese who married locals and were granted privileges in commerce and politics, the locals who gave up their religions to embrace the new faith and take on Portuguese names benefited as well.

above Afonso de Albuquerque.

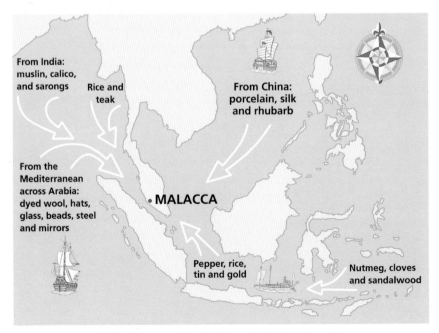

From India: muslin, calico, and sarongs

Rice and teak

From China: porcelain, silk and rhubarb

From the Mediterranean across Arabia: dyed wool, hats, glass, beads, steel and mirrors

• MALACCA

Pepper, rice, tin and gold

Nutmeg, cloves and sandalwood

above Malacca and the countries with which it traded in the fifteenth century.

They were rewarded with houses, land, horses, cattle, allowances and access to the upper echelons of government.

From these mixed marriages a new breed of people evolved. Possessing an exotic blend of Latin and Asian features, they were accepted by the local communities as well as the Portuguese who accorded them many rights and privileges enjoyed by the citizenry of Portugal. These included the benefits and favours of trading as Portuguese merchants, exemption from many tolls and taxes, and citizenship rights in Portugal.

These people identified themselves as Portuguese and occupied a favourable position in the social hierarchy. Many became wealthy and influential. Together with the *casador*s (or 'married ones', a term referring to Portuguese men who were married), they formed an enclave outside A Famosa in what became the prestigious district of Upeh (currently known as Tengkera). In this district the *casador*s established sprawling orchards and large weekend and holiday retreats. The old Cristang saying, *Jenti Tranquerah lantah bandeira'* ('The people of Tranquerah uphold the Portuguese flag') refers to these casadors who were fiercely patriotic to Portugal. They spoke a Creole form of European Portuguese that contained many words borrowed from the local languages of the period. Although it did not have a written form, this Creolized Portuguese persevered and is spoken to this day.

Being the first Europeans to settle in the region, the Portuguese were regarded with suspicion by neighbouring Asian rulers. Furthermore, their missionary objectives did not sit well with the Muslim traders who had been instrumental in the rise of Malacca. They began to shun it in favour of Muslim ports in the region, such as Acheh, Johor, Pasai and Banjarmasin. Without the support of these traders, Malacca began to lose its lustre. Its importance as a major trading centre declined rapidly although it continued to prosper as a way station for Portuguese shipping. The Portuguese tried to ease the tensions but their overtures of friendship were hampered by a vast cultural gap. Their efforts were not well received and they made few friends during their occupation of Malacca. Consequently, they suffered numerous attacks throughout the sixteenth century. Their main harassers included the neighbouring Malay sultanates and the state of Acheh in North Sumatra. The latter proved a formidable enemy and invaded Malacca several times. But it took another European power to dislodge the Portuguese from their fortress.

The Dutch period

By 1602 the Dutch were trading in Batavia, now known as Jakarta. They resented the Portuguese monopoly over the Straits and mounted an unsuccessful attack on A Famosa in 1607. Undaunted by defeat, in 1637 they formed an alliance with the sultanate of neighbouring Johor against the Portuguese and three years later launched a new offensive

left A plan of the fortress built by the Portuguese conquerors of Malacca.

against the fortress. A six-month siege ensued and the Portuguese were literally starved out of their stronghold. Weak and dying, they surrendered in 1641 and Malacca passed into Dutch hands.

Under Dutch rule, life for those of Portuguese and local parentage was difficult, even quite dangerous at times. Religious differences between them and their Protestant masters resulted in persecution. The wealthy among them had their property confiscated and were exiled to islands such as Laran Tukar, Flores and Timor. Those who remained were forced out of their homes to the coast where they had to eke out an existence from the sea. Arrests and torture of suspected papists and anti-Dutch activists were widespread, forcing many to go into hiding. Where once these Eurasians had been proud to be called Portuguese, they now avoided the label and preferred instead to be known as Jenti Cristang or Cristang. Surprisingly, this change of identity found favour with the Dutch who saw the Portuguese as

the enemy, but adopted a neutral attitude towards the Cristang. The Dutch hired a few educated Cristang as clerks for their administration; some Dutch men even wed Cristang women and converted to Catholicism. Obviously, it mattered little that the difference between a Portuguese and a Cristang was only in name. But the heyday of the Cristang was over. Fearful of the Dutch but staunch in their Catholic beliefs, most of the Cristang fled to the jungles and sugarcane plantations along the coast of Malacca to hide and practice their religion free from persecution. At this stage of their history, the Cristang were far removed from the peaceful, privileged life they had known. Poverty and illness, coupled with fear and uncertainty, cast them onto the lower rungs of society.

Although the Dutch had fought hard for control of Malacca, they never made it the base for their trading operations—that was an honour they reserved for Batavia. They regarded their new colony more as a military outpost than a

trading centre. Nevertheless, they assumed monopoly of the Straits and exacted the same kinds of payments from passing ships as had the Portuguese. Disgruntled merchants continued to shun Malacca and its fortunes declined even further.

By 1794 the Dutch were in trouble. The revolutionary armies of France had invaded the Netherlands and were poised to take over Dutch naval bases overseas. To forestall that possibility, the Dutch government-in-exile agreed that Britain would take temporary control of its possessions on the understanding that they would be returned after the war. As a result, Malacca was transferred to the British in 1795.

The British were resolved that when they returned Malacca to the Dutch it would be little more than a useless shell, and so they set about reducing the city and its historic fortress to rubble. Fortunately, the task was not completed and Malacca was saved, ironically, by a young British official of the East India Company named Thomas Stam-

above St John's Fort, built by the Dutch on top of St John's Hill. The Portuguese Settlement began its existence near this hill and was, for a while, called St John's Village.

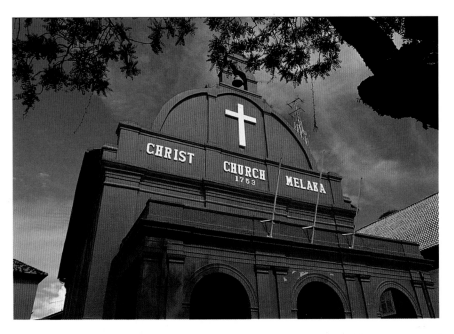

above Christ Church. This church and the imposing red walls of the Stadhuys are a part of the architectural legacy left behind by the Dutch.

ford Raffles, who argued passionately against the destruction of the city. As it turned out, the Dutch did reclaim Malacca in 1818 but ceded it back to the British six years later when they signed the Anglo-Dutch Treaty.

The British era

With Malacca in the south and the island of Penang in the north, the British now had full control of the Straits. Unlike their European predecessors, however, they did not adopt extortionist policies but allowed the ships plying the Straits to come and go without hindrance. Malacca and Penang became free ports, open to all merchants. Peace and prosperity blossomed in the region until the Japanese invaded the Malay Peninsula in World War II.

During the first hundred years of British rule, the Cristang community experienced further decline. Voiceless and insignificant in number, they faced an increasingly uncertain future. Nevertheless, as was the case during Dutch rule, a small number of Cristang who were educated and financially better off managed to rise within the system. Some received large tracts of land in rural areas or on the outskirts of town in return for their services to the British government. These fortunate Cristang tried to help their destitute kin. They formed the Malacca Eurasian Association to obtain places in British-run schools for Cristang children and jobs in the private sector and civil service for adults. Obtaining a 'proper' job with the government became an ambition, if not an obsession, among the poorer Cristang. They took advantage of their European heritage to secure better positions in the British administration than were available to the Asian population. They also encouraged their children to speak English at the expense of the Cristang language, as they believed that the ability to speak English was requisite for a job in the civil service.

It was a time of great social and cultural upheaval for the Cristang, and as they struggled to survive, their culture slid to the edge of extinction. However, in spite of the difficulties they faced, a small group within the community still remembered their heritage, thanks to their religion. Staunch Catholics, this group, who were mostly made up of traditional fisherfolk, availed themselves of the religious freedom granted by the British and revived many of the festivals and rituals associated with their faith and culture. However, these folk were widely scattered throughout the coastal districts of Bandar Hilir, Praya Lane, Kampong Tengah and Alai and were very poor. They could only afford to observe Cristang customs and religious festivals within their own family units. There was little they could do to ensure the survival of the Cristang heritage within the community.

Recognizing that the Cristang culture was in peril of disappearing, two missionary priests proposed to the British government that the poorer Cristang be regrouped in a settlement where they could preserve their culture and way of life. In 1933 the community was given a

---

Porta de Santiago

All that remains of the great Portuguese fortress A Famosa is its famous gateway, Porta de Santiago. Standing as a lonely sentinel, the structure is the centre of many a romantic legend. One such legend tells of a soldier and a nun who kept a nightly tryst by the gateway until they were discovered. The lovers were severely punished for their scandalous behaviour—he was beheaded in front of the gateway and she was buried alive within the very walls that had listened to their whispers. Old Malacca residents maintain that on a certain night when the full moon casts an eerie glow on the boughs of the angsana trees and the sweet smell of frangipani saturates the air, the ghost of the headless soldier can be seen sitting on a cannon, carrying his head in the crook of one arm. Many night revellers claim to have seen the unfortunate soldier pacing in front of the gateway, presumably waiting for his lover.

Another subject of many legends concerns a secret tunnel supposedly built by the Dutch. It is said to be a mile long and to have been used for transporting men and supplies from the fort, via Porta de Santiago, to St John's Fort. Other versions claim that the tunnel led to a vault where the amassed riches of the Malay Sultanate were kept during tumultuous times. It is believed that several treasure hunters once found and entered this tunnel, but it is not known what became of them.

above Porta de Santiago.

piece of swamp land in Ujung Pasir by the British Resident Commissioner. By 1935 the mosquito-infested site had been drained and cleared and several huts with dirt floors and attap roofs had been erected on it. Ten of the poorest Cristang families were allowed to move in. Because it was in the vicinity of St John's Hill, the settlement was initially called St John's Village. The Cristang later changed its name to Padre sa Chang (Priests' Land) in honour of the founding missionaries, Father J.P. François and Father A.M. Coroado. The British called it the Portuguese Settlement.

The Portuguese Settlement

During the early days, conditions in the Settlement were primitive at best and basic amenities were nonexistent. Yet many people moved there willingly, thankful for a roof over their heads. Things improved significantly only after World War II when more houses and a school were built, electricity and water were supplied and sanitation facilities were upgraded.

Today the Settlement is a well-kept, relatively modern housing estate, complete with street lights, telephone poles and macadamized roads. The houses are typically constructed from wood and painted in bright colours. The windows are paneless but have instead steel bars and large wooden shutters. A picture of the Sacred Heart of Jesus or the Virgin Mary hangs above most main entrances and a frond of palm that has been blessed is tucked behind the picture to distinguish a Catholic home. Nearly every home has a *reitori* (altar) in which are placed statuettes of saints along with a crucifix. The walls of the living room are often decorated with pictures of saints and Jesus. Each house boasts a small garden enclosed by a picket or wire fence. Bougainvillaea, roses and other flowers bloom profusely in pots and ceramic jars alongside bushes of screw pine and lemon grass which are used for cooking.

Considered the definitive showcase of the Malacca-Portuguese heritage, the Portuguese Settlement has become a tourist attraction. Much to their credit, the residents have been quick to capitalize on the popularity of their village. Many hold part-time jobs or run businesses that cater to tourists. Nevertheless, a small number of Settlement Cristang remain devoted to the sea despite the option of better paying occupations. To them fishing offers an unhurried way of life with time enough to savour the simple pleasures: mending nets under the shade of ketapang trees, sharing the latest gossip, taking siestas by the sea. By clinging to their traditional lifestyle these fisherfolk do much to maintain public interest in the Settlement. Their presence lends the place considerable authenticity without which the casual visitor would see little more than a façade of cultural shows.

The heart of Cristang culture, however, lies in Roman Catholicism, not in the cultural performances put on for the benefit of tourists. Faith resides deep in the soul of every Cristang and is the singular force that has kept the peo-

right A traditional Cristang house with picket fence and garden.

ple united through more than four centuries of strife and adversity. One religious tradition that is still observed in the Settlement is the reciting of the family rosary. Each day as the sun descends over the horizon, the head of the family prepares the altar for prayer. Other family members stop whatever they are doing and assemble before the altar. Then, kneeling, the family recite the rosary together.

Cristang festivals

Religion also finds expression in the festivals of the Cristang which are either religious ceremonies or celebrations in connection with religious occasions. Examples range from the solemn and pious, such as Festa de Assunta to the boisterous and gay Festa de San Pedro and Intrudo.

Intrudo
The prelude to the Lenten season, Intrudo, is the last day for merriment and feasting. In fact some families strip their larders of all the food that they are fond of to make way for fasting and abstinence during Lent. The Cristang celebrate Intrudo on the Sunday preceding Ash Wednesday.

In the past, Cristang villagers would exchange greetings by teasing and splashing one another with water on the morning of Intrudo.

Water was used because it signifies life and cleanliness. Even those who remained indoors were not spared a drenching: cheeky revellers would call on them and splash them with water. Then the revellers would offer the head of the house a glass of wine to apologize for the 'intrusion' and drink a toast to the family's good health.

In the afternoon men dressed as women and women as men, together with a band of masked merrymakers, went from house to house offering cakes or sweets for sale at inflated prices and for which no change was returned. The highlight of the day was the Branyo Rudya, a troupe of street dancers led by a gaily-dressed group of musicians playing tunes to entice spectators into joining their procession. As the Branyo Rudya moved through the streets, its participants drank, sang and cavorted.

At times wealthy Cristang fami-

left St Francis Xavier is arguably the man most responsible for the spread of Catholicism in India and Southeast Asia. This most famous of Jesuits visited Malacca on five occasions and is said to have performed many miracles there. When he died on the island of Sanchian near Canton in 1552, his remains were brought to Malacca and interred in a vault in The Church of the Annunciation on St Paul's Hill. Nine months later, they were transferred to Goa, India, where they remain to this day.

lies invited the Branyo Rudya into their homes where the *dona de casa* (lady of the house) entertained the whole troupe to a grand and generous spread. Alcohol flowed freely and every imaginable Cristang delicacy was laid out on a long table. Playing host to the Branyo Rudya was a privilege, and the family that did so gained much respect.

For about ten years beginning in 1985 the Cristang in Malacca began to lose interest in celebrating Intrudo. This was a shame because Intrudo has been a traditional festival since the days of the first settlers five centuries ago, and its counterpart, Domingo Gordo, is still celebrated in Portugal.

Happily, this ancient festival did not die out, and in 1995 it was celebrated in a big way once again by the residents of the Portuguese Settlement.

Quaresma

Lent is a forty-day period observed strictly with prayer, fasting, and abstinence from meat on Fridays. Devout Catholics eat only *canje parpa* (rice porridge, p 128) with a salted fish pickle called *pesce tambrinhyu* (p 109) throughout the Lenten season. Lent ends on Easter Sunday and on this day *pang susis* (sweet buns filled with spiced meat, p 149) are served together with hard-boiled eggs for breakfast. In keeping with tradition, some families serve *cari seccu* (a dry mutton curry, p 51) for lunch or dinner.

Festa de San Juang

The Feast of St John begins with three days of prayer during which Cristang families meditate on the life of St John the Baptist who preached the coming of Christ, 'the Light of the world'.

left The compound of a Cristang home lit with candles during Festa de San Juang.

On the evening of 23 June hundreds of white candles can be seen lining the fences, pathways and verandas of devotees' homes along Praya Lane (a street in Banda Praya, site of the first Cristang settlement in Malacca) and in the Portuguese Settlement. The candles, which are lit only once, burn slowly until they flicker and go out one by one.

Children and adults wear green (a colour that denotes the renewal of life) on this day. Even the fishermen who wear pyjamas for their daily attire will put on green ones for the occasion. In keeping with the green theme, *canje mungoo* (p 146), a delicious porridge made from green mung beans, is served in the morning.

In the past it was common for devotees to chant prayers and sing hymns as they climbed St John's Hill. At the top was a chapel where the procession congregated to recite more prayers. The day's activities culminated in the lighting of a bonfire followed by much merrymaking and feasting. The 'picnic' usually ended at night.

Festa de San Pedro

This festival is celebrated on 29 June in honour of St Peter, the patron saint of fishermen. Kept alive for more than five centuries, the festival is still celebrated with grandeur in the Portuguese Settlement by the Cristang, who hold a carnival to mark the occasion.

A celebratory atmosphere pervades the Settlement a week before the festival. To prepare for the carnival, boats are scrubbed clean, repaired and given a new coat of paint. They are then lined up and elaborately decorated to resemble the Portuguese carracks that first sailed into the port of Malacca. Their white sails bear insignia of crosses or pictures of saints. Around Portuguese Square people set up stalls for food, drinks and games. Flags and bunting are put up and members of dance troupes rehearse their performances of traditional dances such as Branyo, Chirkoti and Serampah de Mar.

On the opening day of the carnival a glittering arch of flashing lights greets visitors to the Settlement. Throngs of people wander about in the fairgrounds amidst blaring music. There are competitions for the best decorated boat, for the *langgiang* fisherman (see picture below) who brings in the biggest catch of shrimp and for the best cook of traditional dishes. Other competitions and events are held throughout the week, culminating in the traditional celebration of the Mass for the fishermen and the blessing of their boats by the parish priest on the day of the festival.

above Cristang children in green outfits carry candles in a procession during Festa de San Juang.

right Some Cristang fishermen still use the traditional langgiang method of catching shrimp off the shores of the Portuguese Settlement. Wading chest-deep into the shallows, they push triangular nets (attached to bamboo poles) back and forth until the nets are weighted down with shrimp. Then, with a wide sweep, they lift the nets into the air and shake them vigorously so that the shrimp slide into bags fastened at their waists.

At night everyone is invited to participate in an open-air folk dance extravaganza that marks the end of the year's most colourful event.

Festa de Assunta

Celebrated on 15 August, this feast honours the Mother of God who ascended to heaven. The Cristang of Banda Praya observe the feast with a Mass followed by a candle-light procession to a shrine decorated with flowers and containing a statue of the Mother of God. There the devotees scatter scented petals and leaves about the statue's feet.

The procession begins on the grounds of the Assumption Chapel, which is gaily decorated with bunting, floral streamers, *papuer* (prickly evergreen fern with decorations impaled on its needle-like leaves) and clusters of sugarcane bent into arches. The plant is a reminder of the persecution that the Catholics suffered under Dutch rule and how they hid in the thick foliage of the sugarcane plantations in Banda Canu outside Malacca town to escape their tormentors.

Built in the second half of the nineteenth century in Banda Praya, the Assumption Chapel faced the sea so that fishermen who were going out to sea could stop by the entrance to pray. When the chapel was renovated in 1919 the entrance was repositioned to face inland. The reorientation caused quite a stir among the fishermen. Having for decades practised a tradition begun by their ancestors, they were not prepared to change. So, to appease the fishermen, a shrine was built facing the sea and their beloved statue of the Mother of God was placed in it.

In 1958 the chapel was enlarged and the authorities, sensitive to the community's sentiments, took great pains to place the statue in a niche at the rear of the church so that it faced the sea. Unfortunately, land reclamation activity some years later robbed the statue of the sea; but it looks on, ever faithful to its purpose, and continues to offer the people of Banda Praya divine reassurance.

This statue of the Mother of God, unique for the many amazing stories and miracles associated with it, is more than two hundred years old. For this reason, it is venerated and held very dear by Malacca's Cristang community.

Festa de Santa Cruz

This feast is celebrated on the second Sunday of September to coincide with the Catholic ritual known as the Exaltation of the Holy Cross.

According to legend, a young woman in Kubu dreamt of a wooden cross on three consecutive nights. When the inhabitants of the town learnt of the dream, they decided that it was a vision and were convinced that the cross existed. They searched Kubu and its surrounding area and, on a hillock called Malim

above A parish priest blessing the fishermen's boats during Festa de San Pedro.

left Gaily decorated boats with sails unfurled resemble historical Portuguese carracks.

just outside the Portuguese quarter of the town, they found a wooden cross.

It was only twelve inches high and was growing from the ground. The people tried removing it but it remained fast. Believing this phenomenon to be the will of God, the Cristang of Kubu built a thatched shed over the cross and often went there to pray. Later they erected an altar over the cross and eventually built a chapel on Malim Hill.

Christmas

'Natal ta beng!' ('Christmas is coming!') shout Cristang children as soon as the Feast of All Souls is over and the first Sunday in Advent has been observed. To the Cristang, Christmas is a time for sharing joy and love, paying one's respect to elders, renewing old acquaintances and visiting friends. With all this activity occurring throughout the Yuletide, there is certainly a lot of opportunity for cooking and eating.

Two weeks before Christmas, families are at their busiest, cleaning and dusting, hurrying to get their homes ready for the holiday. Curtains are taken down and washed and floors are given a good scrubbing; if there are terracotta tiles, a coating of lime wash is applied to the grout between the tiles to enhance the lattice pattern they form. Houses without lawns will have their compounds topped with a layer of fresh beach sand.

When the cleaning is almost finished, everyone turns their attention to the Christmas treats. Cooks revive old recipes and begin preparing the traditional favourites: pineapple tarts, *bolu cocu*, *blueda*, *dodol sabang*, *sersagung* and *baje* (see pp 140–152). All day long the house is filled with the aroma of cakes and pastries browning in the oven and the sweet scent of spices escaping from jars of pickled chillies and pots of boiling ham. This is truly the busiest time of the year.

On Christmas Eve, the 'crib' or Christmas crèche (a replica in miniature of the stable at Bethlehem) is assembled. Statuettes of the Baby Jesus, Mary, Joseph, stable animals, shepherds, a hovering angel and the Magi are arranged in the crèche. The Christmas tree, usually a fresh branch lopped off a casuarina, is planted in a pot of sea sand and decorated. Every member of the family hangs at least one Christmas ornament on the tree for luck.

After Midnight Mass on Christmas Eve the family return home to wish each other season's greetings. Younger members kiss the hands of their grandparents and parents, and everyone sits down to supper. *Teem*, a rich soup made from duck or trotters and flavoured with sherry and spices (p 80), *galinhia pai* (chicken pie, p 118), beer-boiled ham, pickles and salad are served.

Impressive as it is, the Christmas supper pales in comparison with an even more sumptuous feast: the

above Galinhia pai (p 118), a favourite at Christmas time, is served after Midnight Mass.

left The Assumption Chapel with the statue of the Mother of God.

Christmas lunch. At this gathering, the head of the family usually proposes a toast to the health and good fortune of all present. Grace is said and everyone tucks into the delicious fare which is accompanied by wine and punch. The menu usually includes rice, roasts, vegetables and salads, curries and mouth-watering relishes and pickles. (See Menu ideas, p 31.) Some homes also serve roast turkey with all the trimmings. Fish and *sambal* (p 60), however, are almost never part of the Christmas fare. The main courses are often followed by a dessert of home-made coconut ice-cream and tinned fruit. On Boxing Day, the family feast assumes a more modest scale, featuring *debal* (p 52), a dish concocted from leftovers, as the main item on the menu.

Weddings

The traditional Cristang wedding is another celebration connected with the church although it also incorporates secular customs and rituals adapted from other cultures. Rarely seen these days, it involves celebrations that run for a week, and—similar to Malay customs—plans for the wedding devolve on the girl's family. Banns are announced in church during the six months of preparations that begin after the engagement.

Invitation to the wedding is usually by word of mouth, but cards are sent to those who live far away. The mothers of the betrothed couple will choose a 'good' day to call on their guests. Should the invitees be away when they call, they will chalk a mark in the form of a cross on the front door to convey the purpose of their visit, and this gesture suffices for a wedding invitation.

One week before the wedding, the *cronchi* (a heart-shaped ornament with a cross on it) is displayed on the front doors of the homes of the betrothed couple.

On the eve of the wedding, a day

right A Cristang couple in their wedding finery. The bride is wearing a saier-cabaier.

referred to as *marra strado* (tying the knot), a special ritual signifying the bride's chastity is observed. Only married women attend this ceremony. The bride, her maids of honour and the matchmaker are invited to take their seats on a dais. A white paper crown, signifying the bride's chastity, is attached to the centre of a canopy above the dais. A mirror, to deflect evil, is placed on the wall behind the chairs on the dais.

In the evening the bridegroom is invited to take a peek at the bride, but before he is allowed to do so, he has to undergo a test. In a jocular manner the matchmaker will tell the tale of a certain 'cow' that has wandered into a neighbour's garden and caused much damage by browsing on the flowers. The groom is asked if he knows who owns the 'cow'. He then replies that he has to see the 'cow' before he can answer. After being shown the bride, who is strapped to a chair, and confirming that the 'cow' is his, the groom is asked to compensate for the damage the 'cow' has done. After the groom has paid the 'penalty'—usually a bottle of brandy—he is allowed to take his 'cow' with him, unstrapping his bride amidst much teasing. Then all those present are invited to the *da comi noibo* (bachelor's dinner party) where only seafood is served.

At the dinner the bride's parents will present a cake and a bottle of wine to the groom's parents. This ritual symbolizes the first marriage of the bride-to-be; the cake and wine are served to relatives on the following day just before the groom leaves for church.

On the morning of the wedding the bride bathes in scented water and has the fine hairs near her hairline shaved off. Then she puts on her wedding ensemble, an elaborate *saier-cabaier* (blouse and skirt in the style of the Malay *sarung kebaya*). The blouse is fastened in front with three ornate brooches of gold and diamonds. The entire outfit of white silk damask with black velvet trimming at the neckline and cuffs is delicately embroidered with floral motifs using threads of silver and gold. To add further grandeur to the spectacular garment and to hint at the family's financial status, the bride is decked with expensive jewellery. She wears white beaded slippers on her feet. Her hair is styled into a *conde* (bun) that is held in place by five large gold and diamond hairpins, and the coiffure is adorned with a string of white jasmine placed on the left side of her head. After the last pin has been attached to her hair, both parents will solemnly place the bridal veil over her head, uttering words of advice as they do so.

Cake and wine are served to everyone and, just before the bridal entourage leaves for church, the bride's father proposes a toast and delivers a poignant speech to draw tears from his daughter's eyes. He does this deliberately so that she will cry for the last time and never shed tears again during her marriage. Her mother wipes the tears with a white handkerchief and quietly chides her daughter for spoiling her make-up. The bride then kneels at her parents' and grandparents' feet. She thanks them for their love and care and asks for their blessing before kissing their hands. Then, accompanied by her father, the bride leaves for church in a *garry* (horse-drawn carriage).

The wedding ceremony proper is simple and straightforward, conducted according to the tenets of the Catholic church. Mass, pipe-organ music and church bells epitomize the occasion. As soon as the ceremony is over, guests adjourn to the bride's house where a reception awaits. This is a joyous occasion filled with speech-making, toasting, dancing and eating. At the end of the reception, the newlyweds leave amidst a shower of petals thrown at them by the guests. On the following Sunday, the couple attend Mass to give thanks. The bride wears her wedding attire without the veil. After Mass they visit all the people who have helped with the wedding, and at night the couple throw them one last dinner to show their appreciation again.

above A conde with a cabilera (hairpiece) and suasa (gold-plated copper) hairpins.

left My grandparents on their wedding day in 1897.

The modern Cristang

Although the Portuguese Settlement has the highest number of Cristang people in Malaysia, it is not the only place where the Cristang are found. After Malaysia won its independence from Britain in 1957, the Cristang availed themselves of opportunities that arose in the form of subsidized or free education and increased employment. Many moved out of the Settlement and other traditional Portuguese areas of Malacca. Some resettled in the coastal areas of states such as Negeri Sembilan, Selangor, Perak and Penang. Others emigrated to countries such as Singapore, Australia and Great Britain.

Since the 1960s the economic status of the Cristang has improved steadily. The average size of a family declined from between ten and twelve people in the 1920s to between six and seven in the 1940s, easing the financial burden. By the 1960s more Cristang children were receiving higher levels of education and securing better jobs. If, in the past, children had to drop out of school after primary education and take on menial jobs to help with the family finances, a large number now stayed on to complete their secondary and tertiary studies and find employment in factories, businesses and the professions. The standard of living was rising.

As the Cristang started enjoying financial security, they became more conscious of the need to preserve and promote their culture. An important result of this awareness was a change in attitude towards the Cristang language, the Creole Portuguese of their ancestors, which, for a long time after Dutch rule, had been associated with the uneducated folk.

The Cristang speak their own language more openly and frequently nowadays. And the young Cristang often colour the language with English, Malay and even Chinese words.

Efforts at promoting Cristang culture gained further momentum when the Malacca government, in developing its tourism industry, featured the period of Portuguese rule in the state's history. This move has created so much interest that a visit to Malacca these days is incomplete without a trip to the sites of Malacca-Portuguese heritage, like Porta de Santiago, The Church of The Annunciation on St Paul's Hill, St John's Hill and, of course, the Portuguese Settlement. With the aid of government funds, the Cristang have revived many long-forgotten festivals and increased the scale on which they celebrate the others. Traditional dances and folk songs have become more and more popular, particularly among the young Cristang. Since the 1980s Cristang culture has been experiencing a renaissance.

In 1983 the federal government declared the Cristang *bumiputras* (indigenous people). This change in status presented the Cristang with new economic opportunities and a number of other benefits that were previously out of reach. Many have invested in high-yield, low-risk government trust funds reserved exclusively for bumiputras.

left A band of Cristang musicians. The Cristang are musically gifted; many supplement their income by performing in pubs and hotels.

right A traditional Cristang dance.

The Cristang identity

Given their origins, consanguinity and association with the Malays, Chinese and Indians of Malaysia, it is fitting that the Cristang have finally gained recognition as an indigenous people.

They are arguably one prototype of a true Malaysian race if such a group indeed exists. There is no telling what a Cristang looks like, for a Cristang is not distinguished by her features or the colour of her skin. Some are extremely fair, almost Caucasian or Chinese in appearance; others have a dark complexion and could be mistaken for Indians; still many more have golden brown skin and could pass as Malays.

The Cristang of my grandmother's generation had much in common with the Malays, especially when it came to attire. For example, Cristang women wore the Malay sarung kebaya, a mid-calf-length blouse worn over an ankle-length skirt, which they called saier-cabaier. (Today an elaborate and much-decorated version of the saier-cabaier is reserved for weddings.) Another similarity between the Cristang women of that generation and their Malay counterparts was the way in which they did their long black hair. They groomed their tresses with coconut oil, and pulled them back tightly before twisting them into a conde (bun). On special occasions, the women donned *cabilera*s (hairpieces) that were secured by *kukupim*s (hairpins) made of gold, silver or *suasa* (gold-plated copper).

The Cristang men of that period wore Western attire for formal occasions but preferred a pyjama-like outfit for daily use—Cristang fishermen even wore this informal garb to church. Today, however, most Cristang men relax in a sarong and put on a Western suit for the office and formal occasions.

The older Cristang also adopted the curious Malay habit of staining their mouths red by chewing betel nut quids called *sirih*. The quids are formed by wrapping a betel nut leaf around a mixture of slaked lime, gambier and chopped betel nuts. Chewing this mixture was not merely a habit, it formed an important part of Cristang etiquette. The implements and ingredients for making the quids were kept in an ornate box called the *boseta de betel*. It was considered a great honour for a guest to be offered the box; however, if the offer was extended to a child, it meant that her presence was not required and she had to leave the room immediately.

To be considered a Cristang, a person must firstly be a Catholic and have a Catholic name. Secondly, a Cristang must have at least one blood ancestor who was a Malaccan-Portuguese (a descendent from a marriage between a sixteenth century Portuguese and local Malaccan of any race). Surnames such as Campos, Dias, Fernandes, Gomes, Lazaroo, Lopes, Nunis, Pinto, Piris, Rodrigues, de Rozario, de Sequeira, de Souza, Varella, and de Vries are a sure sign of a person's Portuguese roots. Some Dutch names are also a part of the list as a result of marriages between seventeenth century Dutch men and Cristang women. Names such as Goonting, Klyne, Marbeck, Van Heusen, Danker, Hendroff, Hendricks and Westerhout are considered Malaccan-Portuguese in origin. And last but not least, a Cristang must be able to speak her own language. Clearly, being Cristang requires much more than having the right bloodline; religious and cultural standards apply as well.

Although there was a time when the Cristang were unsure of their destiny in what was then a newly independent Malaysia—and many responded to this uncertainty by emigrating—they have little doubt of their place in the country today. As Malaysians, the Cristang are optimistic about their future and believe they will progress and prosper along with the rest of the country. The Cristang have indeed come a long way. Certainly, the present generation suffers none of the angst that so preoccupied their predecessors during the 1920s and 1930s. They see no need to conceal their origins and are proud to be Cristang, as my family motto indicates: *Impeh impregah, nang kureh. Adanza gardah ateh mureh!* (Stand firm and never flee. Your inheritance keep until death!)

Cristang cuisine

The early Portuguese, intent on incorporating Malacca's native cuisine into their own, found the cosmopolitan port to be a culinary melting pot. Malaccan cuisine was a hybrid of the many cultures that existed in the city at the time, among them Malay, Chinese, Indian, Arab, Chitty (see below) and Peranakan (see p 17). Combining the ingredients of the local cuisines with Portuguese cooking methods, the Cristang created a collection of dishes that suited their palates. The result was a successful blending of Eastern and Western flavours.

The Portuguese introduced the use of onions, garlic and chillies and imparted their fondness for marinating and preparing food with lime, lemon or vinegar. Today few of the other ethnic groups in Malaysia use as much lime and tamarind juice for preserving and marinating as do the Cristang. They also use tamarind, lemon grass, lime and galangal in imaginative ways to give their curries, sambals, vegetable dishes and soups an exotic flavour. Sometimes they use alcohol to lend a touch of variety to meat or fish dishes. From the Peranakan, the Cristang acquired a taste for sweet-and-sour dishes along with the art of chopping vegetables, which they stir-fry the Chinese way. They also learnt to improve the flavour of their soups by simmering the ingredients. Meat is usually marinated, then sautéed to seal in the juices and impart a richer flavour. Pork is the Cristang's favourite meat; cut into bite-sized pieces, it is usually curried or fried with vegetables.

The early Cristang cooked with coconut oil or lard. Today they use butter, margarine and vegetable oil. Coconut milk is used to enrich curries, cakes, desserts and some vegetable dishes. As a rule, desserts are not served after a meal but offered as snacks or tea-time treats.

Ovens were unheard of in the early Cristang kitchen. The most common appliance then was a firewood or charcoal stove, and cooking methods were simple and largely restricted to simmering, pot-roasting and stir-frying. Although cooking on the traditional stove involved a long and tedious process, the results were nonetheless mouth-watering.

The Cristang take special pride in the way rice is prepared. When properly cooked it has to be white, fluffy, yet grainy. In fact, they hold the skill of cooking rice so dear that a Cristang girl was not considered fit for marriage unless she could serve up a pot of perfectly cooked rice. Cristang women tend to be good cooks, having learnt the art from their mothers and grandmothers. They are not rigid in their approach and interpret recipes according to their family's taste buds. The wife's ingenuity in preparing a daily menu that strikes a balance between spicy, tangy, sweet and sour has produced winners, like debal, *feng*, Teem and *semur* (pp 52, 54, 80 and 123, respectively). Cristang women also make excellent cakes and sweets, and are noted for their pickles (*achar chilli*, p 84).

Given the infusion of modern Asian and European tastes, it is not surprising that Cristang cuisine today is quite different from that of the past. Each family has followed its own gastronomic path, culling from a rich history filled with many influences. Nevertheless, one thing remains unchanged: for the Cristang, a daily meal without rice, curry and sambal is as unsatisfying as a story without an ending.

Chittys

The Chittys are the progeny of unions between Malaccan natives and Indian traders from Choromandel who formed the first foreign settlement in Malacca. The descendants of this little-known community speak only Malay but, unlike most Malays, are not Muslim. Instead, they adhere strictly to an ancient form of Hinduism. The very first aromas of a mixed cuisine in Malacca came from Chitty kitchens. Chitty wives, being of indigenous stock, retained many of the flavours to which they were accustomed. They learnt the Indian art of blending spices and infused local herbs with spices to create innovative dishes that had Indian and Malay overtones.

right A Chitty headman.

above The Sri Poyyatha Vinayagar Moorthi temple, established by the Chittys, is the oldest Hindu temple in Malaysia.

Peranakan

In 1459, in an effort to form ties with the rich and strategic port of Malacca, the Ming Emperor of China betrothed his daughter Princess Hang Li Po to Malacca's ruler, Sultan Mansur Shah. The princess and her entourage of five hundred were given a magnificent palace on a hill outside town. This hill, which became known as Bukit China or Chinese Hill, was the first permanent Chinese settlement in Malacca. It was the members of the princess' entourage who first married Malaccan natives to form the ethnic group known today as the Peranakan (Malay for 'born here'). The *baba*s (the men) and the *nyonya*s (the women) wear Malay attire and converse in a Malay patois but practice the religion of their Chinese ancestry. Like the Chittys before them, the Peranakan too found ways to combine the cuisines of their mixed heritage, adding exotic Chinese herbs and sauces to Malay food. The result is a distinct style of cuisine that is a blend of many tastes. Tangy, spicy and herb-flavoured, it is neither Chinese nor Malay. Cristang cuisine incorporates many elements of the Peranakan style of cooking, especially in the preparation of vegetables.

right The Princess Hang Li Poh Well at the foot of Bukit China.

Fugang Cristang

A CRISTANG KITCHEN

A traditional kitchen

Four decades ago, the ambience of a Cristang village at mid-morning was not unlike that of a huge open-air kitchen. Everywhere one looked one saw people preparing a meal: old ladies sitting in open doorways picking grit from a colander of uncooked rice; at the back of a house, a woman working her granite roller over a granite slab, grinding fresh herbs and spices to make the day's curry paste; three houses away her cousin, scaling and gutting fish and, at the same time, chatting with the women next door; nearby, her young daughter humming to the songs on the radio, pounding chillies, onions and shrimp paste in a mortar. The nosy neighbour was also part of the Cristang village scene; she sauntered from house to house inquiring nonchalantly: *'Qui te cuzhir, nona?'* ('What's cooking, lady?'), and offered hot gossip. As if on a stage, everything and everyone was on display.

Those were the days when Cristang homes did not have enclosed kitchens and cooking was done in an open air-well or in an annexe at the back of the house. The most prominent feature in a Cristang kitchen then was the open hearth with a brick-and-mortar stove fuelled by firewood. On it sat black, round-bottomed earthen pots called *tezaler*s, which are similar to the pots used by Indian chefs. A seasoned tezaler was considered excellent for cooking *cari* (curry) because it imparted a special flavour to the dish. To stir the curry, the Cristang chef used a *culeh de chireta* (a special ladle) that was made of coconut shell or wood. There were also special ladles for cooking *caldo* (soup) and *canje* (porridge).

Every Cristang family owned at least two tezalers, one for meat curries and the other for fish. Other cooking utensils included the *tacho* (a cast-iron

left A midday scene in Jalan Laksamana (fomerly known as Riverside Road), Malacca in the 1840s. The building on the right was the first premises of the Malacca High School.

right A culeh de chireta.

far right A tezaler.

frying pan that also served as a griddle) and two or three *panela*s (deep pans) or *saspan*s that were used for boiling, stewing or making stocks. For stir-frying, the Cristang used the Chinese wok. A brass pan called *grengseng* was used to make pineapple jam, boil *agar-agar* seaweed and cook baje and dodol sabang, two Christmas treats that require long cooking times. (Recipes on pp 142, 143 and 147, respectively.)

The floor of a Cristang kitchen was typically covered with sea sand or laid with red bricks, the second of these treatments most likely the result of Dutch influence; cement floors were also a common sight. In one corner of the small kitchen sat a brick oven over which was built a clumsy-looking funnel that served as an exhaust for smoke. Beside the oven stood a large ceramic jar or barrel filled with water which was used for drinking and cooking. (Some homes did not have taps,

and water had to be carried into the house from community standpipes or wells.) Another water vessel was placed next to the *barleo*, an open-air kitchen sink where crockery was washed and left to dry.

Kitchen furniture included a rough wooden table with broad, heavy wooden benches flanking it. This table was the focus of kitchen activities as well as family gatherings. Another piece of furniture that was typically found in the Cristang kitchen was the meat safe. This was a cupboard with 'see-through' doors made from fine gauge wire mesh that was stretched across a wooden frame; a small wooden knob nailed to the cupboard was used to keep the doors closed. The cupboard had three shelves that served as a store for groceries and cooked food. The wire mesh on the doors allowed air into the cupboard and kept flies out.

The Cristang kitchen also included the pretty egg basket among

above A grengseng.

above An area where crockery is washed and left to dry. To the right of it is a pedra mui tempra or grinding stone.

right A typical Cristang kitchen. The floor is laid with red brick, reflecting the influence of the Dutch, who had their own kitchen floors built in a similar fashion during their occupation of Malacca from 1641 to 1824.

its inventory of foodstuff containers. Made entirely from wire, the basket was usually placed atop the meat safe, out of the reach of children and pets.

Cooked food left on the dining table was covered with a conical food cover woven from screw pine leaves and cane. For convenience, food was sometimes kept in a metal tiffin carrier and family members who returned late for dinner ate out of it. (It is heartening to note that the tradition of eating out of tiffin carriers has been revived in Malaysia; these food containers are now used to pack takeaways as well, a practice that should help reduce the use of plastic bags and containers.)

The coconut grater (a contraption comprising a piece of metal with a curved, serrated head and a tail that was attached to a small bench) was an essential tool. Sharp knives, cleavers, the *pilung tek-tek* (mortar and pestle), the grinding stone and a homemade device for removing fish scales were other important utensils in the Cristang kitchen.

A modern kitchen

The only traces of tradition one is likely to find in the Cristang kitchen these days are the tacho and tezaler. (Apparently, no modern substitutes exist.) Gone are the mortar and pestle and the *pedra mui tempra* (grinding stone, or *batu giling* in Malay) with its heavy roller; in their stead stands that 'Swiss army knife' of kitchen appliances, the ubiquitous food processor. Another casualty of the times, the meat safe has been replaced by the refrigerator; and with the availability of gas ranges, electric stoves and microwave ovens these days, cooking over a hot, sooty fire has truly become a thing of the past.

above A traditional coconut grater.

above A pilung tek-tek.

left A coconut sieve.

left A grater usually used for grating green papaya to make the stuffing for achar chilli (p 84).

left A meat safe with an egg basket on top.

Weights and measures

Most of the quantities in the recipes are stated in metric units; volume, however, is stated in cooking measures, such as teaspoon, tablespoon and cup. This 'mixed' approach has been adopted for practical reasons that are likely to benefit the cook. I have, for instance, found it more convenient to measure out a tablespoon of soy sauce than to obtain the equivalent amount (15 ml) using a graduated cup. On the other hand, many ingredients are sold by weight and not by the cup- or tablespoonful. It therefore makes sense to quantify these ingredients using the most convenient unit of measure. However, it is important to note that the cooking measures stated in the recipes refer to the levelled teaspoon, tablespoon or cup.

To assist the cook further, I have stated the quantities of ingredients such as chillies, garlic, onions, shallots, etc. along with their weights. The careful cook will note that these quantities and weights do not have a consistent relationship. For instance, one recipe may state the weight of 25 shallots as 300 g while another may state it as 500 g. This is to be expected, as the sizes of shallots will vary, as will the sizes of other vegetables. When in doubt, the cook should use weight to obtain more consistent results.

Volume

American	American	Metric
1 tsp.	⅛ fl. oz.	4.9 ml
1 tbsp.	⅓ fl. oz.	14.7 ml
¼ cup	2 fl. oz.	59.2 ml
⅓ cup	2½ fl. oz.	78.9 ml
½ cup	4 fl. oz.	118.3 ml
1 cup	8 fl. oz.	236.6 ml
2 cups	16 fl. oz.	473.2 ml
4 cups	32 fl. oz.	946.4 ml
4¼ cups	34 fl. oz.	1.0 l

Weight

American	Metric
1 oz.	28.4 g
4 oz.	113.5 g
8 oz.	227.0 g
16 oz. (1 lb.)	454.0 g
2.2 lb.	1 kg

Length

American	Metric
1 in.	2.54 cm
3 in.	7.62 cm
6 in.	15.24 cm
12 in. (1 ft.)	30.48 cm

Equivalent measures

2 tsp.	1 tbsp.
4 tbsp.	¼ cup
5⅓ tbsp.	⅓ cup
8 tbsp.	½ cup
16 tbsp.	1 cup

Oven temperatures

°C	°F	British Gas Mark
135	275	1
150	300	2
165	325	3
175	350	4
190	375	5
200	400	6
220	425	7
230	450	8

Abbreviations used

ml	millilitre
l	litre
fl. oz.	fluid ounce
tsp.	teaspoon
tbsp.	tablespoon
g	gram
kg	kilogram
oz.	ounce
lb.	pound
mm	millimetre
cm	centimetre
in.	inch
ft.	foot
sec.	second
min.	minute
hr./hrs.	hour/hours
p/pp	page/pages
m	Malay
c	Cristang
ch	Chinese

Preparasang Cuzinhia

COOKING PREPARATIONS

Basic food preparation techniques

Although their cuisine is simple, Cristang cooks pay particular attention to the way in which they cut their meat and vegetables. Their choice of cutting technique largely depends on the cooking method they are using and the quality of the ingredients. Preparing wholesome and appetizing dishes and serving them in a simple, unpretentious manner is the true object of the Cristang cook. Consequently, they have never emphasized or developed techniques for fancy cutting for decorative purposes.

Generally, all the ingredients in a given dish are cut similarly, whether sliced, diced or chopped. To ensure that they cook evenly and therefore have more flavour, all the ingredients are cut into pieces of the same size; doing this also improves the appearance of the dish.

Cutting meat

The Cristang usually use large chunks of meat when cooking curries, but shred it for stir-frying. Beef is always cut across the grain while other meat can be cut along or across the grain. Although cutting meat into bite-sized pieces is time-consuming, it is an integral part of Cristang cuisine and is essential to making the meat taste good. To the Cristang, bite-sized refers to an amount that fits into half a tablespoon.

Cubing

Begin with a piece of meat about 2.5 cm thick. Cut into strips

2.5 cm wide; then cut the strips into cubes.

Cutting into very small cubes for stir-fried dishes

From slices of meat about 3 mm thick, cut strips of the same length.

Holding several pieces together, cut into cubes.

Mincing or march-chopping

Cut meat into small pieces. Chop with a cleaver, moving the blade from side to side. As the meat spreads,

place the cleaver under it, fold into the centre and continue chopping until desired texture is achieved.

Cook's note This method of mincing is preferable to using an electric meat grinder as the latter tends to render the meat too fine, giving it a mushy texture.

Cutting into slivers

Cut meat into slices 6 mm thick.

Cut each slice into thin strips or slivers about 3 mm wide.

Cook's note To save time, stack up slices and cut. Meat cut this way is suitable for stir-frying with vegetables.

Cutting vegetables

Cristang cooks usually chop vegetables into small uniform pieces so that they cook quickly, retain their crunchiness and absorb the flavours of the seasoning and the oil.

Leafy vegetables such as mustard leaves, spinach or *kangkong* (see water spinach, p 41) are prepared by separating the leaves from the tender stalks. The stalks are cut into uniform lengths and halved; the leaves are left whole or chopped into smaller pieces if they are too large.

Cauliflower and broccoli are separated into florets, while celery and leek are cut across the grain into small diagonal pieces. Long beans are cut into 8-cm (about 3 in.) lengths; they are also sliced diagonally for stir-frying. French beans, four-angled beans and okra are similarly prepared although these are sometimes left whole when they are to be parboiled.

Aubergines are usually halved or quartered and slit through lengthwise; a lattice pattern is then cut into the white pulp. If they are to be cooked in a curry, they are slit ¾ of the way through and their stalks are left intact.

Root vegetables such as carrots, bamboo shoots and radishes are rolling cut or sliced into quarters, rings, sticks and cubes. Gourds and cucumbers are sliced or diced. Cabbages may be quartered, cut into wedges or shredded. Sometimes whole leaves are added to stews and curries or stuffed.

Slicing

Cook's note Certain Cristang dishes call for diced liver or tongue as well. Dicing should produce cubes slightly smaller than bite-sized.

Hold the vegetable at a sixty degree angle; cut, continuing to the end.

Dicing

Slice the vegetables, then cut strips of the same size. Holding several strips together, cut into cubes.

Julienne cutting

Cut vegetables, e.g., cucumber, yam bean or carrots, into thin slices, about 3 mm thick. Stack the slices and cut into narrow strips.

Rolling cut

Hold cylindrical vegetable firmly and cut a diagonal slice from one end. Roll the vegetable a quarter turn towards you and make another diagonal cut. Continue rolling and cutting until the end.

Extracting coconut milk

To obtain thick coconut milk, mix half the warm water the recipe calls for with all the grated coconut. Knead until a white liquid appears.

Squeeze the pulp over a strainer to extract milk. Alternatively, wrap the pulp in muslin and squeeze. For thin coconut milk, add remaining water to the squeezed pulp; knead, then squeeze into a separate bowl.

Cook's note In curries that require coconut milk use 1 tbsp. thick coconut milk when frying the spices or curry paste to prevent burning. Then add all the thin coconut milk and bring it to a boil before adding the meat or vegetables. Add the remaining thick milk last and stir continuously to prevent it from curdling. Thick coconut milk is often added at the end to thicken a dish or poured over desserts to give them a richer flavour. See also p 36.

Extracting tamarind juice

Soak tamarind pulp in warm water, following the proportions given in the recipe. Squeeze firmly to extract juice.

Strain and discard seeds, skin and fibrous matter. To obtain a more piquant taste, use double the amount of tamarind pulp with the same amount of water.

Cook's note Tamarind juice is an essential ingredient in the preparation of many Cristang curries; if it is unavailable, substitute with lemon juice.

Decorating with florets

Remove the bulbous part of the spring onion and trim to 7.5-cm lengths.

Hold down the centre of each length with the index finger and make repeated cuts at both ends, keeping the centre intact.

Put the lengths into a bowl of cold water with ice cubes. This will make them curl, forming florets. Use the florets to garnish roasts or rice dishes.

♠ Chicken stock

ingredients

½ kg chicken carcass or gizzard

2 cm (20 g) ginger, peeled

2 cloves (5 g) garlic, unpeeled

enough water to cover meat plus 1 cup

salt and sugar to taste

method

1 Put all ingredients into a deep pot and bring to a rapid boil. Lower heat and simmer for 1 hour.

2 To serve as a soup, strain, add vegetables such as spinach, mustard greens, gourds, carrots, potatoes or cabbage and cook until tender. Garnish with spring onion and coriander or celery leaves.

Makes 4 cups

🐃 Meat stock

ingredients

½ kg beef shin or veal knuckle

1 tsp. black peppercorns

1 tsp. cloves

1 cinnamon stick, 2-cm length

enough water to cover meat plus 1 cup

method

1 Place all ingredients in a saucepan and bring to a boil. Cover and simmer for 1 hour. Skim off scum, cover and simmer for another hour.

2 Strain and allow to cool; remove the fat that floats to the surface of the stock. If this stock is not used up at once, keep it in the same pot and bring it to a boil every day, adding left over bones or meat and more water as required. Do not keep for more than 3 days.

Makes 6 cups

🦐 Seafood stock

ingredients

½ kg bones and trimmings, such as the head, tail and skin, of any fish

enough water to cover trimmings plus 5 cups

salt to taste

250 g fresh prawns, unshelled

Cook's note Seafood stock does not keep well and should be used the day it is made. The stock makes a tangy soup with lemon grass or tamarind slices added. Prawn stock can be used for seafood dishes and for making the gravy for *laksa Malaca* (p 130).

method

fish stock

1 Boil trimmings in enough salted water to cover plus 1 cup, for 20 min.; skim off any scum that forms. Strain and use immediately.

Makes 4 cups

prawn stock

1 Boil prawns in remaining 4 cups water for 20 min. Remove prawns, reserving liquid. Shell the prawns, reserving the heads and skin. Set the cooked prawns aside for use in other dishes.

2 Grind shells and heads coarsely and wrap in muslin cloth. Immerse the packet in the liquid used to boil the prawns and simmer for 30 min. Strain the stock and use immediately.

Makes 3 cups

Fresh herb curry paste

ingredients

2 stalks lemon grass (use 7 cm from root end)

3 cm (25 g) fresh galangal, peeled and shredded

5 cloves (15 g) garlic, peeled

4 (15 g) candlenuts or 8 (15 g) blanched almonds

20 (200 g) shallots or 2 (200 g) onions, peeled

6 (15 g) dried chillies, presoaked in hot water

5 g fresh turmeric, peeled or ½ tsp. turmeric powder

1 tsp. salt

1 tsp. vegetable oil

method

1 Put all ingredients into a blender and blend for 2 min. to make a smooth, fine paste.

2 Remove and put into a clean, dry bowl or bottle and refrigerate.

Makes 1½ cups

This paste is sufficient for a curry for 4 people.

Dry spice curry powder

ingredients

3 tbsp. coriander seeds

2 tbsp. cumin seeds

1 tbsp. fennel seeds

2 tsp. black peppercorns

2 cinnamon sticks, 6-cm lengths

3 cardamom

pinch of grated nutmeg

5 cloves

1 tsp. turmeric powder

Cook's note To make a curry for 4–6 persons, use 3 tbsp. of the powder. Chillies, onions and garlic are often blended with this powder.

method

1 In a dry frying pan, dry-roast all the ingredients except turmeric, tossing for a few minutes to release aromas and flavours. Be careful not to char the ingredients.

2 Allow the ingredients to cool, then grind to a fine powder in a dry blender or spice mill.

3 Combine the ground spices with turmeric powder and mix well. Place in a dry, clean air-tight jar. Keep in a cool, dry place.

Makes 1 cup

Stew spice powder

ingredients

2 cinnamon sticks, 6-cm lengths

30 cloves

3 star anise

½ dried nutmeg

Cook's note This spice blend may be used for seasoning any meat: add 1 tsp. per kilogram of meat.

method

1 Dry-roast all ingredients until fragrant; while still hot, grind in a dry blender or spice mill to a fine powder. Allow to cool.

2 When the powder has cooled, store in an air-tight container.

Makes 2 tablespoons

Homemade fishballs

ingredients

½ kg soft-fleshed white fish fillets (wolf-herring or
  Spanish mackerel)

5 cups warm water

½ tsp. salt

½ tsp. pepper

1 tsp. sugar

1 tsp. cornflour

preparation

1 Remove skin from fillets. Boil the skin in 4 cups
  of the water. Reduce to 3 cups; strain and set
  aside.

2 Dissolve salt in the remaining water. Pound fish
  flesh in a mortar, adding the salt water gradually
  until the flesh takes on the consistency of a firm,
  smooth paste. If using a food processor, process
  with the salt water until fish is finely mashed.

method: 15 min.

1 Put fish stock from PREPARATION, STEP 1 in a
  deep pot and bring to a boil.

2 Mix fish paste (pounded fish flesh) well with pepper, sugar and cornflour. Take 2 tbsp. of the
  mixed paste and squeeze it through the thumb
  and forefinger until a lump emerges.

3 Scrape this lump off with a wet teaspoon, making
  a fishball about 2½ cm in diameter.

4 As soon as each fishball is formed, gently drop it
  into the boiling fish stock. Repeat until all the
  fish paste has been used up. The fishballs are
  cooked when they are springy when pressed.

5 The cooked fishballs may now be used as required
  in any recipe. Extra fishballs may be cooled and
  kept in a plastic bag in a refrigerator for up to 5
  days. Freezing is not recommended as it tends to
  destroy the springy texture that is the standard by
  which a fishball is judged!

Makes 20–30 fishballs

Cooking methods

In Cristang cookery, the preferred methods for cooking
meat and vegetables include frying, stir-frying, pot roasting or braising, stewing, boiling and flavour-potting.

Frying is a quick cooking method used for small pieces
of meat or fish. To fry a fish, put just enough oil to cover the base of the frying pan. Heat the oil till it smokes,
then slide the fish into the pan and cook on high heat.
When one side of the fish is brown, turn it over once to
brown the other side. Remove the fish when it is cooked
and drain on a paper towel.

Deep frying is not popular in Cristang cookery. In
this method, food is cooked by completely immersing it
in hot or boiling oil.

Stir-frying is a method adopted from the Chinese and is
now widely used by the Cristang, usually for cooking
vegetables. Heat an empty wok over high heat. Put in a
little oil and swirl it around to grease the sides of the pan.
Add onion and garlic and sauté. Then add slivers of meat
and toss until half cooked. Sprinkle with water or stock
and continue tossing until the sizzling stops. Next add
vegetables and other ingredients, such as sauces or seasonings. Continue stirring and tossing the ingredients
until the vegetables are cooked.

Pot-roasting or braising is to the Cristang chef the next
best method for roasting meat if an oven is not available.
Beef, chicken or any other meat is usually marinated in
a mixture of spice paste, freshly pounded herbs, soy
sauce and mustard and placed in a deep pot. A little
stock or water is poured into the pot to keep the meat
moist. The meat is then cooked over low heat and bast-
ed frequently. Pot-roasting produces a succulent piece of
meat that is usually sliced and served with a rich brown
sauce, green peas and boiled potatoes.

Stewing is a slow cooking method suitable for tougher
cuts of meat. The meat is cut into 2.5-cm cubes, sometimes coated in seasoned flour or spice paste, and
browned quickly in hot oil. Water or stock is then added
and the meat is simmered slowly on a low flame. Stews
taste better if allowed to sit for a day. Most Cristang
curries are cooked using this method.

Boiling involves bringing a pot of liquid to boiling point
and maintaining it at that temperature; ingredients are
then added and cooked. Soups and stocks are prepared
using this method.

Flavour-potting refers to a method of flavouring a dish using spices, but without leaving any sediment. The spices are put in a small muslin bag which is then placed into the pot along with other ingredients and removed after the dish is cooked. Whole spices, such as clove, star anise, nutmeg, cinnamon and peppercorn are used in flavour-potting.

Cristang meals

The everyday Cristang meal features a curry or two accompanied by vegetables that are usually stir-fried with small pieces of meat or seafood. And, of course, no meal would be deemed complete without one of the many sambals beloved of the Cristang.

All the dishes are placed on the table at the same time (including soups on the rare occasion they are served) and eaten with boiled rice; sometimes bread or noodles are substituted for rice. Each diner's plate will have small portions of every dish arranged around a steaming mound of rice. Like the Malays, Indians and Chittys, the Cristang use their fingers to eat, although nowadays forks and spoons are preferred. Knives are rarely used at the table, as all the food is bite-sized or soft enough to be broken apart with a fork and spoon.

Formal family gatherings around the traditional long table in a Cristang home mean a huge variety of food and strict attention paid to seating order. The head of the family always sits at the top of the table with his wife on his right; grandfather will be at the other end of the table with grandmother on his right. The children sit in order of seniority beginning with the eldest child on father's left; nobody is allowed to change seats.

If guests are present, the children are fed in the kitchen as only older family members are allowed to sit with the guests. Grace is always said before the host signals the beginning of the meal by offering the platter of rice to the guest of honour. The host is expected to put choice pieces of food on the guest's plate and to frequently urge her to '*Toma mas. Qui foi bergonhia! Fazeh cuma casa ungsong.*' ('Take more. Why be shy! Make yourself at home.')

A standard formal dinner consists of seven or eight dishes: at least two curries, a fried or roasted dish, a pie, cooked vegetables or a salad (usually both), pickles and sambals, noodles, rice and, finally, a variety of cakes for dessert, followed by coffee, the Cristang's favourite beverage. The number of dishes and the richness of the spread is always closely observed, for it is an indication of the host's status within the community. But even more important than variety is the quantity—there must always be a large quantity of food on the table, as the Cristang are traditionally big eaters and have no qualms about asking for seconds. In fact, the host would be quite insulted if there were no requests for a second helping! And, of course, along with all the good food there is bound to be music in some form or other, for the Cristang are a musical people. At heart, they are a people who enjoy themselves in a simple and unpretentious manner.

Menu ideas

Traditional Cristang banquet

Family Sunday fare

Special seafood dinner

A typical Cristang meal

Afternoon tea

Angled luffa gourds

Glossary of special ingredients and staple foods

Nearly every Cristang dish requires the use of one or more kinds of spice or preserved ingredient, such as *belachan* (shrimp paste) or fermented bean. The result is an exciting mix of tastes and flavours. A dish like *singgang mangger* (p 57), for example, is at once pungent and sweet, and Teem (p 80), a beloved Yuletide soup, gratifies the palate with a tangy blend of cinnamon, nutmeg and dried tamarind.

Herbs and vegetables too play an important role in Cristang cooking. Garlic, galangal and lemon grass appear in curries as do chillies, shallots and onions. Gourds, bean sprouts, lady's fingers (okra), spinach and kangkong form a regular part of the Cristang diet and, although less common, the buds of the banana plant and tiger lily are also eaten.

The glossary that follows provides a description of important ingredients and foods that are part of the Cristang culture. Although readers—especially if they are Malaysian—may already be familiar with many of the items here, I have included them for the sake of clarity. In the naming of ingredients it is likely that one term may have been confused with another. This glossary should help avoid ambiguities of this nature. I have included the Cristang name for each item and this is preceded by the letter *c*; where necessary I have also provided the Malay and Chinese equivalents, and these are preceded by *m* and *ch*, respectively.

Belimbing

Black nuts

Bunga telang

Candied winter melon

Candlenuts

Cardamom

Cinnamon

Citrus leaves

Cloves

Coriander

Cumin

Curry leaves

Daun kesom

Daun pegaga

Fennel

Galangal

Gula Melaka

Agar

c: *agar-agar*

A gelatinous extract from several varieties of red seaweed. Available in strips or in powdered form, agar-agar dissolves easily in hot water, hardening to a gel when cooled. It is an excellent thickener for a wide variety of food such as jellies and desserts. Use 1 tsp. agar-agar powder to set 1½ cups of liquid.

Agar-agar seaweed once grew in abundance around the islands off the Malacca coast. It was collected by Cristang fishermen and dried for sale and personal consumption. As a result of unchecked harvesting, however, this group of plants is no longer found in the waters off the coast of Malacca.

Angled luffa gourd

c: *catoler*

m: *petola sanding*

A dark green vegetable of the melon family, identified by its long ridges and elongated shape. The flesh is soft, spongy and sweet; old gourds are tough and may have a bitter taste. To cook it, remove the ridges and the leathery, green skin. Cut it diagonally or into wedges.

Do not discard the skin, for it is delicious; instead chop it into 2-cm pieces and fry with an onion-chilli paste. Add some coconut milk and season to taste. Serve as a side dish, with rice.

Baby mussel

c: *laler-laler*

m: *siput kepah*

A small shellfish with a fine, smooth shell, measuring approximately 1.5 cm across. Baby mussels are brought in by the tide and left along the seashore or in the muddy shoals. At low tide, children and adults comb these areas diligently, scooping up sacks of the tiny creatures. Baby mussels are usually in season just before Christmas. They make a delicious soup (*caldu laler-laler*, p 78) when combined with fresh lemon grass and chillies.

Banana

c: *figu*

The fruit of the banana plant, a giant herb native to Malaysia and the neighbouring archipelago. The stem of the plant consists of a cluster of overlapping, concentric leaf sheaths wrapped tightly. A stalk grows up through the centre of this stem—botanically called a pseudostem—and terminates in a cluster of flowers that each becomes the familiar fruit we eat.

Lily buds

Limes

Mung beans

Mustard seeds

Peppercorns

Screw pine leaves

Shrimp paste

Star anise

Tamarind

Tamarind slices

Turmeric

Water spinach

Whitebait

Wood fungus

Yam bean

The Cristang generally do not peel or slice bananas when serving them. Instead, they are usually left whole and offered in a tray or basket. In Cristang cuisine both the fruit and the bud of the banana are used in savoury dishes such as the traditional banana bud sambal (sambal jantong, p 67). Jerusalem artichokes may be used as substitutes for banana buds.

The large leaves of the banana plant have a place in Cristang cuisine as well. They are used to wrap fish for baking and are also cut into small squares, rectangles or circles to serve as doilies on plates or wrappers for glutinous rice cakes.

Bean curd

c: *taukwa*
m: *tauhu*

A curd product made from soya beans. Originating in China where it has been an important source of protein for thousands of years, bean curd, or tofu, is widely consumed in Asia today. It is available in various forms, including soft and hard bean curd, bean curd puffs, fried bean curd and Japanese bean curd, a variety popular for its smooth texture.

The Cristang use bean curd in braised dishes and soups. Fried bean curd slices (of the firm variety of bean curd) are stir-fried in vegetable dishes or added to sambals. Bean curd puffs are usually stuffed with minced meat or fish paste and added to soups. At times the stuffed puffs are deep fried.

Bean sprout

c: *taugeh*

Tender sprout from the tiny mung bean. Easily grown, this vegetable is available daily in Asian markets and supermarkets. Because of its humble origins and low cost, it is considered a poor man's vegetable. Bean sprouts will keep well for 2–3 days in the refrigerator, in a bowl of water or in a plastic bag. Cristang cooks painstakingly remove the straggly, thread-like root ends before cooking the sprouts in order to enhance their appearance.

Belimbing (m)

c: *bling-bling*

A pale green fruit, about 2.5 cm long, resembling a tiny cucumber with a translucent skin. Appreciated for its sour taste, the fruit is salted and dried when plentiful and used in pickles and as a substitute for tamarind. Fresh belimbing added to certain meat dishes helps to tenderize the meat and increases the acidity of the dish. Salted and dried belimbing is sometimes used in Teem (p 80) in place of tamarind slices. To salt the fruit, prick the skin and rub with salt. Sun-dry until the fruit shrivels up, then store in a glass or earthenware container.

Bitter gourd

c: *marergozu*

An elongated, light green vegetable about 25 cm long. True to its name, the gourd has a bitter taste that is unpleasant to some but appealing to others. To reduce bitterness, cut the gourd in half, discard the pulp and slice thinly. Coat with salt and leave to stand for 15 min.; then knead to extract bitter juices, wash and drain.

Black nut

c: *keluak*
m: *buah keluak*

A hard-shelled, black coloured nut from a tree (*Pengui medulae*) native to Brazil and found in great numbers in the swamps of Indonesia. The nut is collected and exported to Malacca and Singapore, where its black, oily kernel is considered a delicacy.

Always buy ten per cent more nuts than required, as there are often a few bad ones in the lot. Good nuts are heavier and will not rattle when shaken. Soak the nuts overnight and crack open at the scar before cooking. The Cristang use this nut to prepare cari keluak (p 49). This curry is traditionally served with sambal belachan (p 62) to mask the slightly bitter taste of the kernel.

Brinjal

c: *terung*

A large elongated or egg-shaped vegetable, usually purple in colour, also known as aubergine or eggplant. A native of India and China, brinjals were brought to Europe by Arab traders. The Cristang fry this vegetable and add it to curries and sambals. Sometimes cooked brinjal pulp is mixed with minced meat and used as a stuffing for brinjal skins. The stuffed brinjals are then baked or fried.

Bunga telang (m)

c: *bunga telang*

An equatorial creeper (*Clitoria ternatea*, commonly known as butterfly pea) with tiny, deep blue flowers, 3 cm long. Before artificial food colouring was available, the flowers were picked, dried and boiled to extract a blue colouring agent which was used in cakes made of grated tapioca, rice or glutinous rice flour.

Other than colouring food, this flower was also used in the laundry. Washerwomen added two or three fresh flowers to the last rinse of their washing to brighten white fabric.

Candied winter melon

c: *comblanger*
ch: *tungkuey*

The white pulp of winter melon, or wax gourd, is often preserved in sugar and sold in packets. The small pieces of candied pulp belies the size of the vegetable, which happens to be one of the largest in the world. The Cristang soak the candied flesh in boiled water which is then drunk to reduce fever. This preserve is sometimes used in *sugee kek* (p 152) to add moisture.

Candlenut

c: *bokras*
m: *buah keras*

A nut with a hard grey shell enclosing a waxy, cream coloured kernel. The latter is readily available in sundry shops and supermarkets. Candlenuts are used in curries and sambals to alleviate the pungency of chillies and thicken gravy. They should be ground finely before use. Candlenuts are similar in flavour to almonds, which make a good substitute (use two almonds for each candlenut).

Cardamom

c: *cardamungoo*
m: *buah pelaga*

The straw-coloured fibrous pod of a reed-like aromatic plant belonging to the ginger family and occurring in the Malabar region of southwestern India. The small black seeds in the pod are dried and used as a spice. Known as 'grains of Paradise' in fifteenth century Europe, these seeds are used in curries, rice, cordial, cakes and confectionery. They may be used whole or ground. If you prefer the former, bruise the seeds with a mallet before using; if you prefer to grind the seeds, do so just before using, as they lose their fragrance rather quickly. Cardamom is the world's most expensive spice after saffron and vanilla.

Chilli

c: *chilli*

A small and very hot type of pepper, available in a number of colours—usually red and green— which are no indication of its 'fire power'! Cristang cuisine is very adventurous and liberal with the use of chillies. It is chillies that make curries painfully hot, not the spices. To the uninitiated palate, chillies can prove a fiery experience. To reduce the strength of a chilli, remove its seeds, which are the hottest part of the fruit. Deseeding is done by slitting the chilli down one side and scraping the seeds out carefully with a small knife. Shaking the pod vigorously will also dislodge the seeds. Always wash your hands thoroughly in running water after handling chillies; touching the eyes or nose with chilli-stained hands will leave a burning sensation that can last for hours.

Chillies are usually used fresh. Fresh red chillies are added to curries not just for the hot taste but also for the appetizing red colour they impart. Cristang curries that call for fresh as well as dried chillies usually require a proportion of one fresh chilli to two dried ones. Dried chillies must be presoaked in hot water before they are pureed. Green chillies are usually pickled and are sometimes sliced to make a vegetable dish with coconut milk and prawns (*sambal chilli bedri*, p 65).

In Malaysia, pureed chilli or chilli paste, called *cili boh*, may be purchased in grocery shops and markets. Most Cristang cooks make their own cili boh. All that is required is to blend together fresh chillies, salt and oil. The preparation can be kept frozen and used over a period of time.

Chinese spinach

c: *bayam*

A leafy vegetable with broad oval leaves that are either completely green in colour or red in the centre. The Cristang usually add this vegetable to soups. Like English spinach, it is also eaten boiled, tossed in butter and seasoned with salt and pepper.

Cinnamon

c: *pau doce*
m: *kayu manis*

The dried inner bark of the cinnamon tree native to Sri Lanka. It has a sweet penetrating aroma and is available in the form of a stick, a powder or an extract; it is tan in colour. In use since biblical times, this spice was once more valuable than gold and was the most important item in the Dutch East India Company's trade.

In Southeast Asia, the bark of the cassia tree is often substituted for true cinnamon; the former is reddish-brown in colour and has a stronger flavour. Generally, a piece of cassia bark is equivalent to four pieces of true cinnamon.

Citrus leaf

c: *foler lemo purut*
m: *daun limau purut*

The leaf of the kaffir lime tree. Fresh leaves are used in Cristang fish curries and sambals, and are easily available in Malaysia. Dried leaves may be more easily obtained overseas; there is no need to soak them before use. However, if dried leaves have to be sliced, soak them in water for 5–10 min. first.

Clove

c: *krabu*
m: *bunga cengkih*

The sun-dried flower bud of the clove tree. Originating in the Moluccas and used as a spice since ancient times, cloves are popular for flavouring stews, soups and hams. Although they are also available in powdered form, cloves should be used whole whenever possible.

Coconut

c: *cocu*

The fruit of the coconut palm, a tall tree popular for its myriad uses and widely cultivated throughout the tropics. The soft pulp of a young coconut is tasty and can be eaten raw. The liquid inside the fruit is thirst quenching and delicious and may be drunk to relieve diarrhoea. As the coconut matures, its pulp hardens and becomes less palatable. The pulp is usually grated, and in this form it is either squeezed to extract coconut milk or added to dishes. As a rule of thumb, one coconut yields 4 cups or 320 g of grated coconut. The Cristang use coconut milk in a variety of dishes that range from sweet to savoury. After the milk has been extracted, the grated coconut is cooked and given to poultry in a form of a feed called *dedah*.

Coconut oil is another product of the mature coconut. In the past, the Cristang used it for cooking and grooming their hair. They obtained the oil by boiling thick coconut milk.

Coconut milk

c: *leite cocu*

m: *santan*

Extracted from the grated pulp of mature coconuts, this is a thick, rich milk high in cholesterol. It is, however, a beloved ingredient for many curries and desserts. Thick milk is obtained by adding a little warm water to the grated coconut and squeezing it hard. Thin milk is obtained by adding more water and squeezing again. Both types of coconut milk are used in cooking; the thicker form is always added last as it tends to curdle. To further prevent curdling, the dish is stirred continuously once the milk has been added; the dish should also be left uncovered the whole time.

In hot and humid conditions, coconut milk and pulp tend to spoil very quickly and should be kept refrigerated. Thick coconut milk can be deep frozen in the form of cubes for subsequent use.

If fresh coconut milk is unavailable, use the following substitutes:

Tinned coconut milk

This may be purchased in sizes of 200 or 400 ml. The contents of a 400-ml tin are equivalent to the extract obtained from 12 cups of grated coconut. Use tinned coconut milk at full strength if the recipe calls for thick milk. If thin milk is required, mix 2 parts water with 1 part milk to dilute.

Frozen coconut milk sold in blocks

If the recipe calls for thick coconut milk, grate the solid block (as if grating cheese) into a curry that is simmering on low heat. If thin milk is needed, grate 25 g of the frozen coconut milk and dissolve in one cup of warm water.

Desiccated coconut

Add 2 cups desiccated coconut to 1½ cups hot water. Blend at high speed for 1 min. Then squeeze out the milk.

Low fat milk

This can be used as a substitute, especially for making cakes and desserts.

Coriander

c: *kwentru*

m: *ketumbar*

The dried seed of the coriander plant. Used as a spice, it is considered indispensable to Cristang curries. The small, round seeds must be dry-roasted to release their fragrance before they are blended with other spices. The Cristang brew coriander seeds in boiling water to make a tea, *char kwentru*, to bring down high fevers.

Coriander leaf

c: *foler kwentru*

Cristang cooks use the leaf of the coriander plant whole for garnishing dishes and finely chopped for flavouring soups and stews.

Cumin or cummin

c: *ebra brancu*

m: *jintan putih*

The spindle-shaped seed of an aromatic plant belonging to the carrot family. This curry spice is always used together with fennel seeds in Cristang cuisine.

Curry leaf

c: *foler cari*

The leaf of an evergreen bush native to India and Sri Lanka. Commonly grown in Malaysia, this is the ingredient most responsible for giving South Indian curries their distinctive flavour. Not surprisingly, Cristang recipes for curries that have been borrowed from Indian cuisine require the use of this leaf. A sprig from the plant contains about two dozen small, dark green leaves, which can be dried and used when needed.

Daun kesom (*m*)

The leaf of a common herbaceous plant (*Polygonum minus*) that is found throughout Malaysia and known in the country only by its Malay name. Measuring 4–5 cm long and 1 cm wide and pointed at the apex, it is eaten in salads and cooked in curries. The leaf is rich in menthol and gives out a fragrance when crushed or sliced. It is also used medicinally by the Malays to make a decoction that is taken for indigestion and after childbirth.

Daun pegaga (*m*)

c: *foler rabaser*

The leaf of a creeper, also known as dragon plant, which grows wild in equatorial regions. Round and crinkly, this leaf is believed to have medicinal properties. It is used raw in sambals.

Dried prawn
c: *cambrang seccu*
m: *udang kering*

A small prawn that has been sun-dried. Often sold in small packets, dried prawns have a distinctive fishy flavour that cannot be obtained from fresh prawns. Wash thoroughly and soak in hot water for 10 min. before using. However, soaking is not desirable if the prawns are to be pounded and fried in hot oil for use as a garnish.

Fennel
c: *ebra doce*
m: *jintan manis*

The seed of the fennel, an aromatic plant that the Cristang call sweet grass. Slightly whiter and fatter than cumin, it has a sweet fragrance similar to that of aniseed. Fennel seeds are always used with cumin and coriander in Cristang cuisine.

Galangal
c: *lengkuas*

This herb has a ginger-like root with a faint flavour of camphor. The Cristang use it especially in fish curries. Galangal must be used sparingly because, unlike ginger, it imparts a bitter taste when used excessively. Galangal powder and dried slices of galangal are available outside Malaysia. Use the required amount of galangal powder (and no more!) when a recipe calls for it. If this ingredient is unavailable, omit it or replace with lemon grass.

Garlic
c: *arlu*

A bulbous plant probably originating in central Asia, known for its curative properties. Garlic is used with abandon in Cristang curries, soups, and vegetable and meat dishes. Thinly sliced garlic is fried and used to garnish fish and pickled chillies. Care must be taken not to burn the garlic when frying or it will take on a bitter taste. When cooking meat, make sure the garlic and meat are not added at the same time as this will toughen the meat. Add the garlic first and wait until its aroma is released before adding the meat.

Ginger
c: *gingibri*

The underground stem of a reed-like plant found in Asia. Its fibrous roots have a characteristic hot flavour. It is used in various forms in cookery and medicine. When a recipe states that a slice of ginger is needed, cut a slice about 3 mm (⅛ in.) thick. Store fresh ginger wrapped in newspaper in the refrigerator or clean and soak it in an earthen jar filled with sherry; the liquor can be used for cooking later.

Krill
c: *gerago*

A very small, fine shrimp with long whiskers that appears seasonally in the Straits of Malacca. Cristang fishermen use a triangular bamboo pole push-net (langgiang) to trap it. Krill is made into a relish called *chinchaluk* by adding hot boiled rice and salt. The mixture is put in bottles and brandy is added to help it ferment. After 2–3 days the mixture matures and is ready to be eaten as a relish. Chinchaluk is very salty, and the addition of lime juice, shallots and chillies helps reduce the saltiness.

Lady's fingers
c: *bredu dedufemi*
m: *kacang bendi*

Also known as okra, lady's fingers are the immature seed pods of a plant belonging to the hibiscus family. This vegetable exudes a sticky sap when cut. It makes a delectable salad when tossed in a dressing of shrimp paste with lime juice or vinegar, or chilli paste and dried prawns.

Lemon grass
c: *seray*
m: *serai*

A grass native to Southeast Asia and favoured by the Cristang for curries, sambals and seafood soups. It grows in clumps of tall slim reeds. The pale, bulbous part of the plant is usually sliced or finely chopped before it is blended with other spices. If it is unavailable, substitute with lemon zest or with dried lemon peel that has been soaked in hot water.

Lily bud
c: *arguler oru*

The dried bud of the tiger lily. The golden buds are about 10 cm long. Prepare the buds by snipping off the hard knob and tips. Then tie each one into a knot and soak in cool water for at least 15 min.

Lime
c: *limang*
m: *limau nipis*

A citrus fruit closely related to the lemon. Rounded, with light or dark green peel, it is smaller, more fragrant and juicier than a lemon. Cristang recipes often require the use of lime juice; it is most often added to food just before serving. Lemons are an acceptable substitute for this fruit.

Long bean
c: *kachang kumpridu*
m: *kacang panjang*

A variety of bean with an edible pod. Its name is an apt description, for this vegetable grows up to 80 cm in length. It is popular in Cristang cuisine. A high source of protein and fibre, it has an undeserved reputation for causing wind. The Cristang usually slice this vegetable into small diagonal pieces and lengths of 4 cm for curry dishes.

Mung bean
c: *mungoo*
m: *kacang hijau*

The small green seed of a leguminous plant native to India and with the same name. The Cristang transform this humble bean, which is usually sold dried, into an irresistible dessert, called canje mungoo (p 146), by cooking it in palm sugar, ginger and coconut milk. Canje mungoo is an important food served on 24 June each year during the Feast of St John (p 8). Bean sprouts come from this bean.

Mushroom (black or winter)
c: *chindawan*
ch: *tungku*

An edible fungus introduced to Malacca by the Chinese. Believed to be an aphrodisiac and to possess curative properties, it is the most popular type of mushroom among the Cristang. Black mushrooms can be obtained dried or fresh, though the former is preferred by Cristang cooks. The Japanese know this fungus as *shiitake* and prefer it fresh. To use the dried form, first soak in hot water for 30 min.; then remove and discard the tough stems and use the caps as required. The liquid obtained from soaking can be used to prepare a sauce or gravy for the dish.

Mustard seed
c: *biji sawi*

The tiny, dark brown or black coloured seed of the mustard, a herbaceous plant, originating from the Mediterranean region. The Cristang use mustard seeds in garnishes and pickles. To bring out the fragrance of these seeds, fry them in a little hot oil before adding to a

dish. Mustard seeds are also the main ingredient of mustard. For example, the pungent English mustard is made from mustard seeds and turmeric. When mixed with water, two substances present in crushed mustard seeds—myronate and myrosin—release a volatile and piquant essence that gives mustard its unique flavour.

Noodles
c: *mi-tiau*

Long, thin strips of dough made from flour, water and sometimes egg and resembling pasta. The Cristang use three different types:

Kuih tiau farinhia
Traditionally made at home with wheat flour mixed with a pinch of salt and water to form a dough. The dough is fried quickly in a greased flat pan, rolled and then cut up into bite-sized strips with a ladle or a knife. The noodles are then fried again with pounded chillies and other ingredients.

Fresh wheat noodles
Usually available from the market. These noodles, which are usually cooked on auspicious occasions, have a distinct yellow colour from the boric acid that is used to give them their firm texture; they are fried with other ingredients to make *mi annu* (p 130), an elaborate one-dish meal.

Soh hoon or glass vermicelli
Usually added to soups to increase bulk and is an important ingredient in bredu chapchye (p 86), a traditional dish of mixed vegetables. This noodle must be soaked before use.

Nutmeg
c: *nozzer*

The seed of the nutmeg tree native to Indonesia and widely cultivated in Asia. It has a spicy flavour

and aroma and is always used grated. It loses its flavour quickly and should be stored in its shell and used as soon as possible after grating. Nutmeg is a popular spice for flavouring desserts.

Onion
c: *cebola*

A plant whose bulb is used in cooking; technically, the bulb consists of a stem and layers of leaves enclosed in a thin papery skin. The leaves provide food reserves for the shoot that will grow from the centre of the onion. Cultivated for over five thousand years and widely used, the onion is known as the king of vegetables.

The two varieties often used in Cristang cuisine are the Bombay onion, which has a red skin, and the Spanish onion, which has a brown skin. These onions are not the same as shallots but can be substituted for the latter. In Cristang dishes onions are usually cut into quarters or lengths, or sliced into rings and then fried or sautéed and used as a garnish.

Pepper
c: *pimenta*

A condiment derived from the berry-like fruit (peppercorns) of the pepper plant. Depending on the stage of maturity at which the peppercorns are harvested, black, white or even green pepper is obtained. The Cristang use freshly ground black pepper in certain curries and roasts. Ground white pepper is not as important in Cristang cookery.

Rice
c: *arroz*

The grain of the paddy plant, rice is the most important staple in the Cristang diet. It is usually boiled and when properly cooked, should be fluffy, grainy and pure white.

The cooking of rice is an important part of Cristang cookery and the amount of water used makes all the difference between a pot of perfectly cooked rice and a disaster. Cristang cooks put their index finger on the surface of the rice and add water until it comes up to the first flange or joint. Apart from boiled rice, the Cristang also eat rice porridge and fried rice.

Glutinous rice, both the white (*pulut*) and black (*pulut hitam*) varieties, is flavoured with palm sugar, screw pine leaves and coconut milk and made into cakes and sweets.

Sago

c: *sagu*

A starch from the pith of the sago and other palm trees. Available today in hard, dry grains, sago was a major commodity item for several hundred years: Malacca was the centre of the sago trade in the mid-nineteenth century.

The pith is grated to a fine powder and kneaded with water over a strainer through which the starch passes into a trough below, leaving any woody fibre behind. To obtain sago grains, the meal is remixed with water to form a paste which is then rubbed through a sieve.

Salted mustard cabbage

c: *sayur assin*

ch: *hum choy*

Introduced by the Chinese, this is a pickled form of mustard cabbage, a vegetable resembling head cabbage. Preserved in brine, the cabbage has a very salty and sour taste and must be washed and soaked in warm water before use. The Cristang use it sparingly, occasionally in soups. The leaves may be cooked whole or cut up and added to fish curry to give it a piquant taste. The stalks are finely chopped and mixed with young ginger, juli-enned, and slices of shallots and chillies are added to make a mouthwatering relish called *jeruk*.

Salted soya beans

c: *taucho*

ch: *taucheong*

A condiment with the consistency of a paste, consisting of salted soya beans steeped in a light brown sauce. Generally sold in jars, two kinds are available with either whole or mashed beans. Unless specified otherwise, use the kind with whole beans for the recipes in this book.

Screw pine leaf

c: *foler pandan*

m: *daun pandan*

The long dark green leaf of *Pandanus amaryllifalius*. It is used to flavour cakes and sweet porridge, releasing a fragrance when boiled; an extract from this leaf is used to colour food green. The Cristang also use this leaf for flavouring syrup, boiled rice and raw prawns. Besides being used in cooking, screw pine leaves are shredded for a floral pot-pourri called *bunga rampeh,* which is used to scent the bridal chamber and the house on auspicious occasions. Fresh whole leaves kept in cupboards are said to keep cockroaches out.

Sea snail

c: *siput chupaku*

m: *siput sedut*

A mollusc with a dark grey spiral shell, approximately 2.5 cm long. Before cooking, wash the snails thoroughly under a cold running tap. Then snip off a bit of the pointed tip and cook well. To eat it, suck the meat out of the shell.

Semolina

c: *sugee*

A food obtained from coarsely grinding a cereal, mainly wheat, into granules. The Cristang use semolina only for making cakes, particularly the tiered wedding cake. (See recipe for sugee kek, p 152.)

Shallot

c: *cebola keninu*

m: *bawang merah*

A vegetable related to the onion and originating in the Middle East. The flavour of the shallot is more subtle than that of the onion and less pungent than that of garlic. It is widely used in Cristang cookery as an ingredient in curries, usually blended into a paste together with curry spices. One Spanish onion substitutes for 6–8 shallots.

Shrimp paste

c: *belachan*

m: *belacan*

A paste made from shrimps, used to enhance the flavour of fish or sambal dishes. This condiment is almost never used for cooking meat. Many find it hard to believe that such a strong smelling ingredient has such a wide appeal, but it is essential to Cristang cookery. In the past, Cristang women were famous for making this ingredient from scratch, beginning with the fresh shrimps their menfolk caught daily. The women cleaned the shrimps of grit and dried them in the sun before pounding them into a paste.

Most recipes that require belachan also call for it to be toasted. Although vacuum-packed boxes of pretoasted granules are available in supermarkets, this ingredient tastes best if toasted fresh. Take the amount required, wrap it in aluminum foil and toast in a dry wok or pan until the aroma emanating from it is at its strongest. In a simpler method no foil is used, and the paste is toasted until it crumbles into a fine, dry powder.

The toasted paste is the primary ingredient in sambal belachan (see p 62). Believed to have originated in Indonesia, sambal belachan is a necessary condiment for many Cristang at mealtime.

Silver threadfish

c: *karing-karing*

A small fish about 20 cm long and 1 cm wide, found in the seas of South Asia; also called *layor-layor*. Freshly caught fish are cleaned, gutted and carefully slit all the way down to the tail; they are then salted and dried four abreast in a cluster that resembles a duck's feathers. These clusters are dried in the sun for several days and sold in packets of ten. When deep-fried to a golden colour, *karing-karing* has a crisp texture and is an excellent accompaniment to drinks. During colonial days, British planters savoured this snack, which was called Bombay duck, with their *stengah*s (beer).

Soy sauce

c: *soy*

A dark, salty sauce made from fermented soya beans. Generally, Cristang cookery uses two kinds of soy sauces: thin and thick. Soy sauces are used for marinating meat and for seasoning fried fish and a number of vegetable dishes.

Spring onion

c: *foler cebola*

A young bulb onion whose shoots and leaves are eaten. Known as scallions in the United States and shallots in Australia, spring onions make an excellent garnish for soups, fried dishes and roasts. They can be sliced diagonally or into tiny rings or chopped into 2.5-cm lengths; the white bulb can be cut into florets for garnishing (p 26).

Star anise

c: *strela*

m: *bunga lawang*

The dried star-shaped fruit of an evergreen tree belonging to the magnolia family, native to China. This spice has five points with small, shiny seeds in them. The Cristang use it to make stew spice powder and flavour curries. As suggested by its name, star anise contains an aniseed flavour resulting from the presence of an oil similar to that found in anise.

Sugar (palm, rock)

c: *sucre*

Palm sugar is extracted from the sap of the coconut palm. The sap is allowed to dry and solidify into cylindrical blocks which are then wrapped in dried coconut leaves. The sugar has a dark brown colour and tastes of coconut. Locally known as *gula Melaka* (Malacca candy), the Cristang call it *jaggre* and often use it in their sweets and cakes.

Rock sugar is cane sugar allowed to crystallize to pieces the size of big pebbles. Traditionally, this ingredient was used for sweetening syrups and drinks; today, however, castor sugar is preferred.

Sugar cane

c: *cana*

A member of the grass family, producing a sweet sap from which much of the world's sugar is derived. The sap, or sugar cane water as it is known in Malaysia, makes a refreshing and delicious drink.

Tamarind

c: *tambrinhyu*

m: *asam jawa*

The pulp obtained from the pod of a tree belonging to the pea family. It adds an appetizingly sour taste to food. Cristang curries and sambals, particularly fish dishes, require tamarind juice which is obtained by soaking the pulp in warm water. The juice helps to thicken gravies and is a good preservative.

Tamarind slice

c: *tambrinhyu*

m: *asam gelugur*

A sun-dried slice of the large-ribbed fruit of the *asam gelugur* tree. Not to be confused with tamarind or *asam jawa* (see previous entry) for which it is often a suitable substitute, this ingredient is added to soups and fish curries for its sour taste. It is, however, not as full in flavour as tamarind.

Toddy

c: *surer*

An alcoholic beverage made from the fermented sap of the coconut flower. This drink can prove intoxicating if consumed to excess. The Cristang use toddy to make blueda (p 144), a dough cake served on festive occasions.

Turmeric

c: *saffrang*

m: *kunyit*

A tropical herbaceous plant with an aromatic underground stem that is orange in colour. Often dried and crushed to a powder, the stem can be used as a spice and a colourant. The Cristang call this spice *saffrang* because it imparts a yellow colour similar to that of saffron. Nevertheless, in Cristang cookery turmeric is used to flavour curries only and never to colour food. In Malaysia, fresh turmeric may be bought in wet markets. Also grown in many homes, it is ground and blended with other spices and seasonings to make *masala* (spice mix) for curries. The use of turmeric in Cristang cuisine reflects Indian and Goan influence.

Water spinach

c: *kangkong*

A green vegetable with arrow-head-shaped leaves and a hollow stem that thrives in swampy or wet areas in equatorial regions. It is not related to Chinese spinach. True to its name, this vegetable has a high water content and may lose one-third of its original volume during cooking. Select plants that have short stalks with large leaves at the tip, as these are the most tender. The favourite method of cooking this popular vegetable is to stir-fry it quickly with onions, chillies and shrimp paste (belachan); the resulting dish is called *kangkong belachan*.

A tale about Malacca's hero warrior, Hang Tuah, tells of the time he was granted an audience with the Emperor of China. As was the custom, he was warned not to look at the Emperor's face; in fact, all who were in the Emperor's presence had to look down when addressing his Imperial Majesty.

At the royal banquet that evening Hang Tuah asked for a bowl of water spinach, taking great pains to explain that the vegetable had to be served whole and uncut. When the dish was brought to him, the crafty Hang Tuah, on the pretext of feeding himself the unmanageably long strands of the vegetable, lifted his head and caught a glimpse of the Emperor's face. Luckily for Hang Tuah, the Emperor was in good spirits that evening; he burst out laughing and commended Hang Tuah for his ingenuity.

Whitebait

c: *bilis*

m: *ikan bilis*

A tiny fish related to the herring, eaten when 4–5 cm long; the Malaysian answer to anchovy. Whitebait are usually salted and dried whole. Before cooking, discard the heads and dark intestinal tracts. This fish can be deep fried in hot oil and served as a snack.

Wood fungus

c: *ubider ratu*

ch: *mok yee*

An edible black fungus with a convoluted shape and a smooth, thick texture. It is sold dried and must be soaked in water before use; the resulting liquid is useless and should be discarded. Wood fungus has a mild flavour and is eaten for its crunchy texture; it may be cooked whole or shredded.

Yam bean

c: *bangkuang*

m: *sengkuang*

A tuber with sweet, white, juicy and crunchy flesh, belonging to the legume family. It is often eaten raw and is a popular ingredient in salads. Yam bean is also tasty when cooked. It makes a delicious filling in spring rolls when finely shredded and stir-fried with prawns or shredded meat. When buying yam bean, select unblemished ones, preferably those that have moist looking skins. Pick medium-sized tubers instead of large ones; the latter are too fibrous and are no longer tender or sweet.

Substitutes for fresh herbs and spices

Many of the fresh herbs and spices required in the recipes may be purchased in powdered form: turmeric, clove, ginger and even lemon grass, to name a few, may be found in supermarkets or specialist food shops. Consult the table below to work out the equivalent quantities in the event you are unable to obtain fresh ingredients.

Fresh	*Powdered*
5 g cardamom	¼ tsp.
150 g chilli	2 tsp.
20 g cinnamon stick	2 tsp.
10 g clove	1 tsp.
50 g coriander seed	2 tbsp.
10 g cumin	1 tsp.
10 g fennel	½ tsp.
25 g galangal	¼ tsp.
50 g garlic	1 tsp.
25 g ginger	1 tsp.
2 stalks lemon grass	½ tsp.
5 g nutmeg	¼ tsp.
5 g turmeric	1 tsp.

Using powdered ingredients to make fresh herb curry paste (p 28) reduces the bulk of the paste. To make up for this deficiency, use double the quantity of onions and garlic required in the recipe.

Powdered lemon grass or galangal should be used sparingly, as too much will make the dish taste bitter.

Timesaving alternatives

FROM MAGGI

In the past it was common for Cristang cooks to rise at dawn to prepare the spices or stocks they needed for the day's cooking. Painstakingly they would dry-roast and grind their coriander and cumin or cut up a chicken carcass for stock. The work was tedious to say the least.

These days most cooks have neither the time nor the patience to drag out their pilung tek-tek (pestle and mortar) to pound spices and chillies for a curry; nor are they inclined to fuss over the preparation of stocks, a chore that can take several hours. Fortunately, they no longer have to. Advancements in food and packaging technology have made it possible for cooks to obtain the spices and flavouring they need without having to go to such great lengths. Appearing in various forms such as cubes and powders, the products of these advancements come ready for the pot. Although purists might turn up their noses at the notion of using anything 'manufactured' or belonging to the category of 'instant food', these ingredients have become necessary additions to the larders of busy cooks everywhere.

Among the many brands of ready-to-use ingredients available in Malaysia, MAGGI is arguably the most popular. Produced by NESTLÉ, the venerable Swiss food company, MAGGI products have enjoyed a long, successful history in the country. Making its debut in 1969 with tomato ketchup, MAGGI expanded very quickly, introducing its now famous 2-Minute instant noodle range in 1972. Today MAGGI products include a host of prepared dishes and cooking aids, ranging from noodles, sauces, porridge and soups, to a variety of stock cubes, spice mixes and soy sauces.

However, it is not only the wide range and variety that have earned MAGGI products a place in Malaysian kitchens. This achievement is largely a result of the emphasis MAGGI has always placed on quality. Whether it is a simple soy sauce or a secret blend of spices for a dry curry, only the best ingredients go into MAGGI products. For example, MAGGI stock cubes, made from a high quality meat or seafood base, do not impart a starchy taste when added to a dish. I recommend the use of these cubes whenever there is little time to prepare stock from scratch. When using stock cubes in the recipes in this book, first dissolve them completely in hot water, then use as directed in the recipe. Use a quantity of water equal to half the amount of stock required.

MAGGI's toasted belachan (dried shrimp paste) granules are another product that I recommend when the fresh market variety

cannot be obtained. This product is a welcome timesaver for recipes that require belachan to be dry-roasted before further use. Time can also be saved if MAGGI's Rice Porridge is used in place of rice for cooking canje parpa (p 128). Because the recipe requires boiling the rice until it turns into porridge, preparing this dish can take up to two hours; with MAGGI's Rice Porridge, cooking time is reduced to approximately twenty minutes. Further culinary short-cuts are available in the form of MAGGI's Cook-It-Right range of spice mixes. Blends such as MAGGI Rendang Mix or Assam Fish mix do away with the need to dry, grind and roast spices. They may be used in dishes such as singgang cocu and chorka tambrinhyu (pp 55 and 102, respectively) in place of the spice blends prescribed.

Condiments and a range of ten different sauces also figure prominently in the MAGGI stable of products. Probably the best-known among these are MAGGI's Tomato Ketchup and Chilli Sauce which I usually serve to children as a substitute for sambal belachan (p 62). MAGGI's Oyster Sauce may be used for added flavour in place of salt or ordinary soy sauce in dishes such as bredu kachang cung baca, marergozu fretu and baca soy (pp 88, 94 and 135, respectively).

Clearly not all the ingredients mentioned in this book can or should be replaced with convenient substitutes; the cook should try to follow the recipes as closely as possible. However, when substitutes do become necessary (when the original ingredient is unavailable, for instance), it makes sense to use the best. MAGGI products, much to my delight, have consistently maintained their quality and have on more than a few occasions been of tremendous help to me when I unexpectedly ran out of an important ingredient or two.

Botah Fogu

CURRY THRILLERS

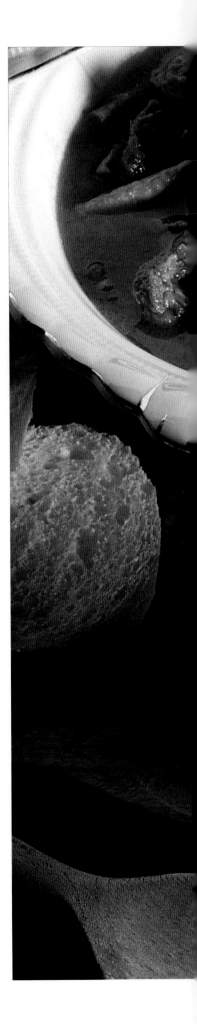

The sharp rhythmic chink of pestle striking mortar, emanating from many a Cristang home in the early morning heralds the start of the day's culinary activities; it is a sure sign that curry paste is being prepared.

Most Cristang cooks have two basic curry pastes in their repertoire. The first is a herb paste which is used in simple, everyday curries. It is made from fresh herbs, such as galangal, lemon grass, shallots, garlic and chillies. The second, called dry spice curry powder, is made from an assortment of spices, such as coriander, cumin, fennel and pepper and is sometimes blended with fresh herbs. Dry spice curry powder is used in meat and poultry curries that are cooked on special occasions.

The successful blending of spices and herbs is an art that requires a considerable amount of patience and practice. To achieve a satisfying and pungent curry flavour, the dried spices must first be roasted to release their fragrance. It is then necessary to blend or grind the herbs or spices to a very fine paste or powder. (See p 28.)

Coconut milk is another important ingredient in Cristang curries. Unlike spice blends which may be prepared days or even weeks in advance and kept until needed, coconut milk should be obtained fresh and used as soon as possible, for it tends to sour quickly. This ingredient imparts a rich, creamy flavour to curries which is difficult to duplicate with substitutes. However, because coconut milk has a high cholesterol content, it is sometimes preferable to use yoghurt and low fat or evaporated milk in its place, especially if a low cholesterol or restricted diet is being observed.

Although certain Cristang curries originated from Malay and Indian recipes, their textures and flavours are quite different from those of their progenitors; examples include cari seccu (p 51), debal (p 52), feng (p 54) and *lardeh* (p 54). Cristang curries generally have a pleasant piquant taste achieved by adding tamarind juice, vinegar, lime juice or sour fruits, such as young mango and unripened pineapple.

Ambiler kachang
Next to the tureen containing the ambiler kachang is a side dish of sambal belachan, a blend of toasted shrimp-paste and chillies (p 62). The fiery sambal is the perfect accompaniment to this sour long bean curry.

Ambiler kachang
(Sour long bean curry)

INGREDIENTS

½ kg stewing beef or any other
meat

200 g long beans or
4 (200 g) brinjals

3 tbsp. tamarind pulp

2 cups water

¼ cup oil

3 tbsp. fresh herb curry paste
(see p 28)

1 tsp. salt

sugar to taste

PREPARATION: 15 MIN.

1 Cut meat into bite-sized pieces.

2 Cut long beans or brinjals
crosswise into 5-cm lengths.

3 Soak tamarind pulp in water and
extract juice (see p 26).

METHOD: 20 MIN.

1 Heat oil in a tezaler (p 19). Put
in fresh herb paste and fry until
fragrant.

2 Add salt and a little tamarind
juice to prevent paste from
burning. Stir.

3 Add meat and stir well to coat
with paste. Add remaining tamarind juice and bring to a boil.
Then pour in enough water to
cover meat. Cover and simmer
for 10 min.

4 When meat is tender, add long
beans and cook for 5 min. Keep
gravy fairly thick; if it becomes
too watery, uncover and boil
rapidly for a few minutes to
reduce liquid.

5 If curry gets too sour, add a little
sugar. Stir and remove from heat.
Let stand for an hour to allow
flavours to develop. Serve with
rice or bread.

Serves 6 to 10

Cook's note This dish tastes better if kept
overnight before serving. Sambal belachan
and soy limang (pp 62 and 96, respectively)
go well with this dish.

To make fruit *ambiler*, use 1 half-ripe
pineapple sliced thickly or 20 peeled
rambutans and 1 kg large prawns.

Fruit ambiler should have a sweet-
and-sour taste and a thin gravy. Add fruit
in METHOD, STEP 4.

Cari Belanda
(Dutch chicken curry)

INGREDIENTS

1½ kg chicken

4 cups (320 g) grated coconut

4 cups warm water

fresh chilli sauce
2 (5 g) fresh red chillies
½ tsp. salt
lime or lemon juice to taste

garnish
5 (50 g) shallots, or ½ (50 g)
onion, peeled and sliced
3 cloves (9 g) garlic, peeled and
sliced thinly
2 (10 g) fresh red chillies, sliced
diagonally

½ cup oil

blended to a fine paste
2 tbsp. coriander powder
1 tbsp. cumin powder
1 tsp. pepper
10 (20 g) dried chillies,
presoaked
20 (200 g) shallots, or 2 (200 g)
onions, peeled
2 tsp. (10 g) turmeric, grated
2 tsp. (12 g) ginger, grated
2 cardamoms
3 cloves (9 g) garlic, peeled
6 (30 g) candlenuts, or
12 (30 g) blanched almonds

6 (300 g) potatoes, peeled and
halved

6–8 (150 g) large cabbage leaves,
left whole

1 tbsp. lime or lemon juice

salt to taste

sugar to taste

PREPARATION: 30 MIN.

1 Cut chicken into large pieces.

2 Soak coconut in warm water and
extract 1 cup thick and 3 cups
thin milk (see p 26).

3 To make chilli sauce, blend
chillies with salt, then add lime
juice to taste. Set aside.

METHOD: 25 MIN.

1 To prepare garnish, fry shallots,
garlic and chillies in 2 tbsp. of
the oil for 2 min. in a small pan;
remove and set aside to drain on
paper towels.

2 In a tezaler (p 19), add remaining
oil and fry blended ingredients
until fragrant and oil rises to the
surface.

3 Add chicken and continue
frying, stirring well for 5 min.

4 Pour in 1 cup of the thin coconut
milk. Cover and simmer until
meat is tender, about 10 min.

5 Add potatoes and remaining thin
coconut milk, followed by thick
milk; stir well.

6 Simmer 5 min., then add
cabbage leaves.

7 Simmer another 5 min., then
add lime juice and salt to taste.

8 If too sour, add a little sugar.
Bring to a boil, then remove
from heat.

9 Garnish with fried shallots,
garlic and chilli from STEP 1
before serving with rice or
noodles.

Serves 6 to 8

Cari Belanda
This Dutch chicken curry—served here with rice—is
mild enough for young palates and for taste buds
unaccustomed to hot curries. The chilli sauce served
with it adds more bite if required.

Cari keluak (right)
This slightly medicinal-tasting dish is fast becoming a best-seller in Nyonya restaurants in Malacca today. The black keluak nuts are in the foreground.

Cari papair cung siput chupaku (below)
The side dish pictured with the cari papair is sambal chinchaluk (p 66), a piquant relish which complements the delicate taste of this curry perfectly.

Cari keluak
(Indonesian black nut curry)

INGREDIENTS

20 Indonesian black nuts,
   presoaked in cold water 3–4 days
   before using

2 tbsp. tamarind pulp

3 cups water

1½ kg chicken or any other meat

½ cup oil

blended to a fine paste
   2 (200 g) onions, peeled and
      quartered
   4 tbsp. fresh herb curry paste
      (see p 28)

1 tbsp. crushed rock sugar
   (optional)

1 stalk lemon grass, bruised

salt to taste

PREPARATION: 20 MIN.

1 Clean presoaked nuts and cut
   open at the smooth part.

2 Soak tamarind pulp in water and
   extract juice (see p 26).

3 Cut chicken into large pieces.

METHOD: 30 MIN.

1 Heat oil in a pan. Put in blended
   ingredients and stir-fry for 2–4
   min. until fragrant. If necessary,
   add 1 tbsp. of the tamarind juice
   to prevent spices from burning.

2 Add 2 cups of the tamarind
   juice, followed by Indonesian
   black nuts and chicken.

3 Simmer, stirring occasionally.
   Add more water if necessary
   until there is enough liquid to
   cover meat and nuts. Cover and
   simmer for 15 min. until meat is
   cooked.

4 Add remaining tamarind juice,
   followed by rock sugar and
   lemon grass. Cover again and

cook for another 15 min. The
gravy should be thick and black.

5 Add salt to taste; stir gently until
   curry boils. Remove from heat.
   Let curry stand for at least 30
   min. before serving.

Serves 6 to 8

Cook's note Always buy at least 10% more
nuts than required as, quite often, there are
some bad ones in the lot. Choose nuts
individually. Good ones are heavier and do
not have a hollow sound when tapped with
the finger, nor do they rattle when shaken.
Pengui medulae, as the black nut is known
scientifically, is a native of Brazil though it
is also grown in Indonesia where it is
seasonally available from wet markets. To
eat the black nut, insert a fork into the
cavity and scoop out the black kernel.

Cari papair cung siput chupaku
(Papaya and sea snail curry)

INGREDIENTS

400 g half-ripe papaya

400 g sea snails or fresh prawns

4 cups (320 g) grated coconut

4 cups warm water

blended to a fine paste
   1 tbsp. dried prawns, presoaked
   1 (5 g) fresh red chilli
   3 (15 g) candlenuts, or 6 (15 g)
      blanched almonds
   20 (200 g) shallots,
      or 2 (200 g) onions, peeled
   2 tsp. toasted shrimp paste
      (belachan)
   2 tsp. coriander powder
   2 tbsp. fresh herb curry paste
      (see p 28)

¼ cup oil

salt and sugar to taste

PREPARATION: 20 MIN.

1 Peel papaya and cut in half
   lengthwise. Discard seeds and
   cut across into thick slices.

2 Wash sea snails thoroughly in
   cold water, discarding any with
   smashed shells. Use a heavy
   chopper to chip off the pointed
   tips of shells. If using prawns,
   rinse well, remove heads and
   leave unshelled.

3 Soak coconut in warm water and
   extract 1 cup thick milk and 3
   cups thin milk (see p 26).

METHOD: 25 MIN.

1 Heat oil in a tezaler (p 19). Add
   thin coconut milk and blended
   paste and bring to a boil, stirring
   continuously.

2 Lower heat, add sea snails or
   prawns and simmer for 10 min.

3 Put in papaya and cook for
   another 5 min.

4 Add thick coconut milk. To
   prevent curdling, stir
   continuously until the gravy
   starts to simmer, then add salt
   and sugar to taste before
   removing from heat. Serve with
   rice.

Serves 4 to 6

Cook's note *Obu trubo* (p 107) makes a good
accompaniment to this dish.

Cari pimenta (right)
Some of the spices used in this peppery
dish are shown here on a large brass tray
of Indian origin.

Cari seccu (left)
This dry mutton curry is a delicate
combination of lime, coconut milk and
toasted grated coconut.

Cari pimenta

(Pepper curry)

INGREDIENTS

1 kg fresh pomfret or skate

1 tbsp. coarse salt

4 (350 g) brinjals, long variety

blended to a fine paste

20 (200 g) shallots, or 2 (200 g)
onions, peeled

2 (10 g) green chillies

1 (30 g) bulb garlic, peeled

2 stalks lemon grass (use 7 cm
of root end)

5 g turmeric, peeled

15 g galangal, peeled

6 (30 g) candlenuts, or 12 (30 g)
blanched almonds

1 tbsp. coriander powder

2 tsp. cumin powder

2 tsp. fennel powder

2 tsp. black peppercorns

2 tsp. toasted shrimp paste
(belachan)

2 tbsp. tamarind pulp

4 cups water

½ cup oil

salt and sugar to taste

PREPARATION: 15 MIN.

1 Cut fish into large pieces. Rub
with coarse salt to remove any
slime and odour. Rinse well,
drain and set aside.

2 Cut brinjals lengthwise into
halves and score the white flesh.
Soak in a bowl of water.

3 Soak tamarind pulp in 2 cups of
the water and extract juice (see
p 26).

METHOD: 20 MIN.

1 Heat oil in a tezaler (p 19). Fry
blended ingredients until fragrant and oil rises to the surface.

2 Pour in ½ cup of the water. Stir
and simmer for 5 min., then add
remaining 1½ cups of water.

3 Add brinjals, fish and tamarind
juice. Stir gently without breaking fish up, then simmer for
5 min.

4 Add salt and sugar to taste. The
gravy should be thin; add more
water if necessary. Serve at once
with rice or bread.

Serves 6 to 8

Cook's note This curry should have a thin
gravy with a greenish colour. Simple
accompaniments such as sambal belachan
(p 62) best complement this dish.

Cari seccu

(Dry mutton curry)

INGREDIENTS

½ kg boneless mutton or lamb

4 cups (320 g) grated coconut and
3 cups warm water; or 2 tbsp.
grated coconut, ¼ cup yoghurt
and 2 cups low fat milk

*mixed together or use 4 tbsp. dry spice
curry powder (see p 28)*

2 tbsp. roasted ground coriander

1 tbsp. roasted ground cumin

½ tbsp. roasted ground fennel

2 tsp. ground black pepper

½ tsp. turmeric powder

blended to a fine paste

25 (250 g) shallots, or 2½
(250 g) onions, peeled

6 cloves (18 g) garlic, peeled

6 (10 g) dried chillies,
presoaked in hot water

30 g young ginger, peeled and
shredded

3 (15 g) candlenuts, or 6 (15 g)
blanched almonds

½ tsp. oil

6 (650 g) potatoes, peeled

1 cup oil

6 cloves

1 star anise

2 cinnamon sticks, 6-cm lengths

3 tbsp. lime or lemon juice

salt to taste

PREPARATION: 10 MIN.

1 Cut mutton into bite-sized
pieces and set aside.

2 Dry-roast 2 tbsp. of the grated
coconut until golden. Set aside.

3 If using coconut milk, soak
remaining grated coconut in 2
cups of the warm water and
extract thick and thin coconut
milk (see p 26).

4 Combine 2 tbsp. thick coconut
milk with spices; mix well to
form a paste. Set aside.

5 If using yoghurt and low fat
milk, mix yoghurt with mixed
spices and blended paste. Set
aside.

6 Boil potatoes whole and drain
well. Fry in ½ cup of the oil until
golden. Set aside to drain on
paper towels.

METHOD: 40–45 MIN.

A (using coconut milk)

1 Heat remaining oil in a tezaler
(p 19). When moderately hot,
add spice mixture and blended
paste. Stir-fry until fragrant and
oil floats to the surface.

2 Add cloves, star anise and
cinnamon sticks. Stir-fry for 1
min. Add meat and 1 tbsp. thin
coconut milk; stir-fry for another
minute. Add remaining cup of
warm water. Lower heat and
simmer until meat is tender,
about 35 min.

3 Pour in remaining thin and thick
coconut milk and bring to a slow
boil.

4 Add fried potatoes and lime
juice. Stir and add salt to taste.

continued on p 52

from p 51, *Cari seccu*

5 Stir curry continuously to prevent coconut milk from curdling. Keep stirring until almost dry, then sprinkle roasted coconut on top. Toss well until coconut is evenly distributed, then remove from heat.

B (using yoghurt and low fat milk)

1 Heat remaining oil in a tezaler. Put in meat and stir-fry for 3 min. Add yoghurt mixture from PREPARATION, STEP 5 and cook for 10 min., stirring well.

2 Add 1 cup of the low fat milk. Simmer until meat is tender, about 35 min. Add remaining cup of milk and stir. Lower heat and add salt to taste. Simmer until gravy thickens.

3 Add lime juice and fried potatoes. Stir until curry is almost dry, then add roasted coconut. Toss well until coconut is evenly distributed, then remove from heat.

This is a dry (*seccu*) curry, so the meat should be just barely coated with gravy. Let stand for 30 min. before serving.

Serves 6 to 10

Debal (Devil curry)

INGREDIENTS

1 kg chicken

1 tsp. thick soy sauce

3 tbsp. vinegar

blended to a fine paste
    1 tsp. oil
    1 tsp. mustard seeds
    30 (300 g) shallots, or 3 (300 g)
      onions, peeled
    3 cloves (9 g) garlic, peeled
    6 (30 g) candlenuts, or 12 (30 g)

    blanched almonds
    3 stalks lemon grass (use 7 cm
      of root end)
    30 g galangal, peeled
    ¼ tsp. turmeric powder
    20 (40 g) dried chillies
      presoaked in hot water, or
      2 tbsp. chilli powder

½ kg roast beef, optional (see p 119)

1 tbsp. tamarind pulp

½ cup water

½ cup oil

30 g young ginger, julienned

2 (200 g) onions, peeled and quartered

4 (10 g) fresh red chillies, slit with stalks retained

1 tsp. mustard seeds

6 (600 g) potatoes, peeled and quartered

optional
    6 (60 g) whole cabbage leaves
    20 (200 g) French beans, sliced
      into two and split

salt and sugar to taste

PREPARATION: 25 MIN.

1 Cut chicken into large pieces and marinade with thick soy sauce, 1 tbsp. of the vinegar and 2 tsp. of the blended paste. Set aside for 20 min.

2 If using roast beef, cut it into bite-sized pieces and set aside.

3 Soak tamarind pulp in ½ cup water and extract 1 tbsp. juice (see p 26).

METHOD: 25 MIN.

1 Heat oil in a tezaler (p 19). Put in strips of ginger; fry till golden brown and remove. Next, sauté onions for 30 sec. and remove. Then sauté red chillies and remove.

2 Put mustard seeds into the same pot. Cover until seeds stop popping. Add remaining paste and fry until oil floats to the top.

3 Drain marinade from chicken pieces and add marinade gradually to fried paste in the pot, stirring continuously to prevent burning.

4 Add chicken and potatoes and toss to coat well with paste. Add 1 tbsp. of the tamarind juice and enough water to cover chicken.

5 Boil rapidly for 10 min., then lower heat. If using cabbage leaves and French beans, add them now. Simmer until vegetables are done and chicken is tender; then stir in remaining 2 tbsp. of vinegar.

6 If using roast beef, add it now, followed by fried ginger, onions and chillies from STEP 1. Cook for 5 min.

7 Add salt and sugar to taste. If necessary, add water to make gravy and stir well. Simmer for 5 min., then remove from heat. Let stand for at least 30 min.; then serve with rice. This dish will taste even better if kept overnight before serving.

Serves 6 to 8

Cook's note Lime or lemon juice may be substituted for tamarind juice. Use 4–5 limes or ½ medium-sized lemon per tablespoon of tamarind juice.

I would like to dedicate this recipe to my sons Julian and Ju Ming, as debal is their favourite dish.

Debal
In the past, every Cristang kitchen had a set of tezalers or earthen pots such as the one in which this devil curry is served. Traditional Cristang cooks believe a well-seasoned tezaler imparts a special flavour to curries, which modern metal pots cannot duplicate.

In the background is an old photograph of the twin towers of St Francis Xavier's Church. The wooden foot-bridge linked the Portuguese fortress with the suburb of Upeh (today known as Tengkera), the commercial quarter of Malacca in the sixteenth century.

Feng (Mixed meat curry)

INGREDIENTS

200 g topside beef

10 cloves

2 star anise

4 cinnamon sticks, 5-cm lengths

2 tsp. salt plus additional to taste

200 g ox tongue

200 g ox liver

1 cup oil

30 g young ginger, julienned

blended to a fine paste
    6 cloves (18 g) garlic, peeled
    30 (300 g) shallots, or 3 (300 g)
      onions, peeled

3 tbsp. vinegar

mixed to a paste with 1 tbsp. of the vinegar and 2 tbsp. water
    4 tbsp. ground coriander
    1 tbsp. ground cumin
    1 tbsp. ground fennel
    2 tsp. ground black pepper
    1 tsp. turmeric powder

sugar to taste

1 tsp. stew spice powder (see p 28)

PREPARATION: 50 MIN.

1 Put beef in a pot with enough water to cover. Add 6 of the cloves, 1 star anise, 2 of the cinnamon sticks and 2 tsp. of the salt. Boil until meat is half cooked, about 10 min., and remove from pot, leaving spices behind.

2 Immerse tongue in the same liquid, adding water, if necessary, to cover meat. Bring to a boil and cook for 25 min. Remove. Scrape skin off tongue and rinse in warm water. Set aside.

3 Add liver to the same liquid and boil for 5 min.; then remove. Reserve liquid, which will be used as stock.

4 Dice beef, tongue and liver into 1-cm square pieces.

METHOD: 30 MIN.

1 Heat oil in a pan and fry ginger strips. Add the remaining cloves, star anise and cinnamon sticks. Fry until fragrant and lower heat.

2 Add blended garlic and shallots followed by spice mixture; stir-fry for 1 min. If paste threatens to burn, add a little of the stock made in PREPARATION, STEP 3.

3 Add beef and tongue and remaining 2 tbsp. of vinegar; stir-fry on low heat until meats are tender, about 10 min.

4 Add diced liver. Cook for 3 min., keeping meats moist by adding a little stock. Add salt and sugar to taste. Stir well.

5 Sprinkle stew spice powder on top and cook for another 2 min. before removing from heat.

6 Let dish stand for at least 30 min. or, for fuller flavour, keep it overnight before serving.

Serves 10

Cook's note Among the Cristang, feng is a must at Christmas and wedding dinners. The secret of this dish's full-bodied flavour lies in the blending and simmering of different meats over low heat and in allowing the dish to sit overnight before serving. The Goan dish *sorpotel* is similar to feng. Traditionally, pig's entrails and offal were used.

Lardeh (Spicy meat curry)

INGREDIENTS

350 g stewing beef

350 g ox liver or tongue

marinade
    2 tsp. stew spice powder
    (see p 28)

    1 tbsp. vinegar
    1 tbsp. thin soy sauce

dry-roasted in a dry, heated pan
    3 tbsp. ground coriander
    1 tbsp. ground cumin
    ½ tbsp. ground fennel

2 tbsp. water

blended to a fine paste
    20 (200 g) shallots, or 2 (200 g)
      onions, peeled
    6 cloves (18 g) garlic, peeled
    10 (50 g) candlenuts, or 20
      (50 g) blanched almonds
    2 tsp. black peppercorns

½ cup oil

6 (15 g) dried chillies, halved

30 g young ginger, sliced thinly

4 cups meat stock (see p 27) or water

salt and sugar to taste

PREPARATION: 25 MIN.

1 Cut meat and liver into bite-sized pieces, mix with marinade and set aside for 20 min.

2 Mix dry-roasted spices with the 2 tbsp. of water. Mix resulting paste with blended ingredients and set aside.

METHOD: 25 MIN.

1 Heat oil and fry liver for 1 min.; remove and set aside to drain.

2 Fry dried chillies and ginger in the same oil. Add paste mixture and fry until fragrant.

3 Drain marinade from meats and add it gradually to paste in pan. Fry for 30 sec.

4 Add beef and toss well to coat with paste. Sauté for 2 min., adding enough stock gradually to cover meat. Simmer until beef is tender, about 15 min.

5 Add fried liver from STEP I. Lower heat and simmer for 5 min. Add salt and sugar to taste and stir. Be careful not to overcook liver; remove from heat as soon as it is tender. Let stand for 10 min. before serving with boiled rice or bread.

Serves 6 to 10

Cook's note The gravy should be thick; hence the use of candlenuts, which are ideal for thickening sauces and gravies.

Mohlyu (Seafood in spicy coconut sauce)

INGREDIENTS

30 fishballs, or 20 (about 300 g) medium-sized prawns and 1 tbsp. coarse salt

5 (250 g) brinjals, long variety

4 cups (320 g) grated coconut and 4 cups warm water; or 1 cup (80 g) grated coconut, 3 cups low fat milk and ½ cup yoghurt

dry-roasted together
    4 tbsp. coriander powder
    2 tbsp. black peppercorns

1 tsp. turmeric powder

20 (200 g) shallots, or 2 (200 g) onions, peeled

1 tsp. toasted shrimp paste (belachan)

2 tbsp. fresh herb curry paste (see p 28)

2 tbsp. vinegar

garnish (optional)
    5 (50 g) shallots, peeled
    3 cloves (9 g) garlic, peeled

½ cup oil

½ tsp. salt plus additional to taste

1 tbsp. lime or lemon juice

1 Rinse fishballs and drain. If using prawns, remove heads, leaving shells intact. Rub with coarse salt to remove any slime and odour. Leave for 5 min.; then rinse well and drain.

2 Slit brinjals lengthwise down the middle, leaving about 5 cm from stalk uncut. Slit each section down the middle again. Each brinjal should now have 4 sections, all attached to the stalk.

3 Dry-roast 1 cup grated coconut until golden. Set aside to cool.

4 Soak remaining coconut in warm water and extract 1 cup thick and 3 cups thin coconut milk (see p 26).

5 Blend dry-roasted coriander and peppercorns with turmeric powder, onions, shrimp paste and dry-roasted coconut.

6 Mix resulting paste with fresh herb curry paste. Moisten with vinegar, stirring well. Set aside.

7 To prepare garnish, fry shallots and garlic in 2 tbsp. of the oil until crispy. Set aside to drain.

8 In the same pan, sauté brinjals for 1 minute. Remove and set aside to drain.

METHOD: 25 MIN.

1 Heat remaining oil in a tezaler (p 19) and add blended ingredients from PREPARATION, STEP 5. Stir-fry for 2–3 min.

2 Add 1 tbsp. thick coconut milk and salt. Stir well.

3 Add thin coconut milk and bring to a slow boil.

4 Add brinjals, and when they are half cooked, add fishballs and simmer.

5 When fishballs are cooked (about 10 min.), pour in remaining coconut milk. If using low fat milk and yogurt, add them now.

6 Stir and season with salt and lime juice to taste.

7 Stir gently once more, then sprinkle garnish on top and remove from heat.

Serves 8 to 10

Cook's note The word *mohlyu* in modern Portuguese means gravy or sauce, so make sure there is plenty of gravy when serving this curry.

Freshly made sambal belachan (p 62) is an excellent accompaniment to this dish.

Singgang cocu (Coconut curry)

INGREDIENTS

1 (1½ kg) dorab, or 1 kg big prawns

1 tbsp. coarse salt

10 (100 g) belimbing

4 cups (320 g) grated coconut

4 cups warm water

½ cup oil

blended to a fine paste
    2 stalks lemon grass (use 7 cm of root end)
    3 (15 g) candlenuts, or 6 (15 g) blanched almonds
    20 (40 g) dried chillies, presoaked in hot water
    25 (250 g) shallots, or 2½ (250 g) onions, peeled
    1 bulb (50 g) garlic, peeled
    5 g turmeric, peeled
    1 tsp. toasted shrimp paste (belachan)

2–3 citrus leaves

salt and sugar to taste

continued on p 57

Mohlyu
A deliciously mild curry of large
prawns or fishballs enriched with
coconut milk and toasted grated
coconut.

from p 55, *Singgang cocu*

PREPARATION: 20 MIN.

1 Cut fish into 5 or 6 thick pieces. Rub all over with coarse salt to remove any slime and odour. Rinse well. If using prawns, remove shells and trim off feelers, leaving heads intact. Rub with coarse salt, leave for 5 min.; then rinse and drain.

2 Remove stalks from belimbing, but leave whole otherwise. Rinse in cold water and drain.

3 Soak grated coconut in warm water and extract 1 cup thick and 3 cups thin coconut milk (see p 26).

METHOD: 25 MIN.

1 Heat oil in a tezaler (p 19). Stir-fry blended ingredients until fragrant. Add 2 tbsp. thick coconut milk and citrus leaves and fry for 1 min.

2 Add thin coconut milk and boil on medium heat for 10 min.

3 Lower heat, add fish and simmer for another 10 min.

4 When fish is half-cooked (or prawns are pink), add belimbing. Lower heat further and simmer for 5 min.

5 Add remaining thick coconut milk, stirring continuously to prevent curdling. Add salt and sugar to taste and when gravy boils, remove from heat and serve immediately with rice.

Serves 6 to 8

Singgang mangger
(Sweet-and-sour mango curry)

INGREDIENTS

5 slices (750 g) wolf herring or mackerel, or 12 (750 g) big prawns, unpeeled with heads intact

1 tbsp. coarse salt

½ cup oil

blended to a fine paste
15 (30 g) dried chillies, presoaked in hot water
2 stalks lemon grass (use 7 cm of root end)
20 g galangal, peeled
5 g turmeric, peeled
30 (300 g) shallots, or 3 (300 g) onions, peeled
1 bulb (60 g) garlic, peeled
6 (18 g) candlenuts or 6 (18 g) blanched almonds
2 tsp. untoasted shrimp paste (belachan)

6 citrus leaves

2 cups water

6 (500 g) green mangoes, halved and deseeded but left unskinned (make sure the fruit are well-scrubbed before halving)

salt and sugar to taste

PREPARATION: 10 MIN.

1 Rub coarse salt all over fish to remove any slime and odour. Rinse well. If using prawns, trim off feelers but leave shells and heads intact. Rub well with coarse salt and leave for 5 min.; then rinse.

METHOD: 20 MIN.

1 Heat oil in a tezaler (p 19) and fry blended ingredients (paste) until fragrant.

2 Add citrus leaves and continue frying paste until oil rises to the surface.

3 Add water and mangoes. Bring to a boil and cook until gravy thickens, about 10 min.

4 Then add fish, lower heat and simmer until cooked. If using prawns, add them and cook till pink.

5 Add salt and sugar to taste before removing from heat. Serve immediately with rice and a vegetable dish.

Serves 4 to 6

Cook's note If mangoes are not available use sour green apples or cooking apples.

The recipe can also be varied by substituting 400 g fresh krill (gerago) for the mangoes. In this variation, the sour taste comes from the use of tamarind juice: Mix 3 tbsp. tamarind pulp with 2 cups water and extract juice. Add the juice in METHOD, STEP 3.

This dish is my cousin Teresa Hendroff's speciality. After tasting it for the first time in a long while, I pleaded with her to part with the recipe. She readily agreed to do so for posterity's sake. Thank you, Teresa!

Vindaloo

(Vinegared meat curry)

INGREDIENTS

1 kg chicken

4 tbsp. dry spice curry powder
(see p 28)

1 tsp. cumin powder

½ tsp. English mustard powder

5 tbsp. vinegar

2 tbsp. fresh herb curry paste
(see p 28)

blended to a fine paste
   6 cloves (18 g) garlic, peeled
   60 g ginger, peeled
   25 (250 g) shallots, or
     2½ (250 g) onions, peeled
   8 (16 g) dried chillies,
     presoaked in hot water

½ cup oil

1 tsp. mustard seeds

2 sprigs curry leaf

1 cinnamon stick, 2½-cm length

1 star anise

4 cardamom

2 cups water or meat stock
(see p 27)

2 (200 g) onions, peeled and
quartered

salt to taste

1 tbsp. lime juice

PREPARATION: 20 MIN.

1 Cut meat into bite-sized pieces.

2 Mix dry spice curry powder,
cumin and mustard powder with
2 tbsp. of the vinegar.

3 Add fresh herb paste and mix
well with a spoon (do not use an
electric blender).

4 Add blended paste to mixture
from STEP 3 and mix thoroughly.
Moisten resulting paste with
remaining 3 tbsp. of vinegar.

5 Marinate meat with 2 tbsp. of
the mixed paste from STEP 4 for
10 min.

METHOD: 25 MIN.

1 Heat oil in a tezaler (p 19). Put
in mustard seeds and cover until
seeds stop popping. Then add
remaining mixed paste from
PREPARATION, STEP 4. Stir-fry
for 1 min.

2 Add curry leaves, cinnamon
stick, star anise and cardamom.
Stir-fry until fragrant and oil
rises to the surface.

3 Put in meat and sauté for 10 min.
Pour in stock, cover and bring to
a boil.

4 Add onions and salt to taste,
reduce heat and simmer until
meat is tender, about 10 min.

5 Continue simmering until gravy
has thickened. Add lime juice
before removing from heat.
Serve with rice.

Serves 8 to 10

Cook's note This is a deliciously pungent
curry with a unique blend of spices and a
tangy taste imparted by the vinegar. It is of
Portuguese-Goan origin and was probably
brought to Malacca during the sixteenth
century by traders from Goa. The original
Goan recipe generally used cubed pork or
prawns simmered in a paste of red chillies,
garlic and cumin.

The Goans had developed their
recipe from the Portuguese *vinhu de arlu*
(p 137). However, unlike vinhu de arlu,
vindaloo contains no alcohol (wine or
brandy) and is considerably spicier.

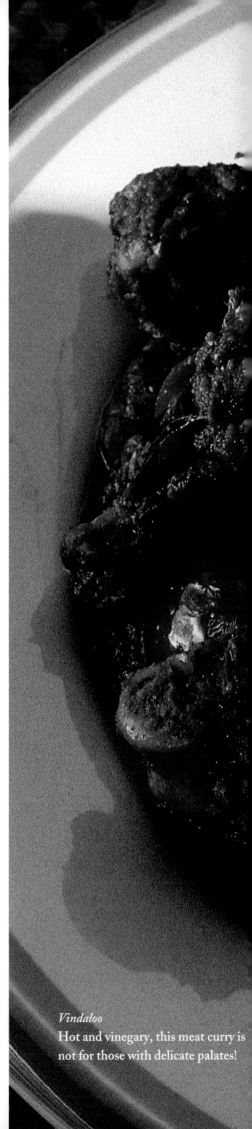

Vindaloo
Hot and vinegary, this meat curry is
not for those with delicate palates!

Diabu Caladu

SPICY SNIPPETS

No traditional Cristang meal is complete without at least one sambal. Always prepared from chillies and inevitably spicy and hot, sambals represent a diverse class of dishes and condiments so well-loved by the Cristang palate that they deserve special mention; these dishes are to a meal what colours are to a photograph. In fact, no other preparation of chillies quite equals the culinary kick of a good sambal.

The well-prepared sambal has a sharp, tart taste that contrasts with the searing pungency of its chillies; it should enhance an oily dish and balance rich curries. The richness of a coconut milk based curry, for instance, can cause a feeling of surfeit, but the sambal offsets this with its pungency and tartness.

Cristang cooks use the pilung tek-tek (mortar and pestle, p 21) to prepare sambal the old-fashioned way; an electric blender is never used! My mother for example, is fastidious about pounding the chillies first, then adding the shallots and finally the toasted shrimp paste (belachan). 'This way,' she tells me, 'the chillies absorb the flavour of the belachan and the sambal will have a delicious fragrance.'

Sambals are eaten either raw or cooked. Raw sambals are combinations of sour fruits or plant shoots with a sambal paste. Lime or tamarind juice is added to increase piquancy, and onions are occasionally included to sweeten the preparation. Cooked sambals are side dishes that complement bland dishes or stand in for curries.

Belachan
Dried shrimp paste or belachan is one of the more important ingredients in a Cristang kitchen and is indicative of the Malay influence in Cristang cuisine.

Sambal belachan 62
(Shrimp paste sambal)

Sambal belimbing 62
(Sour fruit sambal)

Sambal cambrung 62
tambrinhyu
(Tamarind prawn sambal)

Sambal bokras 63
(Candlenut sambal)

Sambal capitang 65
(Captain's sambal)

Sambal chilli bedri 65
(Green chilli sambal)

Sambal chilli-taucho 66
(Green chillies with salted soya bean sambal)

Sambal chinchaluk 66
(Pickled krill relish)

Sambal gerago seccu 67
(Dried krill sambal)

Sambal jantong 67
(Banana bud sambal)

Sambal nanas 69
cung pipineo
(Cucumber and pineapple sambal)

Sambal Tante Juliana 69
(Aunt Juliana's sambal)

Sambal mangger 70
azedu
(Sour mango sambal)

Rabaser 70
(Wild edible shoots with coconut)

Sambal belachan
(Shrimp paste sambal)

INGREDIENTS

6 (30 g) fresh red chillies

4 tsp. untoasted shrimp paste (belachan)

1 (10 g) shallot, peeled

salt and sugar to taste

1 tbsp. lime or lemon juice

2 small limes (optional)

METHOD: 10 MIN.

1 Toast shrimp paste in a dry pan over low heat until brown and aromatic. Set aside.

2 Pound chillies and shallot coarsely. Add salt and sugar.

3 Add toasted shrimp paste and pound again to mix well.

4 Pour lime juice on top. Serve in a small dish garnished with small lime halves.

Serves 4 to 6

Cook's note Care must be taken when toasting the shrimp paste as it will taste bitter if it gets burnt. While pretoasted belachan may be used, it is better to toast the belachan fresh for this sambal. An electric blender can be used instead of the mortar and pestle (p 21); however, this most traditional of sambals somehow tastes better if pounded in the old way.

To make a sandwich filling, add 5 candlenuts and 2 tbsp. dried prawns (washed and drained) in METHOD, STEP 3. Fry the resulting paste in 2 tbsp. oil for 3 min. Season with ½ tsp. salt, 1 tsp. sugar and 2 tbsp. lime juice. Remove from heat and let cool; then spread on buttered bread and top with cucumber slices.

Sambal belimbing
(Sour fruit sambal)

INGREDIENTS

12 (150 g) half-ripe belimbing

blended to a coarse paste
    4 (20 g) fresh red chillies
    5 (50 g) shallots, or ½ (50 g) onion, peeled
    1 tsp. toasted shrimp paste (belachan)

salt and sugar to taste

METHOD: 15 MIN.

1 Cut belimbing across into thick star-shaped slices and place in a deep bowl.

2 Combine salt and sugar with blended paste. Add to sliced belimbing and toss lightly. Serve as a relish with rice and a coconut milk based curry, such as singgang cocu (p 55).

Serves 4 to 6

Sambal cambrung tambrinhyu
(Tamarind prawn sambal)

INGREDIENTS

½ kg medium-sized prawns

1 tbsp. coarse salt

2 tbsp. tamarind pulp

½ cup water

½ cup oil

blended to a fine paste
    10 (100 g) shallots, or
    1 (100 g) onion, peeled
    2 cloves (6 g) garlic, peeled
    2 tsp. toasted shrimp paste (belachan)

1 tsp. thick soy sauce

2 tbsp. grated palm sugar (gula Melaka)

¼ tsp. salt

½ tsp. pepper

PREPARATION: 10 MIN.

1 Shell and devein prawns. Rub with coarse salt to remove any slime and odour, leave for 5 min., then rinse well and drain.

2 Soak tamarind pulp in water and extract juice (see p 26).

METHOD: 10 MIN.

1 Heat oil in a wok over high heat. Put in blended paste and fry until fragrant.

2 Add prawns and cook until pink; lower heat.

3 Pour in thick soy sauce and tamarind juice; simmer for 2 min.

4 Add palm sugar, salt and pepper. Stir until sugar dissolves. The sauce should be thick and shiny and have a sweet-and-sour taste. Remove from heat and serve at once with *Lampries 'landeh* (p 128).

Serves 6 to 8

Cook's note This sambal was traditionally a side dish for children whenever Dutch coconut-flavoured rice was served with dishes that were too spicy for their palates—note the absence of chillies in the recipe. However, if a spicy flavour is preferred, add 2 or 3 fresh red chillies when preparing the shallot-and-garlic paste. Save the prawn heads and shells, as they can be used to make a stock (p 27).

Sambal bokras
(Candlenut sambal)

INGREDIENTS

300 g chicken or any other meat

4 cakes (200 g) firm bean curd

½ cup oil

blended to a fine paste
    20 (200 g) shallots, or 2 (200 g)
        onions, peeled
    6 (18 g) candlenuts, or 12
        (18 g) blanched almonds
    ½ tsp. turmeric powder
    1 tsp. toasted shrimp paste
        (belachan) (optional)
    6 (30 g) fresh red chillies

1 tbsp. lime or lemon juice

1 cup meat stock (see p 27)

2 citrus leaves

salt and sugar to taste

PREPARATION: 15 MIN.

1 Cut chicken into bite-sized
  pieces.

2 Cut bean curd cakes in half; then
  slice into 1-cm thick pieces.

METHOD: 15 MIN.

1 Heat oil and fry bean curd
  pieces. Remove and set aside to
  drain on paper towels.

2 In the same oil, stir-fry blended
  paste until fragrant. Add chicken
  and stir-fry for 2 min.

3 Pour in half the meat stock. Stir
  thoroughly, then add remaining
  stock. Stir well, turning chicken
  pieces to coat thoroughly. Lower
  heat, simmer until chicken is
  cooked and liquid reduced.

4 Add fried bean curd and citrus
  leaves. Season with salt and
  sugar to taste; stir gently and
  remove from heat.

5 Add lime juice just before
  serving with boiled rice or
  noodles.

Serves 4 to 6

Sambal bokras
This sambal has a thick consistency due to its main
ingredient, candlenut, which the Cristang usually use
as a thickening agent.

Sambal capitang (above)
This vinegared chicken sambal is served in an English porcelain tureen that is part of a dinner set presented as a wedding gift to my eldest sister when she got married in 1948.

Sambal chilli bedri (right)
This green chilli sambal is served in a granite mortar, an old kitchen implement that is still used for pounding sambal pastes.

Sambal capitang
(Captain's sambal)

INGREDIENTS

4 (about 1 kg) chicken thighs

1 tbsp. vinegar

1 tsp. thick soy sauce

4 tbsp. lime or lemon juice

1 cup oil

3 (300 g) potatoes, peeled and
quartered lengthwise and boiled

blended to a fine paste
  10 (20 g) dried chillies,
    presoaked in hot water
  20 (200 g) shallots, or 2 (200 g)
    onions, peeled
  2 (6 g) candlenuts, or 4 (6 g)
    blanched almonds
  6 (30 g) fresh red chillies

1 cup water

salt and sugar to taste

3 whole citrus leaves (optional)

PREPARATION: 15 MIN.

1 Cut chicken thighs into joints.
  Marinate with vinegar, soy sauce
  and 2 tbsp. of the lime juice for
  at least 5 min.

METHOD: 15 MIN.

1 Heat oil in a wok and fry
  potatoes until golden in colour.
  Remove and set aside on paper
  towels to drain.

2 In the same wok, fry blended
  ingredients until aromatic.

3 Drain chicken pieces, reserving
  marinade. Add chicken to pan
  and stir-fry for 2 min.; then add
  marinade.

4 Keep frying until more liquid
  appears. Pour in water, cover and
  cook over medium heat until
  liquid is reduced and chicken is
  cooked.

5 Add salt and sugar to taste; stir
  well and remove from heat.

6 Arrange chicken in a dish.
  Mix remaining lime juice with
  gravy from pan and spoon over
  chicken. Arrange fried potatoes
  around dish and garnish with
  citrus leaves. Serve with rice or
  bread.

Serves 4 to 6

Sambal chilli bedri
(Green chilli sambal)

INGREDIENTS

300 g green chillies

2 (200 g) red or green bell peppers

400 g medium-sized prawns, fresh
  or frozen

1 tbsp. coarse salt

2 tbsp. oil

3 cups (240 g) grated coconut

blended to a fine paste
  15 (150 g) shallots, or
    1½ (150 g) onions, peeled
  4 (12 g) candlenuts, or 8 (12 g)
    blanched almonds
  2 tsp. toasted shrimp paste
    (belachan)

3 cups warm water

salt and sugar to taste

PREPARATION: 15 MIN.

1 Slice chillies diagonally into
  1-cm wide pieces and soak in
  cold water. Halve bell peppers
  and remove seeds. Cut into strips
  1 cm wide and slice diagonally
  into diamond-shaped pieces;
  then soak in cold water.

2 Shell and devein prawns. Rub
  with coarse salt to remove any
  slime and odour. Leave for 5
  min.; then rinse well and drain.

3 Toast ¾ cup of the grated coconut in a dry pan until golden and
  fragrant. Mix well with blended
  paste.

continued on p 66

from p 65, *Sambal chilli bedri*

4 Soak remaining coconut in warm water and extract 1 cup thick milk and 1 cup thin milk (see p 26).

METHOD: 10 MIN.

1 Heat oil in a wok. Fry blended mixture from PREPARATION, STEP 3 until aromatic. Pour in thin coconut milk and bring to a boil; then add prawns and cook till pink.

2 Add sliced chillies, bell peppers and salt to taste. Stir, lower heat and simmer gently until gravy thickens.

3 Pour in thick coconut milk. Simmer for 3 min., stirring continuously to prevent milk from curdling.

4 Add sugar to taste, stir well and remove from heat. Serve as an accompaniment with rice or bread.

Serves 6

Sambal chilli-taucho

(Green chillies with salted soya bean sambal)

INGREDIENTS

250 g fresh green chillies

2 tbsp. tamarind pulp

1 cup water

1 cup oil

garnish
> 15 (150 g) shallots, or 1 (150 g) onion, peeled and sliced
> 6 cloves (18 g) garlic, peeled and sliced
> 20 g fresh ginger, peeled and julienned

200 g salted dried ikan bilis (whitebait)

blended to a fine paste
> 10 (50 g) shallots, or 1 (50 g) onion, peeled
> 6 (18 g) cloves garlic, peeled
> 2 tsp. toasted shrimp paste (belachan)

2 tbsp. salted soya beans, mashed

1 cup meat stock (see p 27)

1 large onion, peeled and sliced into rings

sugar to taste

PREPARATION: 20 MIN.

1 Slit each chilli on one side only, taking care not to cut it into separate pieces. Remove seeds, making sure to leave stalk intact.

2 Soak tamarind pulp in 1 cup of the water and extract juice (see p 26).

METHOD: 15 MIN.

1 Heat 2 tbsp. of the oil in a wok. Fry garnishing (shallots, garlic and ginger, separately and in that order) until golden. Set aside to drain on paper towels. Discard oil in wok.

2 In the same wok, heat 4 tbsp. fresh oil over high heat. When oil begins to smoke, put in whitebait. Fry until brown and crisp. Remove from wok and set aside to drain on paper towels. Discard oil in wok.

3 In a clean wok, heat remaining oil. Put in blended paste and stir-fry for 1 min. Then add salted soya beans and fry until fragrant. Add 2 tbsp. of the meat stock, stir and lower heat.

4 Add green chillies and onion rings and toss for 1 minute. Then add tamarind juice and half the remaining meat stock. Cover and simmer for 2 min.

5 Add remaining meat stock and simmer uncovered for another 5 min. When chillies are tender and gravy has thickened, add sugar to taste. Stir and remove from heat.

6 Arrange fried whitebait in a dish. Pour gravy with chillies over the fish; sprinkle fried garnish on top. Serve immediately.

Serves 6 to 8

Sambal chinchaluk

(Pickled krill relish)

INGREDIENTS

sliced finely
> 10 (100 g) shallots, peeled
> 2 (10 g) fresh red chillies
> 1 (5 g) fresh green chilli

4 tbsp. chinchaluk (pickled krill)

4 tbsp. lime or lemon juice

METHOD: 5 MIN.

1 In a glass bowl, toss pickled krill gently with shallots, chillies and lime juice. Serve at once with boiled rice and a curry.

Serves 4 to 6

Cook's note This sharply flavoured side dish, which is eaten raw, best accompanies rice and a coconut milk based fish curry (singgang cocu, p 55).

Sambal gerago seccu
(Dried krill sambal)

INGREDIENTS

200 g dried gerago (krill)

1 tbsp. tamarind pulp

½ cup water

4 (120 g) tomatoes

¼ cup oil

blended to a fine paste
> 25 (250 g) shallots, or 4 (400 g) onions, peeled
> 8 (40 g) fresh red chillies
> 4 (10 g) dried chillies, presoaked in hot water
> 2 (6 g) candlenuts, or 4 (6 g) blanched almonds
> 1 tsp. toasted shrimp paste (belachan)
> 1 stalk lemon grass (use 7 cm of root end)

salt and sugar to taste

1 tbsp. lime or lemon juice

PREPARATION: 15 MIN.

1 Remove grit and place dried krill in a sieve. Pour boiling water over krill and set aside to drain.

2 Soak tamarind pulp in water and extract juice (see p 26).

3 Blanch tomatoes; remove and discard skin. Dice flesh and set aside.

METHOD: 15 MIN.

1 Heat oil in a pan. Put in blended paste and stir-fry until fragrant.

2 Add tamarind juice gradually and cook on low heat for 2 min.

3 Add tomatoes and keep stirring until liquid has reduced, about 5 min.

4 Add krill and stir-fry for 2 min.; then add salt and sugar to taste. Stir well and transfer to a dish. Pour lime juice on top and allow to cool before serving. Serve as a

spread on toast, as a sandwich filling or as an accompaniment to boiled rice and curry.

Serves 6 to 8

Cook's note If dried krill is not available, dried small prawns may be used. However, before using, soak these prawns in warm water until they bloat; then, drain, mince and use in METHOD, STEP 4.

Sambal jantong
(Banana bud sambal)

INGREDIENTS

1 (300 g) medium-sized banana bud, or 1 (250 g) globe artichoke

5 cups (400 g) grated coconut

2 cups water

250 g medium-sized prawns

1 tbsp. coarse salt

blended to a fine paste
> 15 (150 g) shallots, or 1½ (150 g) onions, peeled
> 2 (15 g) fresh red chillies
> 2 tsp. toasted shrimp paste (belachan)

1 tsp. salt

1 tsp. sugar

½ cup prawn stock (see p 27)

1 (80 g) cucumber (optional), sliced thinly

2 tbsp. lime or lemon juice

garnish: sliced fine and mixed together with 4 tbsp. lime or lemon juice
> 6 (15 g) belimbing
> 6 (60 g) shallots, peeled
> 3 (15 g) fresh red chillies
> 50 g ginger, peeled and shredded

PREPARATION: 25 MIN.

1 Strip banana bud of purple outer leaves until the pink-white core is visible.

2 Cut core into halves and cut halves into quarters. Boil pieces of core until half-cooked, about 3 min. Drain and slice into bite-sized pieces.

3 If using artichoke, boil for 40–45 min. in salted water. Drain upside down; then slice bud (or heart) into bite-sized pieces.

4 Soak grated coconut in water and extract thick and thin coconut milk (see p 26).

5 Shell and devein prawns. Rub with coarse salt to remove any slime and odour. Leave for 5 min.; rinse well and drain.

METHOD: 15 MIN.

1 In a tezaler (p 19), combine thin coconut milk and blended paste and bring to a boil. Add salt and sugar, stir well and cook for 1 min.

2 Add prawns and prawn stock. When mixture boils, put in banana bud or artichoke. Simmer until gravy is absorbed and mixture is fragrant.

3 Add thick coconut milk. To prevent curdling, stir continuously until mixture (sambal) boils; then remove from heat.

4 Line a bowl with cucumber slices. Pour in sambal, arrange garnish on top and sprinkle with lime juice. Serve as a salad with rice and a hot curry.

Serves 4 to 6

Cook's note To create the particular blend of flavours for which this sambal is treasured, coconut milk must be used and no substitutes will do.

Sambal jantong (right)
This unusual recipe incorporating banana buds was given to me by my Aunt May who could recall it in great detail at the ripe old age of eighty-seven.

Sambal nanas cung pipineo (below)
The recipe for this pineapple and cucumber sambal comes from my mother, who also donated the serving dish for this photograph.

Sambal nanas cung pipineo (Cucumber and pineapple sambal)

INGREDIENTS

1 (400 g) half-ripe pineapple, or
   250 g canned pineapple cubes

2 (200 g) cucumbers

blended to a fine paste
     5 (20 g) fresh red chillies
     10 (100 g) shallots, or 1 (100 g)
       onion, peeled
     2 tsp. toasted shrimp paste
       (belachan)

1 tbsp. sugar

1 tsp. salt

lime or lemon juice to taste

PREPARATION: 15 MIN.

1 If using fresh pineapple, skin and
remove eyes. Dice the fruit and
place in a deep salad bowl. If
using canned pineapple, drain
well before transferring cubes to
bowl.

2 Cut unpeeled cucumbers lengthwise into quarters; remove seeded
pith and cut each quarter lengthwise into halves. Then slice each
piece diagonally and add to the
pineapple in the bowl.

METHOD: 5 MIN.

1 Add blended paste, sugar and salt
to pineapple and cucumber
pieces; toss well.

2 Before serving, add a dash of
lime juice. Serve with mi annu
(p 130).

Serves 6 to 8

Cook's note This sour dish is called *matah-jelah* in the Cristang language, which means to 'help the food down'. It is especially popular during festive seasons when the food is extra tempting and it is much too easy to overindulge.

Sambal Tante Juliana
(Aunt Juliana's sambal)

INGREDIENTS

400 g Spanish mackerel steaks
   (about 4 thick slices)

1 tbsp. coarse salt

½ tsp. salt

½ tsp. pepper

1 tbsp. plus 1 tsp. tamarind pulp

1 cup water

½ cup oil

blended to a coarse paste
     25 (250 g) shallots, or
       2½ (250 g) onions, peeled
     3 (15 g) fresh red chillies
     9 (18 g) dried chillies,
       presoaked in hot water
     2 tsp. toasted shrimp paste
       (belachan)
     3 (9 g) candlenuts, or 4 (9 g)
       blanched almonds

2 citrus leaves, sliced thinly

salt and sugar to taste

PREPARATION: 15 MIN.

1 Rub fish steaks with coarse salt
to remove slime and odour; rinse
well and drain. Rub with salt and
pepper and set aside.

2 Soak 1 tbsp. of the tamarind
pulp in water and extract juice
(see p 26).

METHOD: 15 MIN.

1 To fry fish steaks, heat oil in a
frying pan, reserving 2 tbsp. To
prevent fish from sticking, add
1 tsp. of the tamarind pulp to
the pan and wait until oil is very
hot before sliding fish in gently;
do not turn until slightly brown
underneath. When fish is cooked
and golden brown, remove and
drain on paper towels. Arrange
on a plate.

continued on p 70

Sambal Tante Juliana
Aunt Juliana's fish sambal goes as well with bread as it does with hot boiled rice. It is pictured here on a Wedgwood plate decorated with Shakespearean characters, a gift from my niece and her husband, Peter and Veronica Burrows.

from p 69, *Sambal Tante Juliana*

2 Discard used oil. In the same pan, heat the rest of the oil and fry blended paste until fragrant.

3 Add tamarind juice gradually, stirring continuously, until all the juice has been added. Simmer for 2 min.

4 Add salt and sugar to taste. When the liquid is boiling add citrus leaves. Lower heat and cook for 1 min., then remove from heat.

5 Spoon sambal over the fried fish. Serve at once.

Serves 4 to 6

Cook's note This old recipe is available thanks to my sister Christie, who learnt it from our grandmother.

Sambal mangger azedu

(Sour mango sambal)

INGREDIENTS

2 (100 g) small green mangoes

blended to a fine paste
  5 (15 g) fresh red chillies
  1 tsp. toasted shrimp paste (belachan)

mixed together until sugar dissolves
  1 tsp. thick soy sauce
  1 tbsp. grated palm sugar (gula Melaka)
  2 tbsp. sugar

PREPARATION: 5 MIN.

1 Skin mangoes and cut into halves. Remove seeds and cut the flesh into cubes.

METHOD: 5 MIN.

1 Place mango in a glass bowl. Add paste made from chillies and toasted shrimp paste. Toss well to coat the mango thoroughly.

2 Add the soy sauce and sugar mixture and toss again. Serve at once as a relish with boiled rice and crispy fried fish (see p 109).

Cook's note Sour green apples may be substituted for mangoes. The tart flavour of this relish complements rich, coconut milk based curries as well as fried dishes.

To check the quality of gula Melaka, pinch a little between the fingers; the best kind always crumbles.

Rabaser

(Wild edible shoots with coconut)

INGREDIENTS

300 g daun pegaga, or watercress

1 cup (80 g) grated coconut

blended to a fine paste
  4 tsp. toasted shrimp paste (belachan)
  5 (15 g) fresh red chillies
  12 (120 g) shallots, or
    1¼ (125 g) onions, peeled
  5 (50 g) shallots, or ½ (50 g)
    onion, peeled and sliced finely

4 tbsp. lime or lemon juice

salt and sugar to taste

PREPARATION: 15 MIN.

1 Discard wilted or damaged leaves of daun pegaga (or watercress, if using).

2 Chop the remaining leaves very fine and set aside. To avoid mashing the leaves, do not use a food processor.

3 Toast grated coconut until brown and fragrant and blend for 30 sec. with the paste made from toasted shrimp paste, chillies and shallots.

METHOD: 10 MIN.

1 Put the blended paste mixture from PREPARATION, STEP 3 in a bowl. Add the daun pegaga and toss well.

2 Pour lime juice on top, add salt and sugar to taste and toss again. Serve immediately with rice or bread and curry.

Serves 4 to 6

Cook's note Known scientifically as *Centella asiatica*, daun pegaga is a wild creeper found only in equatorial regions. This plant is said to have numerous medicinal properties, including the ability to improve blood circulation; juice extracted from its leaves is claimed to sooth sore throats.

My sincere thanks to Mr Gerry Rozario for this recipe.

Sambal mangger azedu
This sour mango and shrimp paste sambal is a variation of an old childhood favourite. Cristang children would pluck guava and pester their mothers to make a sauce exactly like the one in this dish—but without the shrimp paste—to eat as a dip with their fruit.

Pusah Besu

SOUPED-UP YARNS

Soups are not an essential part of Cristang cuisine. However, when they do make an appearance at a meal, they are often served as the first course, especially during formal dinners.

Cristang soups range from light and thin concoctions to hearty, heavily spiced affairs. Teem (p 80) is the traditional soup served for supper after the Christmas Midnight Mass. This anise-cinnamon, wine-flavoured soup cooked with trotters or duck is usually served with homemade crusty breads. Another traditional Christmas soup is a spicy chicken and cabbage soup that is thickened with potatoes and milk; it is often referred to as stew.

Seafood soups figure prominently among the fisherfolk, whose wives whip up delicious preparations with the catch their husbands bring home. In the old days these soups were drunk out of clay mugs called *canecas*. Seafood soups tend to be clear and light, such as the tangy caldu laler-laler (p 78) made from baby mussels and flavoured with lemon grass.

Vegetable soups, made from a variety of greens, are also favoured among the Cristang. However, these soups are rarely completely vegetarian, as Cristang cooks prefer to add substance to them with slivers of meat or an egg.

Caldu bayam
The delicate flavour of this spinach and fishball soup is enhanced with cinnamon and star anise.

Caldu bayam 74
(Spinach and fishball soup)

Caldu bola pesce 74
(Fishball and glass vermicelli soup)

Caldu boloh mai 74
(Angled luffa egg-drop soup)

Caldu pescador 77
(Fisherman's soup)

Caldu galinhia 77
(Old-fashioned chicken soup)

Caldu taucho 78
(Salted soya bean soup)

Caldu laler-laler 78
(Baby mussel soup)

Caldu tauhu cung 78
pesce seccu
(Bean curd and salted fish soup)

Stiu carbra 80
(Mutton stew)

Teem 80
(Anise-and-sherry-flavoured soup)

Caldu bayam
(Spinach and fishball soup)

INGREDIENTS

300 g spinach

20 fishballs (see p 29)

½ tsp. pepper plus to taste

¼ cup oil

blended to a fine paste
    5 (50 g) shallots, or ½ (50 g)
       onion, peeled
    5 cloves (15 g) garlic, peeled

1 star anise

1 stick cinnamon, 5-cm length

6 cups fish stock (see p 27)

1 tsp. sugar

salt to taste

PREPARATION: 10 MIN.

1 Detach leaves and shoots of
   spinach and set aside. Cut stems
   into 5-cm lengths.

2 Sprinkle fishballs evenly with the
   ½ tsp. of the pepper and set
   aside.

METHOD: 15 MIN.

1 Heat oil in a medium-sized pot.
   Put in blended paste and stir-fry
   until fragrant. Add star anise and
   cinnamon stick and stir-fry for
   30 sec.

2 Add stock and fishballs and boil
   for 15 min., adding more water if
   necessary to keep fishballs
   covered.

3 Put in spinach stalks and boil for
   1 min. Add leaves and shoots
   and cook for a further 5 min.;
   then add sugar.

4 Season with salt to taste, stir and
   remove from heat. Serve
   immediately.

Serves 4 to 6

Caldu bola pesce
(Fishball and glass vermicelli soup)

INGREDIENTS

30 g glass vermicelli

3 (30 g) shallots, peeled and
   chopped

¼ cup oil

1 (100 g) onion, peeled and minced

6 cloves (18 g) garlic, peeled and
   minced

1 tbsp. salted soya beans, mashed

3 cups water

2 (100 g) potatoes, peeled and
   cubed

20 fishballs (see p 29)

2 cups fish stock (see p 27)

1 tsp. sugar

salt to taste

1 spring onion, sliced thinly

1 stalk coriander leaves

PREPARATION: 10 MIN.

1 Soak vermicelli in water until
   soft, about 15 min. Cut into
   10-cm lengths.

2 Fry shallots in 2 tbsp. of the oil
   until crisp. Set aside for
   garnishing.

METHOD: 20 MIN.

1 Heat remaining oil in a medium-
   sized pot. Fry onions, garlic and
   salted soya beans until fragrant.

2 Pour in water, add potatoes and
   boil for 4 min.

3 Put in fishballs and boil for a
   further 3 min.

4 Add fish stock, sugar and salt to
   taste. Stir, boil for 3 min. and
   remove from heat.

5 Serve garnished with spring
   onions, coriander leaves and fried
   shallots.

Serves 4 to 6

Cook's note Fishballs may be replaced with
125 g diced lean meat.

Caldu boloh mai
(Angled luffa egg-drop soup)

INGREDIENTS

2 (300 g) angled luffa gourds

4 cups water

2 cups meat stock (see p 27)

6 cloves (18 g) garlic, peeled and
   minced

2 (120 g) eggs, lightly beaten

1 tsp. sugar

½ tsp. salt

4 black peppercorns, crushed
   coarsely

1 stalk coriander leaves

PREPARATION: 10 MIN.

1 Use a vegetable peeler to remove
   ridges on the gourds, leaving the
   skin in between so that the
   vegetable appears striped.
   However, if skin is leathery, as is
   often the case with older gourds,
   remove completely.

2 Hold a gourd firmly on the
   cutting board with fingers at a
   60° angle. Cut 2-cm slices at this
   angle, continuing down the
   length of the gourd. (See rolling
   cut, p 25.) Repeat with other
   gourd.

METHOD: 15 MIN.

1 Put water into a medium-sized
   pot and bring to a boil. Add
   stock and garlic.

2 Add luffa pieces and cook for
   30 sec.

3 To add egg to soup, hold a fork
   about 25 cm above pot with tines
   pointing down; pour egg slowly
   over back of fork, moving both
   hands in tandem in a circular

continued on p 77

Caldu bola pesce
The Cristang first learnt how to make fishball and glass vermicelli soup from the Chinese and have since created their own version, which is presented here.

The *Eurasian Review* in the foreground was a newsletter circulated among the Cristang and Eurasian communities during the 1930s; sadly, it is no longer in print. The photograph in the background is of me at, well, a younger age!

My
Favourite
Recipes

The
EURASIAN
REVIEWS

Caldu boloh mai
The angled luffa egg-drop soup is pictured here in a
tiffin carrier. In the old days, this mode of takeaway was
popular among fishermen and others who were unable
to return home for meals during the day.

from p 74, *Caldu boloh mai*

motion to cover entire surface of soup with egg. Lower heat and cover for 30 sec. to allow egg to set.

4 Add sugar, salt and pepper. Bring soup to a boil; stir twice briskly and remove from heat. Garnish with coriander leaves and serve immediately with buttered toast.

Serves 4 to 6

Caldu pescador
(Fisherman's soup)

INGREDIENTS

400 g (12 to 15) medium-sized prawns

1 tbsp. coarse salt

10 (300 g) fresh squid

200 g white fish fillet

1 tsp. tamarind pulp

9½ cups water

3 slices dried tamarind

2 cloves (6 g) garlic, crushed in their skins

5 (50 g) shallots, or ½ (50 g) onion, peeled and chopped roughly

3 stalks lemon grass, whole, bruised

2 (5 g) fresh red chillies, halved lengthwise

2 tbsp. lime or lemon juice (optional)

1 stalk coriander leaves

PREPARATION: IO MIN.

1 Wash prawns; trim off feelers and legs, leaving heads and shells intact. Rub with coarse salt to remove any slime and odour, leave for 5 min. Rinse well and drain.

2 Carefully pull tentacles and heads away from bodies of squid and discard. Remove innards and any cartilaginous matter. Rub and peel off thin skin. Wash bodies well, taking care to rinse out cavities. Slit bodies open and cut into bite-sized pieces.

3 Cut fish fillet into cubes.

4 Soak tamarind pulp in ½ cup of the water and extract juice (see p 26).

METHOD: 20 MIN.

1 Bring remaining 9 cups of water to a boil in a large (about 4 litres) pot. Put in tamarind slices, garlic, shallots and lemon grass; boil for 3 min.

2 Lower heat, add tamarind juice and simmer for 10 min. Add chillies and simmer for a further 2 min.

3 Add squid and cook for 1 min. Put in prawns and cook for 3 min. Do not overcook. Remove from heat as soon as squid are tender and prawns are pink.

4 Taste and add lime juice if desired. Garnish with coriander leaves and serve immediately.

Serves 6

Cook's note This soup was cooked over a charcoal stove on the beach and shared among fishermen, who would add a splash of brandy as a pick-me-up after a hard day's work. The soup's sharp taste helped whet the appetite and freshen the palate.

Caldu galinhia
(Old-fashioned chicken soup)

INGREDIENTS

1½ kg chicken

2 tbsp. brandy

marinade, mixed well

5 (15 g) cloves garlic, peeled and chopped finely

½ tsp. stew spice powder (see p 28)

½ tsp. ground black pepper

1 tsp. sugar

¼ cup oil

6 cups water

1 tsp. salt

1 egg white, lightly beaten

PREPARATION: IO MIN.

1 Cut chicken into 12 pieces.

2 Add 1 tbsp. of the brandy to the marinade, mixing well. Coat chicken pieces with the mixture and set aside for 5 min.

METHOD: 25 MIN.

1 Heat oil in wok. Put in seasoned chicken and stir-fry for 1 min.

2 Pour in water, cover and bring to a boil. Cook for 20 min.

3 Remove chicken pieces from soup and set aside.

4 Lower heat and add salt; stir well.

5 To remove scum that rises to the surface, add egg white. Stir, and when scum rises to the surface, skim off and remove from heat. The soup should be clear.

6 Just before serving, strain into a tureen. Add remaining brandy and stir well before serving with croûtons.

Serves 4

Cook's note This soup is traditionally recommended to mothers in confinement and to invalids, as it is thought to help restore a person's strength.

The meat from the chicken can be shredded, mixed with salt, pepper and mayonnaise and used as a filling for sandwiches. It can also be fried with onions, stew spice powder and diced potatoes to make the filling for pang susis (p 149).

Caldu taucho
(Salted soya bean soup)

INGREDIENTS

1 red snapper head (about 350 g)

2 (300 g) red snapper cutlets, 2 cm thick

1 tbsp. coarse salt

¼ cup oil

10 (100 g) shallots, or 1 (100 g) onion, peeled and minced

6 cloves (18 g) garlic, peeled and minced

1 tbsp. salted soya beans, mashed

100 g ginger, peeled and sliced thinly

6 cups water

2 (10 g) fresh red chillies, halved lengthwise

1 cup fish or prawn stock (optional, see p 27)

1 tbsp. sugar

1 tbsp. vinegar

2 tsp. lime or lemon juice

PREPARATION: 5 MIN.

1 Rub fish head and cutlets with coarse salt to remove any slime and odour. Rinse well and pat dry with paper towels.

METHOD: 20 MIN.

1 Heat oil in a large pot or wok. Sauté shallots, garlic and soya beans for 30 sec. Add ginger and stir-fry until fragrant.

2 Pour in water and bring to a rapid boil. Lower heat and add chillies and fish. Simmer until fish turns opaque, about 10 min.

3 Add fish stock and sugar; stir well and simmer for 3 min.

4 Remove from heat. Add vinegar and lime juice and stir. Serve immediately with rice and curry.

Serves 6 to 8

Cook's note To eliminate strong fishy odours that cannot be removed by rubbing with coarse salt, cover the fish with tamarind pulp and soak in cool water for 5 min., then rinse.

Caldu laler-laler
(Baby mussel soup)

INGREDIENTS

400 g fresh baby mussels (*laler-laler*)

2 stalks lemon grass

2 (10 g) candlenuts, blended to a fine paste

6 cups water

minced finely
    5 (50 g) shallots, or ½ (50 g) onion, peeled
    4 cloves (12 g) garlic, peeled
    50 g ginger, peeled

½ tsp. sugar

1 tsp. salt

garnish (optional)
    2 (10 g) fresh red chillies, halved lengthwise
    2 limes, or ½ lemon, sliced thinly

PREPARATION: 10 MIN.

1 Wash mussels in cold running water. Discard empty and broken shells.

2 Discard rough blades from lemon grass. Wash thoroughly and tie into knot. Using a kitchen mallet or the side of a cleaver, pound bulb lightly to bruise.

METHOD: 20 MIN.

1 Heat water in a medium-sized pot and bring to a boil. Add minced ingredients.

2 Lower heat, add lemon grass and candlenuts and simmer for 3 min.

3 Put in mussels and boil until their shells open.

4 Add sugar and salt to taste, stir and remove from heat. To serve, remove meat from shells and place in soup bowls. Top up with soup and garnish with pieces of chilli, lime slices and two or three empty shells.

Serves 4 to 6

Caldu tauhu cung pesce seccu (Bean curd and salted fish soup)

INGREDIENTS

1 salted fish head (about 350 g), of any variety

2 cakes (100 g) soft bean curd, quartered

blended to a fine paste
    5 (50 g) shallots, or ½ (50 g) onion, peeled
    4 cloves (12 g) garlic, peeled
    2 (10 g) candlenuts, or 4 (10 g) blanched almonds
    1 (5 g) fresh red chilli

¼ cup oil

4 cups water plus additional

2 cups fish stock (see p 27)

1 tsp. sugar

salt to taste

garnish
    1 stalk coriander leaves

PREPARATION: 10 MIN.

1 Soak salted fish head in cold water for at least 10 min. before using.

METHOD: 15 MIN.

1 Heat oil in a wok and fry blended paste until aromatic.

continued on p 80

Caldu laler-laler
This shell-fish soup is still prepared by Cristang
fishermen out at sea. The Chinese soup bowls are part
of an antique nineteenth century set.

from p 78, *Caldu tauhu cung pesce seccu*

2 Pour in water and add salted fish head. Cover wok and allow water to come to a boil; then uncover.

3 Add bean curd. Lower heat and simmer for 3 min.; then add fish stock and sugar. Be sure to taste soup before adding salt, as both the fish head and stock are salty. If it is too salty, add more water, stir well and boil for 1 minute.

4 Remove from heat, garnish with coriander leaves and serve in individual bowls.

Serves 4 to 6

Stiu carbra (Mutton stew)

INGREDIENTS

½ kg lamb shank or boneless mutton, or 340 g corned beef

2 (200 g) onions, peeled

¼ cup oil

4 cloves (12 g) garlic, peeled and minced

1 tsp. stew spice powder (see p 28)

1 tsp. ground black pepper

2 cinnamon sticks, 5-cm lengths

1 pinch rosemary (optional)

2 cups water or meat stock (see p 27)

½ cup elbow macaroni (optional)

2 (160 g) carrots, diced

½ (250 g) cabbage, quartered

1 tsp. sugar

salt to taste

PREPARATION: 15 MIN.

1 Cut meat into bite-sized cubes.

2 Mince 1 of the onions and cut remaining one into quarters.

METHOD: 1 HR. 30 MIN.

1 Heat oil in a medium-sized pot. Sauté minced onion and garlic. Add stew spice powder, pepper, cinnamon sticks and rosemary; stir-fry until fragrant.

2 Add meat and sauté for 1 min.; then add water and bring to a boil.

3 When meat is tender, add macaroni and cook uncovered for 5 min.

4 Add carrots, cabbage and remaining onion. Continue simmering uncovered until vegetables are cooked, about 4 min.

5 Add sugar and salt to taste, stir and remove from heat. Serve immediately with bread or rice.

Serves 6 to 8

Cook's note Just after World War II when meat was expensive, Cristang families (like most others in Malaysia) substituted tinned corned beef for expensive and difficult to obtain fresh meat. The tinned meat was curried, stewed or fried. Fried corned beef was a popular sandwich filling. To make it, fry the corned beef with 1 large onion (sliced), 2 fresh red chillies (sliced) and a beaten egg. Toss well and remove from heat.

Teem (Anise-and-sherry-flavoured soup)

INGREDIENTS

2 kg duck, cut into large pieces

¼ cup oil

2 star anise

2 cinnamon sticks, 5-cm lengths

½ tsp. stew spice powder (see p 28)

1 tsp. grated nutmeg

10 cups water

1 bulb (60 g) garlic, whole and unpeeled

3 dried tamarind slices, or 6 dried belimbing (see *Cook's note*)

1 (100 g) onion, peeled and quartered

1 tsp. sugar

4 tbsp. sherry, or 2 tbsp. brandy

METHOD: 40–50 MIN.

1 Heat oil in a large pot. Add star anise, cinnamon sticks and stew spice powder; stir-fry for 30 sec.

2 Add duck and fry with spices for 1 min. Add grated nutmeg and toss well.

3 Pour in water and bring to a boil. Add garlic, tamarind slices and onion. Cover pot and boil until meat is tender, about 30 min.

4 Check liquid level. If necessary, top up with more water to cover ingredients. Boil for another 30 min.

5 Add sugar. If too salty, add more water and remove tamarind slices.

6 Remove from heat. Add sherry while soup is hot and serve immediately with crusty bread or croûtons.

Serves 6 to 8

Cook's note Dried belimbing is made by coating the fruit in coarse salt and drying it in the sun until it shrivels and turns brown. The dried fruit is used to add a tang or sourness to soups as well as to substitute for tamarind or lime juice.

To make croûtons, cut 2 slices of crustless white bread into 1-cm cubes and deep fry in ½ cup very hot oil till golden. Drain thoroughly on paper towels. Make a batch in advance and store in an air-tight container; they will come in useful whenever soup is served and will keep for a week.

Traditionally, trotters are used to make this soup. Nevertheless, duck makes an excellent substitute and I have included it in this recipe for the benefit of those who do not eat pork.

Teem
Christmas would not be Christmas for the Cristang
without Midnight Mass followed by a hearty supper of
this rich soup.

Furiada Bedri

GREEN MENTIONS

Like most ethnic cuisines in Asia, Cristang food uses a wide variety of vegetables that includes leafy greens, wild edible roots, mushrooms and, to some extent, flowers and sour fruits. Apart from their nutritional value, vegetables add variety and bulk to dishes and provide welcome relief after a 'fiery' encounter with a sambal or curry.

The Cristang appreciation for vegetables is a result of Malacca's historical role as a trading centre and cultural crossroads: merchants from India and the Middle East brought beans, lentils, brinjals and okra, while traders from nearby islands introduced roots, spices and herbs; and the Europeans brought with them potatoes, onions, garlic and cabbage.*

Cristang cooks are not fastidious about the vegetables they serve, as long as they are fresh. A Cristang mother is equally at ease serving up a dish of bean sprouts or the locally popular water spinach, kangkong, as she is presenting a selection of exotic greens. Often fruits such as mango, papaya and pineapple are added to curries, and hibiscus and sweet pumpkin flowers are used in several traditional side dishes. Cabbage leaves are used to wrap fish cutlets or minced meat, and yam bean is usually shredded for stuffing. Yam bean is the main ingredient for bredu chapchye and pongtey (pp 86 and 94, respectively), two dishes adopted from the Peranakan (p 17) people that are now part of the Cristang culinary heritage.

The most popular method of cooking vegetables is stir-frying Chinese-style, with flavour borrowed from a starter of shallots, garlic, candlenuts and fresh chillies sautéd until fragrant; occasionally belachan is used as well. Vegetable dishes usually include fine strips of meat or small prawns although egg blended with a little water, salt and pepper may be used as a substitute for meat.

*Source: *Journal of the Malayan Branch of the Royal Asiatic Society* 13, part 4 (August 1934): 8.

Achar chilli
This pickle of chillies stuffed with shredded papaya is usually served with beer-boiled ham at Christmas.

Achar chilli (Chilli pickle)

INGREDIENTS

preparation 1 (requires 1 week)
2 medium-sized green papayas
(½ kg each)
1 tbsp. salt
1 pinch slaked lime

preparation 2 (requires 1 day)
50 (½ kg) shallots, peeled
8 cups cool boiled water
5 pinches slaked lime
4 (400 g) medium-sized
cucumbers
4 tbsp. salt

pickling sauce:
blended to a fine paste
½ tsp. oil
5 (15 g) cloves garlic, peeled
5 (50 g) shallots, or ½ (50 g)
onion, peeled
1 tsp. turmeric powder

1 cup water
5 cups white vinegar
3 cups sugar
1 tsp. salt or to taste

papaya stuffing:
blended to a fine paste
1 tsp. oil
5 (50 g) shallots, or ½ (50 g)
onion, peeled
2 (10 g) candlenuts, or 4 (10 g)
almonds, roasted
2 tbsp. dried prawns, soaked
in ½ cup vinegar for 10 min.
and drained

3 tbsp. sugar or to taste
½ tsp. salt or to taste

50 (300 g) fresh green chillies
8 cups cool boiled water
1 pinch slaked lime
¼ cup oil
100 g ginger, peeled and julienned
2 (100 g) bulbs garlic, peeled and
sliced thinly

2 tsp. mustard seeds
10 cabbage leaves (from a 100-g
cabbage), quartered
salt and sugar to taste

PREPARATION I: I WEEK

1 Peel papayas, halve and remove
seeds. Grate flesh and mix with
1 tbsp. salt and a pinch of slaked
lime.

2 Place a 1-kg weight on grated
papaya and leave for 20 min. to
extract juice. Then squeeze fruit
well to remove any remaining
juice; spread out and dry in the
sun for 1 week.

PREPARATION 2: I DAY

1 Prick shallots all over with a fork.

2 Pour boiled water into a deep
pot. Add a pinch of slaked lime
and soak shallots for 10 min.
Drain, place on a tray
and dry in the sun for 1 day.

3 Cut ends off unpeeled cucumbers. Then cut cucumbers into 5-
cm lengths. Halve each piece
lengthwise, remove seeded pith
and halve again. Make two small
slits on one side of each piece.

4 Arrange cucumber pieces into 3
or 4 layers on a tray, sprinkling
1 tbsp. salt and a pinch of slaked
lime between each layer. Let
stand for 20 min.; then drain off
all liquid and dry in the sun for
1 day.

PREPARATION 3: 45 MIN.

1 To make pickling sauce, heat oil
in a deep pot. Put in blended
paste and stir-fry until fragrant.
Add water, vinegar, sugar and
salt. Simmer until sugar dissolves
and a thick syrup forms. Set
aside to cool before using.

2 To make papaya stuffing, heat oil
in a wok. Put in the blended
paste and fry until fragrant;
lower heat.

3 Add 1 cup of pickling sauce and
simmer for 2 min. Put in dried
papaya and add more sauce
gradually until papaya bloats.
Add sugar and salt to taste. Stir
continuously to prevent mixture
from burning. Remove from heat
and set aside to cool.

4 Holding each chilli by the stalk,
slit in the middle, making sure
not to cut through completely.
Remove and discard seeds.

5 Pour boiled water into a deep pot
and add a pinch of slaked lime.
Soak deseeded chillies for 5 min.
Drain and dry in the sun for
5 min.

METHOD: 20 MIN.

1 Heat ¼ cup oil in a clean wok.
Put in ginger and garlic and fry
until golden. Remove and set
aside. Put mustard seeds into the
same oil, cover and cook until
seeds stop popping; then fry for
30 sec. Remove and set aside.

2 Stuff each chilli from PREPARA-
TION 3, STEP 4 with 2 tsp. of the
papaya stuffing from PREPARA-
TION 3, STEP 2. Place stuffed
chillies into a clean glass or
earthen jar. Add dried shallots
(from PREPARATION 2), cucumber and cabbage leaves.

3 Sprinkle fried ginger, garlic and
mustard seeds over vegetables.

4 Pour in pickling sauce until level
is 5 cm above vegetables. Close
jar tightly and store in a cool
place for 2 days before serving as
a side dish with rice or noodles
or as a snack with drinks.

Serves 8 to 10

Cook's note Only the Cristang people
pickle chillies in this manner. Because of
the time-consuming preparation, the
pickles are made in huge batches, enough
to last throughout a festive season.

When all the vegetables have been eaten, the pickling sauce is used in Ambiler kachang or Debal (pp 46 and 52, respectively). Slaked lime is used to add crunchiness to the vegetables; it may be omitted.

My sister Teresa (Mrs B. Gomes) is an expert at making this dish that is the epitome of Cristang cuisine; the recipe I have included is hers. Thank you, Teresa!

Batata caldu leite cocu
(Sweet potato in coconut milk)

INGREDIENTS

4 (400 g) sweet potatoes
  (orange coloured variety)
400 g water spinach (kangkong)
200 g medium-sized prawns
1 tbsp. coarse salt
1 cup prawn stock (see p 27)
3 cups (240 g) grated coconut
3 cups warm water

¼ cup oil

blended to a fine paste
    15 (150 g) shallots, or
      1½ (150 g) onions, peeled
    5 cloves (15 g) garlic, peeled
    2 (6 g) candlenuts, or 4 (6 g)
      blanched almonds
    2 (5 g) fresh red chillies
    2 tsp. toasted shrimp paste
      (belachan)

salt and sugar to taste

PREPARATION: 20 MIN.

1 Peel sweet potatoes and cut into wedges. Soak in water until needed.

2 Remove and keep only leaves, shoots and tender stems of spinach; discard other parts.

3 Remove shells and heads of prawns and set aside. Rub shelled prawns with coarse salt to remove any slime and odour.

continued on p 86

Batata caldu leite cocu
This rich and fragrant dish goes particularly well with sambal belachan (p 62).

from p 85, *Batata caldu leite cocu*

Leave for 5 min.; then rinse well and drain.

4 Prepare prawn stock using shells and heads from STEP 3 (see p 27).

5 Soak grated coconut in water and extract 1 cup thick and 2 cups thin coconut milk (see p 26).

METHOD: 20 MIN.

1 Heat oil in a deep pot. Add blended paste and stir-fry.

2 Pour in thin coconut milk and boil for 5 min.

3 Reduce heat, add sweet potatoes and simmer for 5 min. Then add prawns and cook until they turn pink.

4 Add water spinach stalks, followed a minute later by shoots and leaves.

5 Pour in prawn stock. Add thick coconut milk, stirring continuously to prevent milk from curdling. Season with salt and sugar to taste.

6 When gravy begins to bubble, lower heat, simmer for 3 min. Remove from heat and let stand for 5 min. before serving with rice.

Serves 4 to 6

Cook's note Half a small cabbage (cut into wedges) and 2 brinjals (halved and sliced thickly diagonally) may be substituted for the sweet potatoes and water spinach. This recipe is dedicated to my sister Minnie (Mrs Bill Kennedy), who loves this dish.

Bendi pas'agu
(Boiled lady's fingers)

INGREDIENTS

6 (100 g) lady's fingers (okra)

70 g dried prawns

4 cups hot water

1 tsp. vinegar

1 pinch baking soda

blended to a coarse paste
7 (70 g) shallots, or ½ (50 g) onion, peeled
3 cloves (18 g) garlic, peeled
3 (15 g) fresh red chillies
1 tsp. toasted shrimp paste (belachan)

1 tbsp. lime or lemon juice

salt and sugar to taste

3 (20 g) shallots, sliced thinly

PREPARATION: 10 MIN.

1 Cut tips off lady's fingers, leaving rest of vegetable intact.

2 Discard heads and grit in dried prawns. Rinse and soak in 1 cup of the hot water until soft; then drain. Add to blended paste and blend for 30 sec. using an electric blender.

METHOD: 15 MIN.

1 Bring remaining water to a boil in a stainless steel or porcelain pot with vinegar and a pinch of baking soda. Scald lady's fingers, remove and immerse immediately in cold water. Drain and set aside.

2 Mix blended paste from PREPARATION, STEP 2 with 1 tsp. of the lime juice. Add salt and sugar.

3 Arrange lady's fingers in a glass dish and spread paste on top. Sprinkle with more lime juice if desired.

4 Sprinkle sliced shallots on top and serve as a side dish,

accompanying rice and a fish curry.

Serves 2

Cook's note Adding baking soda to the scalding water preserves the green colour of the lady's fingers. The vinegar prevents the pods from breaking open and reduces the slime that accumulates in this vegetable as it cooks. Careful handling and short cooking times are also effective against the accumulation of slime.

Use stainless steel, porcelain or glass cookware as the vegetable will discolour aluminium utensils. The discolouration is harmless but unsightly, and it will bleach the vegetable.

Bredu chapchye
(Traditional mixed vegetables)

INGREDIENTS

30 g edible wood fungus

30 g dried lily buds

30 g glass vermicelli

3 (15 g) strips soft bean curd sheet, 30 cm long each

½ (200 g) cabbage

½ (150 g) yam bean

100 g dried prawns

1 cup hot water plus additional for soaking wood fungus

¼ cup oil

blended to a fine paste
10 (100 g) shallots, or
1 (100 g) onion, peeled
7 cloves (21 g) garlic, peeled

2 tbsp. salted soya beans

½ cup water

½ tbsp. sugar

salt to taste

garnish
1 spring onion, chopped finely
1 stalk celery, chopped finely

continued on p 88

Bendi pas'agu
This boiled lady's fingers and sambal paste dish is pictured with an antique carved floral chain (top). The eighteenth century chain of Dutch origin was used as a pot hanger.

from p 86, *Bredu chapchye*

PREPARATION: 15 MIN.

1 Soak wood fungus in hot water and lily buds and glass vermicelli in separate bowls of warm water until each ingredient bloats, about 10 min.; then discard water.

2 Cut rough ends and stalks off wood fungus; snip tips off lily buds and tie a knot with each strand. Wash both ingredients well to remove grit and sand and set aside. Cut vermicelli strands in half and soak again.

3 Cut bean curd strips into 7-cm lengths and soak in cool water for 5 min.; then discard water.

4 Separate cabbage leaves and discard those that are wilted; cut remaining leaves into halves and set aside.

5 Slice yam bean thinly, then cut each slice into quarters. Set aside.

6 Remove dirt and grit from dried prawns and soak in ½ cup of the hot water for 10 min. Then drain off liquid and set it aside. Rinse dried prawns and soak in cool water.

METHOD: 15 MIN.

1 Heat oil in a wok. Put in blended paste and stir-fry for 1 minute. Add salted soya beans and stir-fry until fragrant.

2 Add dried prawns and liquid from PREPARATION, STEP 6. Simmer for 2 min., stirring occasionally. Add remaining hot water.

3 Add wood fungus, lily buds and yam bean slices. Stir well. Cover, lower heat and cook for 4 min.

4 Add vermicelli and bean curd strips. Stir gently and cook covered for another 3 min.

5 Add the ½ cup of water if necessary to prevent ingredients from burning. Add cabbage leaves, stir and cook until liquid starts bubbling, about 4 min.

6 Add sugar and lower heat. Using two ladles, toss well to mix ingredients. Season with salt before removing from heat.

7 Sprinkle garnish on top and serve hot with rice and curry.

Serves 4 to 6

Cook's note This is a popular festival dish among Malacca's Peranakan people.

═══════════════

Bredu chilli mustardu
(Green chilli with mustard)

INGREDIENTS

200 g fresh medium-sized prawns

1 tbsp. coarse salt

1 tbsp. tamarind pulp

1 cup water

¼ cup oil

blended to a coarse paste
    10 (100 g) shallots, or
        1½ (150 g) onions, peeled
    2 tbsp. mustard seeds
    ¼ tsp. turmeric powder
    2 tsp. toasted shrimp paste
        (belachan)
    3 (15 g) candlenuts, or 6 (15 g)
        blanched almonds
    20 g dried prawns, presoaked

salt to taste

300 g fresh green chillies, sliced
    thick

sugar to taste

PREPARATION: 15 MIN.

1 Remove heads and shells from prawns, leaving tails intact.

2 Rub with coarse salt to remove any slime and odour. Leave for 5 min.; then rinse well and drain.

3 Soak tamarind pulp in water and extract juice (see p 26).

METHOD: 15 MIN.

1 Heat oil in a pan. Put in blended paste and sauté until fragrant.

2 Pour in tamarind juice and stir, then add prawns and stir-fry until they turn pink.

3 Season with salt, add sliced chillies and simmer for 5 min.

4 Add sugar to taste. Simmer until very little liquid remains and remove from heat.

Serves 4 to 6

Cook's note Meat (pork or beef) may be substituted for prawns; add in METHOD, STEP 2 before pouring in tamarind juice.

═══════════════

Bredu kachang cung baca (Long beans with beef)

INGREDIENTS

300 g long beans

300 g lean beef or any other meat,
    or 100 g small prawns

¼ cup oil

blended to a fine paste
    4 (12 g) cloves garlic, peeled
    5 (25 g) shallots, or ¼ (25 g)
        onion, peeled

½ tsp. freshly ground black pepper

1 tbsp. salted soya beans, mashed

½ cup meat stock (see p 27)

1 tsp. thick soy sauce

salt and sugar to taste

PREPARATION: 15 MIN.

1 Slice beans diagonally into 4-cm lengths.

2 Slice beef into thin, matchstick-length strips.

3 If using prawns, trim off feelers but do not shell or remove heads.

continued on p 91

Bredu kachang cung baca
This long bean and meat dish is served in a colourful nineteenth century Peranakan plate. The copper containers in the background are miniatures of those used by Portuguese farmers to cook stews for their farmhands after a bountiful harvest.

Cebola enchimintu
This mild stuffed onion dish makes a good introduction to Cristang cuisine, especially for those who are unaccustomed to Asian flavours.

from p 88, *Bredu kachang cung baca*

4 Rub with coarse salt to remove any slime and odour. Leave for 5 min.; then rinse well and drain.

METHOD: 10 MIN.

1 Heat oil in a wok over high heat, put in blended paste and black pepper and sauté until fragrant.

2 Add mashed salted soya beans and stir-fry for 3 min.

3 Put in beef slices, or prawns if using, and stir-fry, adding 2 tbsp. of the stock to prevent ingredients from burning. Cook for 3 min.

4 Add long beans and remaining stock. Cover and cook until beans are done.

5 Add soy sauce and salt and sugar to taste. Cook until sugar dissolves, then remove from heat. Serve immediately.

Serves 4 to 6

Cook's note French or runner beans may be substituted for long beans.

Traditionally, pork fat was cut into tiny cubes, rubbed with salt and deep fried to a crisp. The resulting oil was used to cook this dish; the lard crisps were then sprinkled over the cooked vegetables just before serving.

Cebola enchimintu
(Stuffed onions)

INGREDIENTS

6 medium-sized Spanish onions of equal size (100 g each)

stuffing: mixed well
    200 g minced beef
    100 g minced prawns
    1 tbsp. fine breadcrumbs
    1 tbsp. chopped coriander leaves
    (optional)
    ½ tsp. stew spice powder (see p 28)
    ½ tsp. paprika or chilli powder

½ tsp. sugar
½ tsp. salt

1 (60 g) egg, beaten

a little oil or butter

½ cup water or meat stock (see p 27)

1 tbsp. flour

3 tbsp. milk

2 tsp. thick soy sauce

½ tsp. thin soy sauce

½ tsp. black peppercorns, coarsely ground

salt and sugar to taste

a splash of brandy (optional)

1 tbsp. fine bread or cracker crumbs

PREPARATION: 15 MIN.

1 Cut roots and tops off onions; peel and boil in slightly salted water for 2 min. Drain and set aside to cool.

2 When onions are cool, scoop out centres using a teaspoon; the cavities created should be large enough to take 2 tsp. of stuffing. Save scooped out flesh.

3 Chop onion flesh and add to mixed ingredients for filling. Beat egg and add to mixture, making sure to mix well.

4 Heat oven to 150°C (300°F or gas mark 2).

5 Fill cavities of onions with 1 or 2 tsp. of the filling. Dot the top with oil or butter.

METHOD: 25 MIN.

1 Arrange onions in a heat proof dish and bake for 25 min.

2 Meanwhile, prepare gravy. Heat water in a pan and gradually stir in flour, taking care to dissolve lumps.

3 Add milk, thick and thin soy sauces and stir over low heat for 5 min.

4 Season with black pepper and salt and sugar to taste; remove from heat when gravy has thickened.

5 Arrange baked onions in a serving dish. Add a splash of brandy to gravy and stir well. Spoon gravy over onions.

6 Sprinkle bread crumbs on top and serve immediately.

Serves 6

Coubes gulung
(Cabbage rolls)

INGREDIENTS

1 slice white bread, 1½ cm thick

½ cup milk

mixed well
    300 g minced beef
    200 g minced prawns

½ tsp. stew spice powder (see p 28)

½ tsp. pepper

1 (½ kg) medium-sized cabbage

1 egg

2 tsp. cornflour

¼ cup oil

chopped fine
    1 (100 g) onion, peeled
    3 cloves (9 g) garlic, peeled
    1 (80 g) carrot
    2 slices yam bean

1 tsp. salt

1 tsp. sugar

1 cup meat stock (see p 27)

6 pieces thread, 18-cm lengths

garnish
    1 spring onion, sliced
    1 fresh red chilli, chopped

PREPARATION: 15 MIN.

1 Soak bread in milk for 2 min. Squeeze dry, break up and

continued on p 92

from p 91, *Coubes gulung*

incorporate with meat and prawn mixture. Season with stew spice powder and pepper and leave to marinate for 5 min.

2 Immerse cabbage in boiling water until it is pliable, about 10 min. Separate leaves and pare down hard stem and spine of each leaf until it is easily folded. Set aside.

3 Beat egg and cornflour together, making sure to dissolve lumps.

METHOD: 25 MIN.

1 To cook filling, heat oil in a pan. Put in onion and garlic and sauté until fragrant. Add yam bean and carrot and fry for 3 min.

2 Add meat mixture (from PREPA-RATION STEP 1) and cook for 3 min., removing any excess oil that appears. Add salt, sugar and 2 tbsp. of the meat stock.

3 Cook, stirring occasionally until all liquid is absorbed. Remove filling from heat and set aside.

4 Place one boiled cabbage leaf on a plate. Place 2 tbsp. (or less) of the filling about 2½ cm from the end of the leaf closest to you. Lift that end over the filling and roll once. Fold in left and right sides, then continue rolling till the end of the leaf. Secure by wrapping a piece of thread around each roll three times.

5 Repeat until all filling has been used up. You should have about 7–8 rolls. Stack rolls in a deep dish and set aside.

6 To make gravy, pour remaining meat stock into a small saucepan and gradually bring to a boil.

7 When stock begins to boil, pour in egg-and-cornflour mixture, stirring well. When gravy thickens, remove from heat and pour over cabbage rolls.

8 Steam rolls for 5 min. Sprinkle with garnish and serve at once with a roast, curry and rice.

Serves 4 to 6

Epuk-epuk sayor
(Vegetable turnovers)

INGREDIENTS

5 black mushrooms, presoaked in hot water

shortcrust pastry
    2 cups flour, sifted
    3 cups hot water
    2½ tbsp. butter, or margarine
    pinch of salt

4 cups plus 3 tbsp. oil

2 cakes (50 g) firm bean curd, diced

2 (200 g) onions, peeled and chopped finely

6 cloves (18 g) garlic, peeled and chopped finely

1 cup shredded yam bean

½ cup shredded carrot

1 tsp. thick soy sauce

1 tsp. pepper

1 tsp. stew spice powder (see p 28)

3 tbsp. meat stock (see p 27)

1 tsp. salt

2 tsp. sugar

chilli-vinegar sauce:
blended together; adjust sourness with
lime juice and vinegar
    6 (25 g) fresh red chillies
    1 bulb (60 g) garlic, peeled
    ½ tsp. salt
    1 tsp. sugar
    lime or lemon juice and vinegar
    to taste

PREPARATION: 20 MIN.

1 Dice black mushrooms into small cubes .

2 To make shortcrust pastry:
  i Dissolve butter in hot water. Add salt, followed by flour. Knead well to form a soft pliable pastry.
  ii Divide pastry into balls about 2½ cm in diameter. Set aside.

METHOD: 30 MIN.

1 Heat 3 tbsp. oil in a wok. Put in diced bean curd and fry until golden; remove and drain.

2 In the same oil, sauté diced mushrooms for 1 min. Add chopped onions and garlic and stir-fry until fragrant.

3 Put in yam bean, carrot, pepper and stew spice powder and stir-fry for 1 min. Add meat stock and stir. Cover and cook over low heat for 5 min.

4 Add salt and sugar; cover and cook until liquid is absorbed, about 2 min.

5 When all liquid has been absorbed, add fried bean curd. Toss mixture gently. Remove from heat and set aside to cool before using.

6 Flatten pastry balls from PREPA-RATION, STEP 2 evenly until they are about 10 cm in diameter each. Place 2–3 tsp. of the cooked vegetables in the centre of the pastry. Fold over and seal by fluting the edges, using thumb and index finger. Place turnover on a tray. Repeat until all pastry has been used.

7 Heat remaining oil in a wok. Deep fry 3–4 turnovers at a time until golden all over. Remove and drain on paper towels. Serve hot as a snack with the chilli-vinegar sauce.

Makes 20 turnovers

Foler cebola cung taukwa (Fried spring onions with bean curd)

INGREDIENTS

2 cakes (100 g) firm bean curd

20 spring onion leaves

¼ cup oil

5 (50 g) shallots, or ½ (50 g) onion, peeled and chopped

4 cloves (12 g) garlic, peeled and chopped

10 g ginger, peeled and shredded

1 tbsp. salted soya beans, mashed

2 tsp. thick soy sauce

4 tbsp. meat stock (see p 27)

salt and sugar to taste

PREPARATION: 10 MIN.

1 Cut bean curd into strips 1 cm thick.

2 Cut spring onion leaves into 2½-cm lengths.

METHOD: 10 MIN.

1 Heat oil in a wok over moderately high heat. Fry bean curd until golden and crispy. Remove and drain on paper towels.

2 Add shallots, garlic and ginger to the same oil. Sauté for 10 sec.

3 Add salted soya beans and sauté for a further 10 sec.

4 Add spring onions, soy sauce and meat stock. Stir well. Cook for 2 min. Add fried bean curd from STEP 1 above.

5 Season with salt and sugar. Remove from heat and serve at once.

Serves 4 to 6

Foler cebola cung taukwa
This dish of fried spring onion with bean curd reflects the great influence Chinese cooking techniques have had on Cristang cuisine, especially in the preparation of vegetables.

The plate is resting on pieces of antique Chinese wood carving; the skeins of coloured silk thread are a reminder of the old days when silk was one of the most important trading goods brought by the Chinese merchants to Malacca.

Marergozu fretu
(Fried bitter gourd)

INGREDIENTS

2 medium-sized bitter gourds (about 100 g each)

1 tbsp. salt plus additional to taste

200 g medium-sized prawns

1 tbsp. coarse salt

¼ cup oil

6 cloves (18 g) garlic, peeled and chopped

1 (100 g) onion, peeled and chopped

1 tbsp. salted soya beans, mashed

1 tbsp. thick soy sauce

½ cup water

2 tbsp. sugar

PREPARATION: 20 MIN.

1 Wash gourds and halve them lengthwise. Discard pith and seeds. Slice across thinly and sprinkle with 1 tbsp. of the salt. Rub well and leave for 20 min. Squeeze slices and discard liquid to remove bitter taste. Rinse well and drain.

2 Shell and devein prawns. Rub with coarse salt to remove any slime and odour. Leave for 5 min.; then rinse well and drain.

METHOD: 10 MIN.

1 Heat oil in a frying pan. Put in garlic and onions and sauté until soft.

2 Add mashed salted soya beans and stir-fry for 30 sec.

3 Add bitter gourd, thick soy sauce, water and sugar to make gravy. Cook until vegetable is soft. Lower heat.

4 Add prawns; cover and cook for 2 min.

5 Season with remaining salt or to taste before removing from heat.

Serve at once as an accompaniment to rice and a meat dish.

Serves 6 to 8

Mohlyu gingibri doce cung taukwa
(Bean curd in sweet ginger sauce)

INGREDIENTS

4 cakes (200 g) firm bean curd

1 tbsp. tamarind juice

1 cup plus 3 tbsp. water

1 tbsp. cornflour

½ cup oil

30 g ginger, peeled and sliced finely

4 cloves (12 g) garlic, peeled and sliced finely

blended to a paste
    6 cloves (18 g) garlic, peeled
    10 (100 g) shallots, or 1 (100 g) onion, peeled

2 tbsp. salted soya beans, mashed

1 tbsp. sugar

1 tbsp. vinegar (optional)

PREPARATION: 10 MIN.

1 Rinse bean curd and leave to drain in a colander. Do not cut.

2 Soak tamarind pulp in 1 cup of the water and extract juice (see p 26).

3 Mix cornflour to a smooth paste with remaining 3 tbsp. of water.

METHOD: 25 MIN.

1 Heat oil in a wok. Put in bean curd cakes one at a time and fry until golden brown. Remove and drain on paper towels.

2 In the same oil, fry ginger and garlic until crispy and golden brown; remove and drain. Discard 2 tbsp. of the oil.

3 In the same pan, fry blended paste for 30 sec. Add salted soya bean and 1 tbsp. tamarind juice. Stir until fragrant.

4 Add sugar, cornflour paste from PREPARATION, STEP 3 and fried ginger and garlic from STEP 1. Cook for 1 min. If gravy becomes too thick, add water.

5 Taste and, if preferred, add vinegar. Stir well, remove from heat and serve at once.

Serves 4

Pongtey (Yam bean stew)

INGREDIENTS

2 medium-sized yam beans (about 200 g each)

1 kg chicken or any other meat

1 piece (200 g) sugar cane, 15 cm long (optional)

½ cup oil

blended to a fine paste
    12 (120 g) shallots, or 1 (100 g) onion, peeled
    1 bulb (60 g) garlic, peeled
    50 g ginger, peeled

2 tbsp. salted soya beans, mashed

1 tbsp. thick soy sauce

2 cups water or meat stock (see p 27)

4 (400 g) potatoes, peeled and quartered

1 stalk coriander leaves

salt to taste

PREPARATION: 10 MIN

1 Peel and halve yam beans. Cut across into slices 1 cm thick, then cut each slice into four.

2 Cut chicken into bite-sized pieces.

3 Skin sugar cane and cut into 5-cm lengths.

continued on p 96

Mohlyu gingibri doce cung taukwa
Bean curd in an unusual sweet ginger sauce.

from p 94, *Pongtey*

METHOD: 30 MIN.

1 Heat oil in a pan. Put in blended paste and stir-fry until fragrant. Add salted soya beans and fry until oil rises to the surface.

2 Add chicken and thick soy sauce. Stir to coat meat well. Pour in water and cook for 10 min.

3 Add sugarcane, potatoes and yam bean. Cover and continue cooking until meat and potatoes are cooked, about 15 min.

4 When meat is cooked, add in a few sprigs of coriander leaves. Taste and season with salt. Remove from heat and serve at once with hot rice.

Serves 4 to 6

Salade dumingu
(Fresh vegetable Sunday salad)

INGREDIENTS

2 (200 g) potatoes
1 (150 g) head of lettuce
1 (350 g) pineapple, sliced, or 6 slices tinned pineapple, drained
1 tbsp. salt
1 (100 g) onion, peeled and sliced into rings
2 (120 g) hard-boiled eggs, sliced
3 (125 g) tomatoes, cut into wedges
1 (80 g) cucumber, sliced unpeeled

salad dressing
   1 tsp. prepared English mustard
   2 tbsp. condensed milk
   ½ tsp. pepper
   a pinch of salt
   2 cloves (6 g) garlic, peeled and chopped
   1 tbsp. vinegar

PREPARATION: 15 MIN.

1 Boil potatoes in their jackets; peel and slice thickly (½ cm).

2 Separate lettuce leaves and arrange on a salad platter.

3 Skin pineapple and remove eyes. Rub fruit with 1 tbsp. salt; then rinse. Remove core and slice into rings. Alternatively, cut fruit into quarters lengthwise, remove hard core and cut flesh into triangles.

METHOD: 15 MIN.

1 Arrange pineapple pieces on the plate of lettuce. Then layer the potato, onion, egg, tomato and cucumber alternately around the dish; cover and chill.

2 In a deep bowl, mix ingredients for salad dressing, leaving out vinegar. Stir until smooth, then add vinegar gradually and stir well.

3 Just before serving, sprinkle dressing on salad. Serve as an accompaniment to rice, curry and braised meat (see seybah, p 139).

Serves 6 to 8

Soy limang
(Brinjals in lime and soy sauce)

INGREDIENTS

4 (400 g) brinjals, long variety

mixed well
   1 tsp. black pepper, freshly ground
   ¼ tsp. stew spice powder (see p 28)
   ½ tsp. salt

2 tbsp. lime or lemon juice, or 1 tbsp. tamarind pulp and ½ cup water
1 cup plus 1 tbsp. oil
1 (100 g) onion, peeled and sliced thickly
2 (6 g) fresh red chillies, sliced thickly
½ tsp. sugar

mixed together into a smooth paste
   1 tbsp. thick soy sauce
   1 cup water
   1 tsp. cornstarch

½ tsp. salt

PREPARATION: 10 MIN.

1 Cut brinjals into 7-cm lengths and halve each piece lengthwise. Score the white flesh of each piece.

2 With index finger, spread spice mixture over scored surfaces of each piece and set aside.

3 If using tamarind instead of lime juice, soak tamarind pulp in water and extract juice (see p 26).

METHOD: 15 MIN.

1 Heat the 1 cup of oil in a pan. Put in 3 or 4 slices of the brinjal and fry with coated surfaces face-down until brown. Remove and drain on paper towels. Repeat until all slices have been fried; discard oil.

2 To make sauce, heat the 1 tbsp. of oil and sauté onion and chillies until soft. Add sugar and stir until it is dissolved.

3 Add soy sauce-and-cornstarch mixture. Simmer for 3 min. Add salt and stir.

4 Add lime or tamarind juice, stir once and remove from heat.

5 Arrange fried brinjals on a plate and pour sauce on top. Serve at once as a side dish with rice and curry.

Serves 6 to 8

Salade dumingu (right)
It was my duty every Sunday to prepare this salad and the homemade dressing, which was concocted by my late father. The wooden carving on which the salad is displayed is part of a door from a Dutch cupboard.

Soy limang (below)
This dish of brinjals in a lime and soy sauce is resting on a reproduction of a 1671 painting by the Dutch artist Valentyne which shows the fortress that the Portuguese built in Malacca, A Famosa.

Comir Noibu

SEA MYTHS

Staunchly Catholic, the Cristang community of old adhered to the Church ruling of abstaining from meat on Fridays. Even when an auspicious occasion fell on a Friday, no meat was served. However, fish and other seafood were permitted, and Cristang chefs developed delicious recipes for them.

Many of these recipes may be sampled at the elaborate spread of the Comir Noibu, a dinner party hosted by the parents of the bridegroom on the eve of a wedding. Traditionally held on a Friday, the Comir Noibu includes nearly every seafood dish or delicacy known to the Cristang.

Living so close to the sea has given the Cristang a discerning palate for seafood—only the freshest ingredients will do. To ensure that this standard is not compromised, the fishermen in the Portuguese Settlement take their *praus* (small boats) out to sea at night and return in the morning to land their catch on the beach.

A Cristang fisherman's eagle eye misses little when he sorts out his catch. If he finds a crab with a cross on its shell, he sets it free immediately. This crustacean, known locally as the St Francis Xavier crab, is considered sacred by Cristang fishermen. Legend* has it that St Francis Xavier was sailing past Malacca when his boat was caught in a storm. As the sea raged, the frightened crew pleaded with St Francis Xavier to pray for them. The Saint agreed, and when he ended his supplications, he dipped his crucifix into the turbulent sea. Immediately the storm abated. Unfortunately, as he was performing this miracle, the crucifix slipped from its cord and fell into the water. St Francis was disconsolate at the loss of his most treasured possession. After the boat had landed, the Saint and his friend were on the beach when they noticed a large crab making its way towards them. It was holding the lost crucifix in its claws! The crab approached the Saint who promptly retrieved his beloved cross. Overcome with joy, he knelt down in prayer and blessed the crab by making a sign of the cross on its back.

It is not known what happened to the crab after it performed its good deed, but to this day crabs bearing the impression of a cross on their carapaces can be found in the Straits of Malacca; many believe them to be the progeny of the crab that had reunited St Francis with his crucifix. People who have eaten this species of crab say that the meat is exceptionally tasty; the shell is never discarded, for it is considered lucky to own one.

*Source: *Orient Conquistado a Jesu Christo pelos Padres de Companhia de Jesus*, First Edition, 370–1 (quotation from James Broderick in *St Francis Xavier*, p 263).

Cambrang cung cana
This prawn and sugarcane dish is a delightful combination of textures and tastes. It is served on a bed of pomelo and pomegranate pips. The antique trinket box with floral motifs in the background is nineteenth century Chinese.

Cambrang cung cana
(Prawn on sugarcane)

INGREDIENTS

½ kg medium-sized prawns

1 tbsp. coarse salt

1 stick (300 g) sugarcane, 30 cm long

marinade, mixed well
> 4 cloves (12 g) garlic, peeled and chopped finely
> 1 tsp. salt
> 1 tsp. ground black pepper
> 2 tsp. baking powder
> 1 tbsp. white wine
> 2 tbsp. rice flour

blended to a fine paste
> 8 (50 g) shallots, or ½ (50 g) onion, peeled
> 2 (10 g) fresh red chillies
> 1 tsp. spring onion, chopped
> 1 tsp. sugar
> 1 (5 g) candlenut, or 2 (5 g) blanched almonds

garnish
> 2 tbsp. pomelo and pomegranate pips

PREPARATION: 40 MIN.

1 Shell prawns and devein. Rub with coarse salt to remove any slime and odour. Leave for 5 min.; then rinse well and drain. Mix thoroughly with marinade and let stand for 30 min.

2 Peel sugarcane and cut into 10-cm lengths. Cut each length into quarters.

3 Puree marinated prawns in a blender and mix with rice flour.

4 Add blended paste to pureed prawns and mix well.

5 Divide mixture into 12 portions. Mould each portion around the centre of a piece of sugarcane, leaving about 5 cm of the sugarcane exposed at each end.

METHOD: 30 MIN.

1 Half-fill a large pot with water and bring to a boil. Place prepared sugarcane in water and simmer for 15 min. Remove and drain thoroughly.

2 Using a charcoal or electric grill or an oven, grill sugarcane until prawn mixture turns golden. Alternatively, heat 1 cup oil and deep fry 2 sticks of sugarcane at a time for 3 min. Drain on absorbent paper.

3 Sprinkle garnish on top and serve immediately with chilli sauce (see seybah, chilli sauce, p 139).

Serves 4 to 6

Carengguezu cung chilli taucho (Fried crabs with chillies and salted soya beans)

INGREDIENTS

3 (450 g) medium-sized fresh crabs

1 cup oil

chopped finely
> 5 (15 g) fresh red chillies, deseeded
> 20 (200 g) shallots, or 2 (200 g) onions, peeled
> 1 clove (3 g) garlic, peeled
> 30 g ginger, peeled

1 tsp. ground black pepper

1 tbsp. salted soya beans, mashed coarsely

1 cup water

½ tsp. sugar

PREPARATION: 20 MIN.

1 Remove carapaces and gills (spongy grey matter) of crabs. Chop each crab into quarters. Remove claws and break shell with a mallet or blunt edge of a cleaver.

METHOD: 20 MIN.

1 Heat oil in a wok. Fry crab pieces for 3 min. Remove and drain on a paper towel.

2 Remove all but 2 tbsp. oil. Add chopped ingredients and black pepper. Stir well, add salted soya bean and stir-fry until fragrant.

3 Add crab pieces and toss for 3 min. Add water and cook covered for 10 min.

4 Add sugar, stir and remove from heat. Stand for several minutes before serving.

Serves 6

Cook's note In Malaysia it is customary to eat crabs with the fingers, even in restaurants.

Traditionally, finger-bowls containing diluted Chinese tea with slices of lemon in them were used to clean the fingers after the meal.

Chicharru soy limang
(Hardtails in lime sauce)

INGREDIENTS

½ kg fresh hardtail or horse mackerel (4–5 whole fish)

4 tbsp. coarse salt

blended to a coarse paste
> 10 (100 g) shallots, or 1 (100 g) onion, peeled
> 4 cloves (12 g) garlic, peeled
> 4 (20 g) fresh red chillies
> 2 (10 g) candlenuts, or 4 (10 g) blanched almonds

1 cup oil

1 (100 g) onion, peeled and sliced

2 (10 g) fresh red chillies, sliced

1 tbsp. thick soy sauce

½ cup water

1 tbsp. vinegar

continued on p 102

Chicharru soy limang
This piquant dish of hardtails in a gravy of lime juice and thick soy sauce is typical of the way the Cristang combine Portuguese and local ingredients in their cuisine.

from p 100, *Chicarru soy limang*

1 tsp. sugar

salt to taste

1 tbsp. lime or lemon juice

PREPARATION: 15 MIN.

1 Gut fish and rub all over with coarse salt to remove any slime and odour. Rinse well and drain.

2 Coat each fish with blended paste and place some of the paste inside stomach cavity.

METHOD: 20 MIN.

1 Heat oil in a wok and fry fish, two at a time. Remove to a deep plate.

2 Remove oil, leaving ½ tbsp. in wok. Reheat and sauté onion. Add chilli and stir-fry.

3 Pour in thick soy sauce and water and simmer for 3 min.

4 Add vinegar and sugar; cook until sugar dissolves. Taste and add salt if necessary.

5 Pour sauce over fish and sprinkle with lime juice. Serve immediately with rice and ambiler kachang (see p 46).

Serves 4

Chorka tambrinhyu

(Tamarind squid)

INGREDIENTS

200 g medium-sized whole squid

1 tbsp. tamarind pulp

1 cup warm water

1 tbsp. white wine

1 tbsp. tomato sauce

1 tsp. prepared mustard

1 tsp. sugar

¼ cup oil

blended to a fine paste
    2 (10 g) fresh red chillies
    6 (12 g) dried chillies, presoaked in hot water
    3 cloves (9 g) garlic

1 tsp. thick soy sauce

1 cucumber, sliced into rounds (optional)

PREPARATION: 20 MIN.

1 Carefully pull tentacles and heads away from bodies of squid. Cut off tentacles for later use; discard heads. Remove innards and any cartilaginous matter. Rub and peel off thin skin. Wash bodies well, taking care to rinse out cavities. Slit bodies open and cut into bite-sized pieces.

2 Soak tamarind pulp in water and extract juice (see p 26).

3 Combine wine, tomato sauce, mustard, sugar and 1 tbsp. of the tamarind juice in a bowl. Mix thoroughly. Pour over squid pieces (including tentacles), mix well and set aside to marinate for at least 10 min.

METHOD: 10 MIN.

1 Heat oil in a pan and fry blended paste until fragrant.

2 Add marinated squid pieces and stir gently until squid is half-cooked, about 5 to 10 min. Add remaining tamarind juice and simmer until half the liquid is absorbed.

3 Add thick soy sauce and stir well. The dish should have a sweet and sour flavour that is also spicy.

4 Arrange squid on sliced cucumber. Pour any sauce remaining in pan over squid and serve at once with rice and curry.

Serves 4 to 6

Chuan-chuan

(Fried fish in ginger sauce)

INGREDIENTS

1 kg whole pomfret, sea bream or snapper

2 tbsp. coarse salt

mixed well
    1 tsp. salt
    1 tsp. pepper
    1 tsp. plain flour, sifted

1 tbsp. plus 1 tsp. tamarind

2 cups water

1 cup plus 2 tbsp. oil

50 g young ginger, julienned

2 (10 g) fresh red chillies, sliced finely

blended to a coarse paste
    10 (100 g) shallots, or 1 (100 g) onion, peeled
    6 (18 g) cloves garlic, peeled

2 tbsp. salted soya beans, mashed

5 black mushrooms, presoaked and sliced finely (optional)

1 tsp. thick soy sauce

sugar to taste

garnish
    1 stalk spring onion
    1 sprig coriander leaves

PREPARATION: 20 MIN.

1 Gut fish and rub with coarse salt to remove any slime and odour. Rinse well and dry with paper towels.

2 Make two 3-cm diagonal slits on both sides of fish and rub with mixture of salt, pepper and flour. Set aside.

3 Soak 1 tbsp. of the tamarind pulp in 1 cup of the water and extract juice (see p 26). Set aside.

continued on p 105

Chorka tambrinhyu
This simple village dish of tamarind squid is served with boiled rice on an antique Portuguese plate. The type of crab shown here is known to the Cristang as St Francis Xavier's crab and is found in the Straits of Malacca; note the cross-shaped pattern on its back. (See legend, p 98.)

Chuan-chuan
The sauce made from salted soya beans, chillies, ginger and tamarind transforms an otherwise ordinary fried fish into an exotic dish.

from p 102, *Chuan-chuan*

METHOD: 25 MIN.

1 Heat 1 cup of the oil in a frying pan to fry fish. To prevent sticking, add 1 tsp. tamarind pulp to the pan and wait until the oil is very hot before sliding fish in; do not turn fish until it is slightly brown underneath. When fish has browned evenly, remove and drain before arranging on a plate.

2 Discard used oil. In the same pan heat remaining 2 tbsp. of oil and sauté ginger and chilli over medium heat for 30 sec. Remove and set aside.

3 Put in blended paste and fry until fragrant. Add salted soya beans and continue frying for 1 min. Add a little water to prevent burning.

4 Pour in remaining cup of water and simmer for 3 min. Add tamarind juice; sauce should taste slightly sweet with a hint of sourness. If too sour, add sugar.

5 Add mushrooms and fried chillies and ginger from STEP 2 to sauce. Cook for 2 min.

6 Remove from heat and pour over fish. Garnish with spring onions and coriander leaves and serve with rice.

Serves 4

Gerago pikkadel
(Krill fritters)

INGREDIENTS

300 g fresh krill or baby shrimp

2 tbsp. plain flour, sifted

2 tsp. salt

2 tsp. black pepper

5 (300 g) eggs

2 tbsp. water

1 (100 g) onion, peeled and chopped

1 (5 g) fresh red chilli, chopped

1 tsp. sugar

2 cups oil for deep frying

garnish
    1 (220 g) cucumber, sliced
    1 head lettuce, leaves separated

PREPARATION: 15 MIN.

1 Remove grit and scraps and place krill in a sieve. Pour water on krill and set aside to drain.

2 To remove krill feelers, dip a pair of chopsticks in krill and twirl. Discard feelers that wind round chopsticks. Repeat if necessary.

3 Mix flour, salt and pepper in a bowl. Add eggs and beat well to form a batter. Add water and mix again.

4 Add onion and chilli to batter, followed by krill and sugar. Mix well.

METHOD: 15 MIN.

1 Heat oil in a deep pot or wok.

2 Drop 1 ladleful of the batter into the hot oil one at a time and deep fry until golden and crisp.

3 Drain fritters on absorbent paper. Cut into quarters and place on a bed of lettuce and cucumber and serve with chilli sauce. (See seybah, chilli sauce, p 139.)

Serves 8 to 10

Cook's note When the shoals of gerago or krill make their annual appearance in the Straits of Malacca the sea turns a delicate pink. The sight of this delights the Cristang fisherfolk for it means they will soon be enjoying homemade fermented krill (chinchaluk) and shrimp paste (belachan). The excess krill is turned into this fritter, which is a popular snack.

Doppar (White pomfret in egg sauce)

INGREDIENTS

½ kg whole white pomfret (*pampal*)

1 tbsp. coarse salt

mixed well
    ½ tsp. stew spice powder (see p 28)
    ½ tsp. pepper
    ½ tsp. salt

2 cups water

1 cup fish stock (see p 27)

2 tbsp. white vinegar

2 tbsp. butter

1 (100 g) onion, peeled and sliced

3 tbsp. plain flour, sifted

2 (120 g) eggs, lightly beaten

garnish
    1 stalk spring onion, chopped
    1 stalk coriander leaves

PREPARATION: 10 MIN.

1 Gut fish and rub with coarse salt to remove any slime and odour. Rinse well and drain. Score fish on both sides and rub thoroughly with mixture of stew spice powder, pepper and salt.

METHOD: 15 MIN.

1 Put water, fish stock and vinegar into a deep pot. Slide in fish and bring to a slow boil.

2 When flesh is white and opaque, remove fish. Reserve stock.

3 Place fish on a plate. While still warm, rub all over with 1 tbsp. of the butter and set aside.

4 In a pan, heat remaining butter and sauté onion. Pour in fish stock from STEP 2 and add flour gradually, stirring continuously until a thin sauce forms.

continued on p 107

Doppar
This dish of white pomfret in egg sauce used to be
served on special occasions such as weddings and grand
celebrations. Today, it is reserved for convalescents
who require light but nutritious meals.

from p 105, *Doppar*

5 Gradually add egg to sauce, stirring continuously. Do not allow sauce to boil.

6 When sauce has thickened, remove from heat and pour over buttered fish. Garnish with spring onion and coriander leaves and serve with rice or bread.

Serves 2

Karing-karing fretu
(Fried silver threadfish)

INGREDIENTS

tossed well together
    12–15 dried silver threadfish (karing-karing)
    1 tsp. sugar
    1 pinch chilli powder

1 cup oil

3 limes or 1 lemon, cut into wedges

4 (40 g) shallots, peeled and sliced

METHOD: 10 MIN.

1 Heat oil in a wok until it is smoking. Put in threadfish and fry until golden and crispy. Drain on paper towels.

2 Sprinkle lime juice over fish and serve garnished with raw sliced shallots.

Serves 4

Cook's note This dish makes an excellent snack with beer or whiskey. It can also be served with rice and curry. Silver threadfish is known as layor-layor in Cristang; once it is dried, it is known as karing-karing. (See glossary, p 40.)

Obu trubo (Fish roe relish)

INGREDIENTS

150 g fish roe

1 cup water

½ tsp. salt

blended to a fine paste
    5 (50 g) shallots, or ½ (50 g) onion, peeled
    2 (10 g) fresh red chillies
    2 (10 g) candlenuts, or 4 (10 g) blanched almonds

1 tbsp. lime or lemon juice

1 tbsp. oil

PREPARATION: 10 MIN.

1 Boil fish roe in water with salt until soft. Remove from liquid and set aside. Reserve liquid.

METHOD: 5 MIN.

1 Heat oil in a pan and fry blended paste for 2 min. or until aromatic. Add liquid from PREPARATION, STEP 1 and simmer for 2 min.

2 Slide in roe gently and continue to simmer for 2 min. or until very little moisture is left.

3 Arrange fish roe on a dish. Sprinkle lime juice on roe and serve at once with rice and a hot curry.

Serves 2

Pesce assa (Spicy grilled fish)

INGREDIENTS

½ kg whole snapper (or sea perch or bream)

4 tbsp. coarse salt

3 tsp. turmeric powder

1½ tsp. salt

2 tbsp. tamarind pulp

½ cup water

½ cup oil

blended to a fine paste with 1 tsp. oil
    6 (12 g) dried chillies, presoaked in hot water
    3 (15 g) fresh red chillies
    12 (120 g) shallots, or 1¼ (120 g) onions, peeled
    4 cloves (12 g) garlic, peeled
    4 (20 g) candlenuts, or 4 (20 g) blanched almonds
    2 tsp. (25 g) toasted shrimp paste (belachan)
    2 stalks lemon grass (use 7 cm of root end)
    30 g galangal, peeled

1 tsp. sugar

banana leaves for making parcels

2–3 citrus leaves, shredded finely

1 tbsp. lime or lemon juice

PREPARATION: 20 MIN.

1 Gut fish and rub all over with coarse salt to remove any slime and odour. Rinse well and pat dry.

2 Make shallow, diagonal cuts on both sides of fish; season with turmeric and 1 tsp. of the salt. Set aside.

3 Soak tamarind pulp in ½ cup water and extract juice (see p 26.)

4 Heat oil in a pan and stir-fry blended paste for 2 min., taking care not to overcook. Add remaining salt and sugar and tamarind juice. Continue stir-frying till all moisture has been absorbed.

METHOD: 40 MIN.

1 Soften banana leaves by holding them over a low flame—be careful not to singe leaves. Lay fish on leaves and cover with stir-fried paste. Sprinkle shredded citrus leaves on top and wrap into a parcel. Secure with tooth picks.

continued on p 109

Pesce assa
Traditionally, this dish is prepared by wrapping the fish in banana leaf and cooking over hot coals placed in a hole in the ground.

from p 107, *Pesce assa*

2 Wrap again with aluminium foil
if desired, making a neat long
parcel.

3 Bake or grill parcel for 20 min.
on each side or until fish flakes
easily. Sprinkle lime juice on fish
and serve hot with rice.

Serves 2 to 4

Pesce binagre
(Salted fish in vinegar)

INGREDIENTS

300 g dried salted horse mackerel
or rayfish

½ cup plus 1 tbsp. oil

5 (50 g) shallots, or ½ (50 g)
onion, peeled and sliced thinly

2 cloves (6 g) garlic, peeled and
sliced thinly

2 (10 g) fresh red chillies, sliced

2 tbsp. vinegar

½ tsp. sugar

METHOD: 10 MIN.

1 Heat ½ cup of the oil until very
hot. Slide in fish carefully and fry
until crisp. Remove.

2 Discard oil. In same pan, heat
1 tbsp. fresh oil and sauté
shallots, garlic and chillies for
about 30 sec.

3 Add vinegar and sugar and stir
until sugar dissolves.

4 Pour sauce on fried fish and serve
immediately with hot rice and a
coconut milk based curry, such as
cari Belanda (p 46).

Serves 2

Cook's note Salted fish roe may be
substituted for the salted fish.

Pesce fretu (Fried fish)

INGREDIENTS

½ kg Spanish mackerel steaks

1 tbsp. coarse salt

blended to a paste
  4 (20 g) fresh red chillies
  3 (15 g) candlenuts, or 6 (15 g)
    blanched almonds
  10 (100 g) shallots, or
  1 (100 g) onion, peeled
  2 (6 g) cloves garlic, peeled

1 tsp. salt

1 tbsp. plus 1 tsp. tamarind pulp

½ cup water

1 cup oil

1 tsp. brown sugar

PREPARATION: 10 MIN.

1 Rub fish steaks with coarse salt
to remove any slime and odour.
Rinse well and drain.

2 Mix blended paste with salt and
use to coat both sides of fish
steaks.

3 Soak 1 tbsp. of the tamarind
pulp in water and extract juice
(see p 26).

METHOD: 10 MIN.

1 Heat oil in a frying pan to fry
fish. To prevent fish from
sticking, add 1 tsp. tamarind
pulp to pan and wait until oil is
hot before sliding fish in; do not
turn fish until it browns underneath. When fish is evenly
golden brown, remove and drain.

2 Remove oil. In the same pan,
add tamarind juice and simmer
for 2 min. Then add brown sugar
and stir well. Remove from heat.

3 Arrange fish on a plate and
spoon sauce on top. Serve
immediately with rice.

Serves 4

Cook's note The fish can also be battered
before frying by dipping it in beaten egg
and coating with seasoned breadcrumbs or
flour. For a different flavour, rub the fish
with curry or chilli powder or with garlic
and tamarind pulp before frying.

Pesce tambrinhyu
(Pickled tamarind fish)

INGREDIENTS

½ kg dried salted fish (dorab or wolf
herring)

5 tbsp. whole coriander seeds, or
3 tbsp. coriander powder

1 tbsp. cumin

1 tbsp. fennel

1 tbsp. ground black pepper

4 cups plus 2 tsp. white vinegar

blended to a fine paste
  20 (40 g) dried chillies,
    presoaked in hot water
  20 (200 g) shallots, or
  2 (200 g) onions, peeled
  5 g turmeric, peeled

2 bulbs (120 g) garlic, peeled and
mashed finely

1 tbsp. English mustard powder or
prepared English mustard

2 tsp. salt

1 cup oil

4 tbsp. tamarind pulp

ADVANCE PREPARATION: 24
HRS.

1 Cut salted fish into 7-cm square
portions. Wash and dry in the sun
for one day or leave in oven on
very low heat until completely dry.

PREPARATION: 40 MIN.

1 In a dry, heated pan, put in
coriander, cumin, fennel and
black pepper in that order, dry-
roasting each spice for a few

continued on p 110

from p 109, *Pesce tambrinhyu*

minutes before adding another. Remove roasted spices and, while still warm, blend together with 2 tsp. of the vinegar to form a thick paste.

2 Mix together spice paste, blended paste and mashed garlic using a spoon. Stir in mustard and salt and mix thoroughly. Do not use a food processor.

3 Put this mixture (marinade) in a *pasu* (clay pot) or porcelain bowl. Do not use a metal container as marinade could react with the metal. Place salted fish in container and coat well with marinade.

4 Soak tamarind pulp in remaining 4 cups of vinegar and extract juice (see p 26). Pour juice over fish and toss lightly. Cover and keep in refrigerator for one week, stirring daily.

SERVING METHOD

1 Heat oil in a pan and deep fry the quantity of fish required (about 2 pieces per person).

2 Fry 2–3 pieces at a time on high heat until crisp. Remove, drain and arrange on a plate.

3 Remove oil from the pan, retaining 1 tbsp. Fry 1 tbsp. marinade until fragrant. Spoon fried marinade over fish and serve at once with boiled rice or canje parpa (p 180).

Serves 10 or more

Cook's note Pesce tambrinhyu is a traditional dish eaten by the Cristang during Lent when Catholics fast and abstain from eating meat. This recipe was given to me by Aunt Julia Zarzadias, a late family friend. So popular was her pesce tambrinhyu that connoisseurs from as far away as Penang and Singapore used to order it from her for Lent.

Pesce kertouk
(Fish parcels)

INGREDIENTS

8 (400 g) large leaves of Chinese white cabbage

¼ cup oil

blended to a fine paste
    4 (20 g) candlenuts, or 8 (20 g) blanched almonds
    10 (100 g) shallots, or 1 (100 g) onion, peeled
    2 (10 g) fresh red chillies

Salt and pepper to taste

4 snapper or sea bass cutlets, each weighing 120 g

2 cups fish stock (see p 27)

1 tbsp. white wine

fish sauce, mixed well
    1 tbsp. thick soy sauce
    2 tbsp. lime or lemon juice
    1 (5 g) fresh red chilli, sliced

PREPARATION: 25 MIN.

1 Blanch Chinese cabbage leaves quickly. Immerse in cold water. Remove and drain.

2 Heat oil in a pan and fry blended paste. Add salt and pepper, sauté for 1 min. and remove from heat.

3 Lay two Chinese cabbage leaves on a plate, making sure they overlap. Place a fish cutlet on top. Spread a portion of cooked ingredients from STEP 2 on cutlet and wrap into a parcel. Tie each parcel with a piece of thread. Wrap other cutlets in the same manner.

METHOD: 15 MIN.

1 Place fish parcels in a saucepan and add enough fish stock to cover.

2 Simmer for 10 min., making sure parcels remain completely immersed in stock. If necessary, add more stock or water.

3 Add white wine and stir.

4 Just before serving, remove threads. Place parcels in a deep dish and spoon stock over. Serve with fish sauce.

Serves 4

Tante Maria-se achar pesce seccu
(Aunt May's salted fish pickle)

INGREDIENTS

5 pieces (300 g) dried salted fish

½ cup oil

mixed with 1 tbsp. vinegar to form a paste
    3 tbsp. cumin powder
    3 tbsp. fennel powder
    3 tbsp. coriander powder
    3 tbsp. chilli powder
    3 tbsp. turmeric powder

blended together
    50 g ginger, peeled
    1½ bulbs (90 g) garlic, peeled
    1 (100 g) onion, peeled

1½ cups vinegar

1 kg sugar

ADVANCE PREPARATION: 24 HRS.

1 Rinse fish and cut into cubes. Drain well then dry in the sun for 1 day or leave in oven on very low heat until completely dry.

METHOD: 15 MIN.

1 Heat oil in a pan and fry fish until crisp. Remove and drain.

2 Using the same oil, fry spice paste and blended ingredients together. Add 1 tbsp. of the vinegar and keep stirring continuously over low heat. Add more oil if necessary and

continue stirring until oil floats to the top.

3 Add remaining vinegar and sugar. Stir well until sugar has dissolved. Taste for sweetness and add more sugar if necessary. The dish should taste sweet and sour.

4 Cool cooked paste completely. In a clean, dry jar, add a little fried paste, followed by some fish. Repeat, alternating between paste and fish, until both are used up. Keep for a week before serving.

Serves 10 or more

Cook's note Dried mango and two local berries, belimbing and *rumenya*, can be substituted for the salted fish.

Pesce kertouk (above)
This delicately-flavoured dish of fish wrapped in Chinese cabbage is served on an antique Portuguese plate.

Tante Maria-se achar pesce seccu (below)
This lip-smacking pickle of salted fish and tamarind was Aunt May's speciality.

Mezza De Noiba

COCK-AND-BULL STORIES

To the Cristang, meat used to mean anything from poultry, beef and pork to wild boar, tiger or even flying fox, when they were in season. After moving into the Portuguese Settlement, however, most Cristang were content with less exotic fare, such as chicken, duck, geese and other livestock kept in the backyard. Live turkeys, purchased a few months earlier, were fattened for Christmas, and hens were reared for their meat and eggs throughout the year. Geese were also kept in the yard, although more for their excellent ability to keep watch—they tend to make a lot of noise at first sight of a person approaching their territory—than for their meat.

Although meat is readily available these days, meals featuring this ingredient are unusual and reserved for Sundays, special occasions and family celebrations. On normal occasions, however, Cristang families are likely to eat small quantities of meat as an ingredient in curries, for example. They believe that meat eaten in large quantities causes illness, and, accordingly, they limit their consumption of it. However, the Cristang make it a point to feed a rich chicken soup (made only from home-reared chickens) to mothers who have just delivered or who are still lactating.

A thrifty people by nature, the Cristang do not waste any part of the animal. Intestine, gizzard and liver are used for sambals or vegetable dishes. Tripe is used in curries, feet in soups and the brain, heart and liver in a number of other delectable dishes. Feng, lardeh and *figdu tempradu* are some of the dishes the Cristang make from offal.

Ardi bafa cung tempra
Baked duck is given the Cristang touch with a rich
blend of coriander, lemon grass and coconut milk.

Ardi bafa cung tempra
(Baked spiced duck)

INGREDIENTS

2 kg young duck

blended to a fine paste
> 2 tbsp. roasted coriander seeds
> 5 (10 g) dried chillies,
>   presoaked in hot water
> 1 (100 g) onion, peeled
> 2 cloves (6 g) garlic, peeled
> 5 g turmeric, peeled
> ½ tsp. salt
> 1 tsp. sugar

1 cup (80 g) grated coconut

1¼ cup warm water

½ tbsp. tamarind pulp

½ cup oil

1 stalk lemon grass, sliced thinly
(use 7 cm of root end)

salt to taste

PREPARATION: 20 MIN.

1 Cut duck into large pieces and reserve giblets. Rub duck with half of the blended paste and set aside.

2 Soak grated coconut in ¼ cup of the water and extract 1 cup thick coconut milk (see p 26).

3 Soak tamarind pulp in remaining cup of warm water and extract juice (see p 26).

METHOD: 1 HR.

1 Heat oil in a wok. Put in lemon grass and fry till golden. Add remaining blended paste and fry until fragrant.

2 Add duck pieces and toss until brown.

3 Heat oven to 175°C (350°F or gas mark 4).

4 Pour half of the thick coconut milk and all the tamarind juice into the pan. Cook until duck is tender and gravy thickens, about 30 min.

5 Add salt to taste, stir and remove duck to a baking dish. Pour remaining coconut milk over duck and bake for 50 min. Baste with pan juices occasionally to keep duck moist. Serve immediately with rice, sambal belachan and sambal nanas cung pipineo (pp 62 and 69, respectively).

Serves 6 to 8

Baca pimenta fretu
(Pan-fried pepper steak)

INGREDIENTS

400 g sirloin steak

marinade
> 1 tbsp. thick soy sauce
> 1 tbsp. Worcester sauce
> 2 tsp. black peppercorns,
>   coarsely crushed
> 2 cloves (6 g) garlic, peeled and
>   chopped finely
> 1 tsp. brandy (optional)

4 (400 g) potatoes, peeled

1 tsp. cornflour

2 tbsp. water

3 tbsp. butter

¼ cup oil

1 (100 g) onion, peeled and sliced into thick rings

salt and sugar to taste

2 tbsp. tinned green peas, drained

PREPARATION: 25 MIN.

1 Cut meat into thin slices. March-chop (see p 24) lightly with blunt side of cleaver to tenderize meat; do not mince!

2 Knead meat slices in marinade for 1 min. Let stand for 20 min.

3 Boil potatoes, drain and let cool. Slice lengthwise into quarters and set aside.

4 Add cornflour to water and stir well to make a thick, smooth mixture.

METHOD: 10 MIN.

1 Heat butter and oil in a pan. Put in 2–3 slices of beef at a time and fry on high heat. Fry each slice for about 1 min. on each side. Remove to a plate.

2 In the same pan, sauté onion rings until soft. Pour in cornflour mixture and simmer for 2 min. Add more water if sauce thickens too much. Add salt and sugar to taste.

3 When gravy begins to bubble, add potatoes and peas. Simmer for 2 min.; then remove from heat.

4 Arrange meat in the centre of a plate and potatoes around it. Spoon sauce over and sprinkle with peas. Serve with bread or rice, and a salad.

Serves 4 to 6

Baca pimenta fretu
The Cristang have taken this very European dish of
pepper steak and added their own twist to it with a dash
of soy sauce and lots of garlic.

Figdu tempradu
(Liver seasoned with spices)

INGREDIENTS

½ kg ox liver

1 tsp. salt plus additional to taste

2 tbsp. vinegar

1 tsp. pepper

3 cups water

blended to a paste
>   2 (200 g) onions, peeled
>   4 cloves (12 g) garlic, peeled
>   3 (15 g) candlenuts, or 6 (15 g) blanched almonds
>   2 tsp. black pepper
>   4 (10 g) dried chillies, presoaked in hot water
>   3 tbsp. coriander powder
>   1 tbsp. cumin powder
>   2 tsp. fennel powder

½ cup oil

1 (100 g) onion, peeled and sliced thickly

½ cup water

1 tbsp. lime or lemon juice

PREPARATION: 40 MIN.

1 Put liver into a wok with 1 tsp. of the salt and all the vinegar, pepper and the 3 cups of water. Cook for 5 min. Drain and let cool; then cut into thin slices.

2 Coat slices with blended paste and marinate for 30 min.

METHOD: 10 MIN.

1 Heat oil in a wok and put in onion rings, reserving a few for garnishing later. Sauté for 30 sec. Remove to a plate.

2 In the same wok, stir-fry liver for 2–3 min. with any remaining marinade. Season with salt to taste.

3 Add the ½ cup of water to keep liver moist and simmer for 5 min. Remove from heat and transfer to a plate. Spoon gravy over liver.

4 Sprinkle sautéed onions and lime juice on liver. Top with raw onion rings. Serve at once with rice and a coconut milk based dish, such as singgang cocu (p 55).

Serves 6 to 8

Galinhia assa ne saspan (Chicken pot roast)

INGREDIENTS

1 kg chicken

marinade, mixed well
>   1 tsp. salt
>   1 tsp. black pepper
>   2 tsp. stew spice powder (see p 28)
>   1 tbsp. thick soy sauce

2 tbsp. butter

2 (100 g) boiled potatoes, sliced thinly

3 cups chicken stock (see p 27) or water

1 cinnamon stick, 2½-cm length

1 cup oil

2 tbsp. tinned green peas, drained

PREPARATION: 10 MIN.

1 Rub whole chicken thoroughly with marinade and set aside.

2 Heat butter in a pan. Put in potatoes and sauté until golden. Set aside.

METHOD: 45 MIN.

1 Heat stock in a deep saucepan. Add cinnamon stick and bring to a boil.

2 While waiting for stock to boil, heat oil in another deep pan. Put in whole chicken and fry for 5 min., turning it from time to time, being careful not to break skin.

3 Transfer chicken to boiling stock. Cover and simmer until meat is cooked, about 25 min.

The liquid should have reduced by this time.

4 Arrange chicken on a plate and spoon any gravy left in pot over chicken.

5 Garnish with potatoes and peas and serve with rice.

Serves 6 to 8

Galinhia fretu
(Fried chicken)

INGREDIENTS

1 kg chicken

marinade, mixed well
>   2 cloves (6 g) garlic, peeled and chopped finely
>   ½ tsp. salt
>   ½ tsp. pepper
>   1 tsp. prepared English mustard
>   1 tsp. stew spice powder (see p 28)
>   1 tsp. sugar
>   1 tbsp. thick soy sauce
>   1 tbsp. Worcester sauce

1½ tbsp. butter

1 cup oil

½ cup water

2 (200 g) onions, peeled and sliced

sauce, mixed well
>   2 tsp. cornflour
>   1 tbsp. thick soy sauce
>   ½ cup water
>   salt and sugar to taste

2 tbsp. white wine

1 tbsp. lime or lemon juice

garnish (optional)
>   4 (400 g) large potatoes, boiled and quartered
>   2 tbsp. tinned green peas, drained

continued on p 118

Figdu tempradu
This simple yet highly spiced dish of liver is served on a
plate from a 45-year old dinner set of British origin.

from p 116, *Galinhia fretu*

PREPARATION: 20 MIN.

1 Cut chicken into 8 pieces.

2 Combine marinade with 1 tbsp. of the butter; mix well.

3 Coat chicken pieces thoroughly with marinade. Let stand for 10 min.

METHOD: 20 MIN.

1 Heat oil in a pan. Put in chicken pieces and sauté for 5 min.

2 Add any remaining marinade into pan. Pour in water and cook until liquid evaporates.

3 Stir-fry chicken for a further 2 min. When cooked, remove from heat and arrange in a dish.

4 In a clean pan, heat remaining ½ tbsp. of butter and fry onions until brown. Pour in thick-soy-sauce-and-cornflour sauce and cook till sauce thickens. Add wine and season to taste with salt and pepper before removing from heat.

5 Pour sauce over chicken. Garnish with boiled potatoes and tinned peas and sprinkle lime or lemon juice on top before serving. Serve with rice, boiled noodles or bread.

Serves 4 to 6

Cook's note Fried or pot roasted chicken used to be standard Sunday fare among the Cristang. The Sabbath has always been a day for family gatherings and good food, followed by a relaxing siesta.

Galinhia pai
(Chicken pie)

INGREDIENTS

Chicken stew (see next recipe)

2 (120 g) eggs

shortcrust pastry
    400 g plain flour
    pinch of salt
    250 g butter (keep refrigerated
      until needed)
    1 egg yolk
    ½ cup cold water

1 tbsp. brandy or sherry (optional)

3 rashers (beef) bacon, fried crisp

4 (200 g) frankfurters, fried

a little evaporated milk for glazing

PREPARATION: 30 MIN.

1 Cook chicken stew. Set aside to cool.

2 Meanwhile, boil eggs until hard. Remove shells and cut eggs lengthwise into halves; set aside.

3 To make shortcrust pastry:
  i Sieve flour and salt together in a bowl.
  ii Add butter and rub in until a breadcrumb consistency is obtained. Add egg yolk and a little of the cold water. Mix to form a pliable dough. Knead lightly. Chill pastry dough while preparing rest of pie.

METHOD: 40 MIN.

1 Heat oven to 175°C (350°F or gas mark 4).

2 Transfer stew into a medium-sized pie dish (about 25 cm in diameter at the base). Stir in brandy if using.

3 Arrange hard-boiled eggs on top, followed by bacon. Place frankfurters along sides of dish.

4 Roll out chilled pastry on a lightly floured board to form a crust large enough to cover mouth of pie dish and about ½ cm thick. Moisten rim of dish with water and cover dish with pastry.

5 Trim pastry edges and flute with a fork. Use any leftover pastry to make decorative shapes for top of pie. Prick holes in pastry using a fork to allow steam to escape.

6 Brush with a little milk and bake until pastry is golden in colour, about 20 min. Remove and glaze with milk again. Serve immediately with a salad and wine.

Serves 4 to 6

Cook's note Chicken pie has always been part of the Christmas eve midnight supper menu, along with Teem (p 80) and beer-boiled ham.

Galinhia stiu
(Chicken stew)

INGREDIENTS

1 kg chicken

½ tsp. salt plus extra to taste

½ tsp. pepper plus extra to taste

¼ cup oil

2 (200 g) onions, peeled and quartered

½ star anise

6 cloves

1 cinnamon stick, 2½-cm length

1 tsp. stew spice powder (see p 28)

1 tsp. black pepper

3 cups water

1 (50 g) carrot, sliced diagonally

3 (300 g) potatoes, peeled and quartered

6 (60 g) large cabbage leaves, halved lengthwise

2 tbsp. milk (optional)

1 Cut chicken into bite-sized pieces.

2 Season chicken with half each of the salt and pepper. Let stand for 5 min.

METHOD: 20 MIN.

1 Heat oil in a wok. Put in onions and sauté until soft. Add star anise, cloves and cinnamon stick. Fry till fragrant, then add stew spice powder and black pepper; mix well.

2 Put in chicken and stir-fry over high heat until light golden in colour. Add 1 cup of the water, cover and cook for 5 min. Add carrots, potatoes and the remaining water and bring to a boil.

3 Add chicken stock, reduce heat and simmer for 5 min. Add cabbage and cook another 3 min. Season with salt and pepper to taste.

4 Just before serving, add milk and stir well. Serve with rice or bread and two other dishes.

Serves 6 to 8

Cook's note This stew is used for the filling for galinhia pai (p 118). One kilogram of ox tail may be substituted for the chicken; if using ox tail, increase the pepper to 2 tsp. In another variation, the milk may be replaced with 30 ml of brandy or cognac.

Lingu baca bafa
(Braised ox tongue)

INGREDIENTS

1½ kg ox tongue

½ cup oil

3 cloves (9 g) garlic, peeled and crushed

sauce, mixed well
    2 tsp. stew spice powder
        (see p 28)
    2 tbsp. thick soy sauce
    2 tbsp. Worcester sauce
    1 tsp. brown sugar
    salt to taste
    1¼ cup medium dry sherry,
        or 1 cup meat stock (see p 27)

3 cups hot water

1 cup meat stock (see p 27)

1 tbsp. cornflour

1 cup water

PREPARATION: 35 MIN., 1 DAY IN ADVANCE

1 Place ox tongue in a large pot with enough water to cover and bring to a boil.

2 Reduce heat and simmer for 30 min. Rinse tongue under cold water and scrape off thick outer layer or skin.

METHOD: 1 HR. 45 MIN.

1 Heat oil in a large, heavy saucepan. Put in garlic and brown for 1 min. Add tongue and brown for 2 min. on either side.

2 Pour in sauce and cook for 2 min.

3 Add hot water and meat stock and bring to a gradual boil over a low flame. Simmer for about 1½ hrs.

4 Check liquid level; it should cover tongue. If necessary, add more water.

5 When tongue is tender, there should be a little gravy left in the pot. Remove tongue and slice thinly. Reserve gravy.

TO SERVE

1 Before serving, make sure tongue is warm; heat it in an oven if necessary.

2 Heat gravy in a pan. To thicken, mix cornflour with water, stir into gravy and simmer for 1 min. before removing from heat. Pour gravy over tongue and serve at once with rice, curry and a vegetable.

Serves 4 to 6

Ros befe casamintu
(Wedding roast beef)

INGREDIENTS

1½ kg beef fillet

marinade
    5 (15 g) cloves garlic, peeled
        and chopped
    1 (100 g) onion, peeled and
        chopped
    ½ tsp. stew spice powder
        (see p 28)
    1 tsp. thick soy sauce
    1 tsp. vinegar
    ½ tsp. salt
    pinch of sugar

3 tbsp. black peppercorns, cracked

egg and vinegar sauce
    5 tbsp. white vinegar
    2 cloves
    2 cloves (6 g) garlic, peeled and
        crushed
    ½ tsp. sugar
    5 (125 g) egg yolks
    1 spring onion, sliced into
        rounds

1 cup oil

1 bulb lemon grass, bruised
    (use 7 cm of root end) (optional)

1 cup meat stock (see p 27), or
    water

PREPARATION: 20 MIN.

1 Rub beef thoroughly with marinade and set aside.

continued on p 120

from p 119, *Ros befe casamintu*

2 Roll beef in peppercorns and set aside for 20 min.

3 Prepare egg and vinegar sauce: Boil vinegar, cloves, garlic and sugar in a small saucepan. Lower heat and simmer for 1 min. Remove from heat and cool.

4 Beat egg yolks until thick and creamy. Add cooled vinegar sauce 1 tsp. at a time to yolks, beating after each addition. Repeat until all vinegar sauce is used up. Pour mixture into a shallow dish, sprinkle with spring onion and set aside.

METHOD: 50 MIN.

1 Heat ½ cup of the oil in a large pan. Put in beef, brown evenly on all sides and remove.

2 Heat remaining oil in a deep pot. Put in lemon grass and fry until fragrant.

3 Pour in stock and bring to a boil. Lower heat and put beef into pot. Close lid and roast for 30 min. or to preferred degree of doneness. Baste regularly to prevent meat from drying.

4 When meat is cooked, remove from heat. Spoon any remaining gravy in pot over meat to keep it moist.

5 Slice beef and arrange on a plate. Serve with egg-and-vinegar sauce and *arroz manteiga* (see p 128).

Serves 4 to 6

Cook's note An alternative to pot roasting the beef is to bake it in an oven for 40 min. at 165°C (325°F or gas mark 3) or until the preferred degree of doneness is achieved. Serve in the manner described above.

Satei goreng
(Fried satay)

INGREDIENTS

1 kg sirloin steak

4 (320 g) cups grated coconut

3½ cup warm water

3 tbsp. dried spice curry powder (see p 28)

blended to a fine paste
    15 (150 g) shallots, or
      1½ (150 g) onions, peeled
    6 cloves (18 g) garlic, peeled
    10 (30 g) candlenuts, or
      18 (30 g) blanched almonds
    2 stalks lemon grass (use 7 cm of root end)
    15 g galangal, peeled
    5 g turmeric, peeled
    2 tsp. toasted shrimp paste (belachan)
    10 (20 g) dried chillies, pre-soaked in hot water

½ cup oil

salt and sugar to taste

4 (100 g) peanut brittle biscuits, pounded, or 6 tbsp. chunky peanut butter

garnish
    1 (60 g) cucumber, sliced into rounds
    1 (100 g) large onion, peeled and sliced into rings

PREPARATION: 40 MIN.

1 Cut steak into slices 1 cm thick. Pound with a mallet to make slices wafer thin.

2 Soak grated coconut in 1 cup of the warm water and extract 1 cup thick coconut milk (see p 26).

3 Soak tamarind pulp in ½ cup of the warm water and extract juice (see p 26).

4 Combine 1 tbsp. of the coconut milk with dried spice curry powder and mix thoroughly.

5 Mix resulting paste with blended paste. Add tamarind juice gradually to make a thick marinade.

6 Knead beef slices in marinade for 1–2 min. and let stand for 30 min.

METHOD: 30 MIN.

1 Heat oil in a frying pan until smoking hot. Add 3–4 beef slices and stir-fry until meat is a little charred at the edges. Remove fried meat and put in another 3–4 slices. Repeat until all meat is cooked.

2 Lower heat. Put all beef slices back into pan and add remaining 2 cups of water to prevent burning. Add salt and sugar to taste and simmer for 20–25 min.

3 Remove beef and add peanut brittle biscuits to remaining gravy in pan and stir. The gravy should be thick; if it is too watery, boil uncovered to reduce liquid. Remove from heat.

4 Serve beef hot with plain boiled rice, cucumber, onion rings and peanut gravy.

Serves 6 to 8

Cook's note This dish is one of the most popular among the Cristang living in Kuala Lumpur. It is usually served for Sunday lunch when the whole family is gathered and on special occasions. This recipe was given to me by Mr Gerry Rozario, who enjoys cooking for guests, friends and his 'orphans'.

Satei goreng
Satay is a common dish in most parts of Malaysia, but only the Cristang fry the meat and add peanut brittle to the sauce to create an unusual and delicious variation.

Semur
(Ox tongue and beef stew)

INGREDIENTS

½ kg ox tongue

1 tbsp. Worcester sauce

2½ tbsp. thick soy sauce

3 tbsp. malt vinegar

½ kg stewing beef

2 tsp. stew spice powder (see p 28)

4 cloves (12 g) garlic, peeled and crushed

¼ cup oil

1 cinnamon stick, 2½-cm length

2 star anise

6 cloves

2 (200 g) onions, peeled and quartered

3 cups water

4 (400 g) potatoes, peeled and quartered

1 cup meat stock (see p 27)

6 (20 g) cream-crackers or semi-sweet biscuits, finely crushed, or 4 tbsp. breadcrumbs

1 tbsp. red wine (optional)

PREPARATION: 50 MIN.

1 Scald tongue in boiling water and scrape off skin. Place tongue in a pan with enough water to cover and a little salt; boil for 30 min. (Or cook for 5 min. in a pressure cooker with the same amount of water.) Remove and let cool. Slice against grain.

2 Mix Worcester sauce with 2 tbsp. of the thick soy sauce and 1 tbsp. of the vinegar. Coat tongue well with this mixture and marinate for 10 min.

3 Meanwhile, cut stewing beef into bite-sized pieces and marinate with remaining soy sauce and vinegar and all the stew spice powder and garlic. Set aside for 10 min.

METHOD: 25 MIN.

1 Heat oil and fry cinnamon stick, star anise, cloves and onions.

2 Put in marinated beef and stir-fry for 1 min. Add 2 cups of the water and bring to a boil.

3 Put in seasoned tongue. Stir well and add remaining cup of water. Simmer for 8–10 min.

4 Add potatoes and cook for another 5 min. Pour in meat stock and stir.

5 Make sure liquid covers meats; add more water if necessary. Simmer until meats are tender and potatoes are cooked, about 15 min.

6 Add crushed biscuits to thicken gravy. Stir, add red wine and stir well once again. Remove from heat and let stand for at least 20 min. before serving with rice or bread. This dish tastes better if kept overnight.

Serves 6 to 8

Semur
Vinegar and blended spices add an exotic touch to this ox tongue and beef stew. The dish goes very well with fresh warm bread and the pictured side dish, sambal belachan (p 62). The tablecloth in the foreground is of Portuguese origin. To the right of the semur is a brass weight traditionally used by Cristang fishermen to weigh their catch.

Dali Cung Mung

CEREAL SAGAS

Although rice has been cultivated in Asia for over seventy centuries, it was only first introduced into Malacca by the Chinese traders in the fifteenth century. By the time the Portuguese arrived, the cereal was already a staple food of the people there. Eventually, the Portuguese who settled in Malacca—the forefathers of the Cristang—also incorporated rice into their daily diets.

Although other grains are included in the Cristang diet (and they are normally consumed in the form of noodles), it is rice that is the most important staple food. Indeed, the Cristang describe rice as 'seed pearls,' and believe that the grain symbolizes life's blessings; to be able to eat *arroz branco* (white rice) is to be able to afford the luxuries in life. For this reason, when eating rice it is considered vital to 'grab one's blessings' with one's fingers rather than pick at the precious food with a fork and spoon.

The Cristang cook rice and noodles in a variety of ways, creating different flavours and textures that reflect indigenous as well as foreign influences. The rich *arroz gordu* (p 126), for instance, is a Portuguese dish that combines rice with a variety of meats and sausages. The Dutch-inspired lampries 'landeh (p 128) is an inviting concoction of coconut-flavoured rice served with egg, cucumber slices and sambal belachan. Lampries 'landeh is similar to the Malay breakfast dish known as *nasi lemak* or coconut-flavoured rice. These dishes, along with mi annu (p 130), a lavish noodle concoction, are usually served on festive occasions. Rice porridge or canje parpa (p 128) introduced by the Chinese is usually served to invalids and babies, and rice porridge made from black glutinous rice is offered to mourners at a funeral. Leftover plain boiled rice and noodles also find their way to the dining table in a Cristang home: fried with a chilli, onion and shrimp paste mixture, they make a delicious meal at breakfast.

Arroz gordu

In the old days, this rice dish always made an appearance at Cristang banquets, especially wedding feasts.

Traditionally, Cristang women would arrive for these feasts with their hair elaborately coiffured and adorned by the large, ornate antique gold pins seen in the background . The gold brooch next to the pins is from a set of three used for fastening the front of the saier-cabaier (the Cristang version of the Malay sarung kebaya). In the background is my parents' wedding photograph.

Arroz gordu
(Jumbo rice)

INGREDIENTS

1 kg chicken

350 g long grain rice

1½ (150 g) large onions, peeled

1 cup oil

5 cloves (15 g) garlic, peeled and
chopped

2 (100 g) carrots, diced

200 g minced beef

1 tsp. sugar

1 tsp. salt plus additional to taste

garnish
 200 g cocktail sausages
 2 slices (30 g) white bread,
  cubed
 1 tbsp. almond slivers
 ½ tbsp. raisins
 1 sprig parsley, or 1 tsp. spring
  onion, chopped

2 tbsp. margarine

1 onion, sliced

4 tbsp. tomato paste

2 tomatoes, diced

2 (120 g) eggs, hard-boiled and
sliced

2 cinnamon sticks, 6-cm lengths

2 star anise

6 cloves

2 bay leaves

1 tbsp. tomato sauce (optional)

PREPARATION: 40 MIN.

1 Cut chicken into 8 pieces and
make chicken stock (see p 27).
Allow stock to cool; then remove
chicken pieces. Reserve 8½ cups
of the stock.

2 Wash rice in cold water. Rinse
twice and drain in a colander for
10 min.

3 Meanwhile, dice 2 of the onions;
slice the other one thickly.

4 Heat 2 tbsp. of the oil and fry
garlic until golden. Discard
garlic. Put diced onions and
carrots into the same oil. Sauté
for 3 min. Add minced beef,
sugar, 1 tsp. of the salt and ½ cup
of the chicken stock from PREPA-
RATION, STEP 1. Stir-fry until
beef is cooked, about 5 min.
Remove and set aside.

5 In the same pan, heat remaining
oil and fry sausages for garnish;
remove and set aside. Fry cubed
bread to make croûtons. Remove
and drain on paper towels.

6 In a clean pan, heat 1 tbsp. of the
margarine and sauté sliced onion
until soft. Add tomato paste and
diced tomatoes. Stir-fry for 1
min.; remove from heat and set
aside.

METHOD: 25 MIN.

1 Heat remaining margarine in a
wok. Put in cinnamon sticks, star
anise and cloves and fry until
fragrant. Add rice and fry for 2
min. Remove from heat.

2 Pour remaining chicken stock
into a deep pot or rice cooker.
Add fried rice and bay leaves.
The stock should come to about
2½ cm above the level of the
rice; add more water if necessary.
Cover and boil for about 15 min.
The rice is cooked when it is
fluffy and grainy and all the
liquid has evaporated.

3 Stir tomato sauce into hot rice,
making sure to mix well. Add
fried mixture of sliced onion,
tomato paste and tomatoes from
PREPARATION, STEP 6. Stir again
and add salt to taste. Cover for
10 min. to allow rice to absorb
flavour of ingredients.

4 Place chicken pieces on a platter.
Spread rice over chicken and top
with stir-fried mixture of diced
onions, carrots and minced beef

from PREPARATION, STEP 4.

5 Arrange garnish of egg, sausages
and croûtons on top and sprinkle
with almond, raisins and parsley.

Serves 8 to 10

Arroz Macau
(Macau rice)

INGREDIENTS

300 g long grain rice, washed and
drained

2 chicken drumsticks, about 300 g
each

5 cups water

¼ cup oil

5 cloves (15 g) garlic, peeled and
chopped

1 (100 g) onion, peeled and
chopped

10 g ginger, peeled and shredded

4 black peppercorns, coarsely
crushed

½ tsp. stew spice powder (see p 28)

5 black mushrooms, soaked and
sliced finely

3 (180 g) eggs, beaten lightly

1 spring onion, chopped into
rounds

PREPARATION: 30 MIN.

1 Put chicken drumsticks and
water in a small but deep pot
and boil until chicken is tender,
about 20 min. Remove chicken
and set stock aside to cool.

METHOD: 15 MIN.

1 Heat oil in a wok. Put in garlic,
onion and ginger. Stir-fry for
30 sec.

2 Add peppercorns, stew spice
powder and mushrooms. Stir-fry
for another 30 sec.

3 Add rice and toss to coat with oil.

continued on p 128

Arroz Macau
This rice dish from Macau goes very well with sambal
bokras (p 63), pictured at right. In the top left corner is
a black and gold bamboo basket from Macau.

from p 126, *Arroz Macau*

4 Transfer rice into a deep pot or rice cooker. Add 3½ cups of the cooled chicken stock from PREPARATION, STEP 1. Cook until rice is soft and grainy, appears glossy, and all liquid has been absorbed. Set aside to cool.

5 Heat oven to 165°C (325°F or gas mark 3).

6 Pour eggs over cooled rice and toss well to coat thoroughly. Using a spoon, transfer rice into a ring mould, packing gently. Bake in oven for 5 min. to cook eggs.

7 Remove mould from oven. Carefully remove rice from mould and transfer to a platter. Top with spring onion and serve with galinhia assa ne saspan (p 116), a curry and a sambal.

Serves 6 to 8

Cook's note Meat from the chicken drumsticks used to make the stock can be shredded and added to a stir-fried vegetable dish. The shredded meat can also be mixed with salt, pepper and mayonnaise to make a delicious sandwich filling.

Arroz manteiga
(Butter rice)

INGREDIENTS

300 g long grain rice, washed and drained

2⅓ cup water

2 cloves (6 g) garlic, peeled and chopped

1 cinnamon stick, 2½-cm length

4 cloves

1 tsp. salt

8 tbsp. butter

1 tbsp. evaporated milk

1 tbsp. raisins (optional)

METHOD: 20 MIN.

1 Put rice and water into a deep pot and bring to a boil.

2 Add garlic, cinnamon stick, cloves and salt and continue boiling, keeping pot covered. When a fragrance emits from pot, lower heat and continue cooking until rice is soft and grainy, appears glossy, and all liquid has been absorbed.

3 Stir rice, remove from heat and keep covered for 10 min. to allow steam to cook rice further. Uncover and fluff up rice with a fork.

4 Stir in butter, evaporated milk and raisins. Serve at once with a curry or a hot sambal.

Serves 2 to 4

Cook's note Thinly sliced Chinese sausages or chunks of luncheon meat can be added for variety: add 2 Chinese sausages or 1 tin of luncheon meat to the cooked rice in METHOD, STEP 3.

Canje parpa
(Rice porridge)

INGREDIENTS

150 g broken or ordinary rice, rinsed and drained

8 cups water

salt to taste

METHOD: 10 MIN.

1 Put rice and water into a deep pot and bring to a boil. Lower heat and simmer uncovered until rice grains break open. The porridge should remain a little watery; add more water if it dries. Add salt and serve hot with pesce tambrinhyu (see p 109).

Serves 2 to 4

Cook's note This dish is served when the Cristang observe Lent. To make the porridge more palatable, add minced meat, fish or prawns when the porridge is boiling. Serve with chopped spring onion and crisp fried shallots; young ginger, julienned, is usually added if fish is used. Season with soy sauce and pepper.

Lampries 'landeh
(Dutch coconut-flavoured rice)

INGREDIENTS

To make meat stock

2 chicken thighs (about 200 g each)

300 g topside beef

200 g ox tongue

200 g ox liver

4½ cups water

300 g long grain rice

3 cups (240 g) grated coconut

1 cup warm water

1 (100 g) onion, peeled and chopped

1 (60 g) cucumber, peeled and sliced

1 banana leaf

¼ cup oil

Feng (cooked a day in advance; see PREPARATION 1, STEP 2)

Sambal chilli bedri (see PREPARATION 2, STEP 1)

PREPARATION 1: 1 HR.
(COMPLETED A DAY IN ADVANCE)

1 To make meat stock, bring water to a boil in a deep pot. Put in ox tongue; 10 min. later, add beef and 10 min. after that, chicken thighs. Boil together for 10 min. more; then remove meats from pot. Put in liver and cook for 5 min.; then remove and cool. Reserve liquid to use as stock.

2 Dice all boiled meats and use them to make feng (see p 54).

PREPARATION 2: 45 MIN.

1 Make sambal chilli bedri (see p 65).

2 Wash rice and drain it.

3 Soften banana leaf by holding it over a flame; be careful not to singe it. Remove midrib and cut leaf into 4 equal pieces.

4 Soak grated coconut in warm water and extract 1 cup thick coconut milk (see p 26).

METHOD: 35 MIN.

1 Heat oil in a wok. Put in onion and sauté until soft. Add rice and toss well. Transfer rice to a deep pot or rice cooker. Add 3½ cups of the meat stock (made in PREPARATION I, STEP I) and bring to a boil. Cover and simmer until all liquid has been absorbed. Let stand covered for 10 min.; then fluff up rice with a fork.

2 Heat oven to 165°C (325°F or gas mark 3).

3 Place a ladleful of cooked rice on a piece of banana leaf. Pour 2 tsp. of the thick coconut milk over it. Arrange 1 tbsp. each of feng and sambal chilli bedri around the rice. Fold leaf to form an oblong package and secure ends with toothpicks.

4 Bake no more than 4 packages of lampries at a time for 5 min. Serve with more feng, sambal chilli bedri and sliced cucumber.

Serves 4 to 6

Cook's note This dish is known as *lomprijst* in Dutch.

Lampries 'landeh
Although this dish of rice and meat when arranged on a banana leaf looks typically Indian, it is Dutch in origin. Unlike the Indian banana leaf rice, the ingredients are wrapped in the leaf and baked to impart the sweet aroma of the leaf to the rice.

Laksa Malaca
(Noodles in spicy coconut sauce)

INGREDIENTS

600 g rice vermicelli

400 g medium-sized prawns

1 tbsp. coarse salt

200 g bean sprouts

20 (240 g) bean curd puffs

3 cups (240 g) grated coconut

2 cups warm water

½ cup oil

blended to a paste

    20 (200 g) shallots, or 2 (200 g)
      onions, peeled

    1 bulb (60 g) garlic, peeled

    5 g turmeric, peeled

    5 g ginger, peeled

    5 stalks lemon grass (use 7 cm
      of root end)

    5 (50 g) candlenuts, or 10
      (15 g) blanched almonds

    6 (30 g) fresh red chillies

    2 tsp. toasted shrimp paste
      (belachan)

    1 tbsp. coriander powder

9 sprigs daun kesom

salt to taste

sugar to taste

20 fishballs (see p 29)

6 (30 g) fresh red chillies

1 (80–100 g) cucumber

PREPARATION: 1 HR.

1 Soak rice vermicelli in cool
water for 1 hr.

2 Rub unshelled prawns with
coarse salt, leave for 5 min.; then
rinse well and drain. Put prawns
in a pot with enough water to
cover and boil for 5 min.
Remove prawns and reserve
liquid to be used as stock.

3 Remove heads and shells of
prawns and set prawns aside.
Pound heads and shells and add
resulting liquid to prawn stock.

Boil stock for 10 min. and top
up with 2 cups of water. Strain
and set aside.

4 Break off and discard roots of
bean sprouts and blanch sprouts
in boiling water; set aside.
Blanch bean curd puffs and set
aside.

5 Soak grated coconut in the 2
cups of warm water and extract
thick coconut milk with 2 cups
of water and thin coconut milk
with 3 cups of water (see p 26).

METHOD: 15 MIN.

1 Heat oil in a deep pot. Fry
blended ingredients till aromatic.
Add 5 sprigs of the daun kesom,
thin coconut milk, salt and
sugar. Simmer for 5 min.

2 To make gravy, add prawn stock
and fish balls and bring to a boil.
Gradually pour in thick coconut
milk, stirring continuously to
prevent curdling. Reduce heat
and simmer for 3 min. Stir once
more, then remove from heat
and set aside.

3 Blend 2 sprigs of the daun
kesom with chillies to make a
chilli sauce. Add salt to taste and
set aside.

4 Peel, core and slice cucumber
into fine rings. Shred remaining
sprigs of daun kesom.

TO SERVE

1 Blanch rice vermicelli in hot
boiling water. Drain and put
into individual bowls. Top each
bowl with some of the bean
sprouts. Pour some gravy from
METHOD, STEP 2 into each bowl.

2 Garnish each bowl with prawns
from PREPARATION, STEP 3, followed by cucumber rings and a
pinch of shredded daun kesom.
Serve with chilli sauce from
METHOD, STEP 3.

Serves 6 to 8

Mi annu (Birthday noodles)

INGREDIENTS

400 g chicken or any other meat
with some fat

1 bulb (60 g) plus 2 cloves (6 g)
garlic, peeled

10 (100 g) shallots, or 2 (200 g)
onions, peeled

1 tbsp. thick soy sauce

3 cloves

1 cinnamon stick, 2-cm length

1 tsp. salt plus additional to taste

3 tsp. sugar plus additional to taste

3 cups water

200 g Swatow mustard cabbage

2 (120 g) eggs

1 cup oil

300 g small prawns, shells and
heads removed

200 g bean sprouts, roots removed

pepper to taste

3 tbsp. salted soya bean, mashed

½ kg yellow noodles, or cooked
spaghetti

garnish

1 (5 g) fresh red chilli, sliced

1 (80 g) cucumber, peeled and
julienned

PREPARATION: 30 MIN.

1 Cut chicken (or any other meat,
if using) into 4 large pieces.
Place in a wok.

2 Chop 2 cloves of the garlic and
2 of the shallots coarsely. Add to
chicken, along with soy sauce,
cloves, cinnamon and 1 tsp. each
of the salt and sugar. Mix well.

3 Add water, stir thoroughly and
bring to a boil. When chicken is
cooked, remove from heat and
cool. Debone and slice meat into
slivers. Return meat to liquid in
wok and keep until needed.

4 Cut off leaves of mustard cabbage and trim stalks into 5-cm lengths.

5 Blend remaining shallots and garlic to a fine paste.

6 Beat eggs well and fry to make an omelette. Cut into fine strips and set aside.

METHOD: 30 MIN.

1 Heat 2 tbsp. of the oil in a wok. Fry half of the blended shallot-garlic paste until fragrant.

2 Add mustard cabbage stalks and a little water to steam the vegetable.

3 Add prawns and cook until pink. Add mustard cabbage leaves and bean sprouts. Season with salt, sugar and pepper to taste; stir well. When vegetables are half-cooked, remove to a dish.

4 In the same wok, heat remaining oil. Add remaining shallot-garlic paste and salted soya beans and stir-fry for 3 min.

5 Add noodles and fry for 5 min., tossing well. Lower heat, add half-cooked vegetables and toss well again.

6 Strain liquid from meat cooked in PREPARATION, STEP 3 and add to noodles. Stir well and season with salt, sugar and pepper accordingly before removing from heat.

7 Dish noodles onto an oval platter. Top with slivers of meat from PREPARATION, STEP 3. Spoon remaining gravy from wok over dish.

8 Arrange strips of omelette, red chillies and cucumber on top of noodles. Serve at once, on their own or with sambal nanas cung pipineo (p 69).

Serves 8 to 10

Mi annu
This birthday noodle dish is shown here with sambal nanas cung pipineo, an accompaniment that has just the right touch of piquancy to complement this rich dish.

Matah Bontade

TOOTHSOME TRIVIA

This category comprises a miscellany of Cristang dishes that are seldom discussed; their recipes are hardly ever exchanged eagerly or handed down with great ceremony. These are the everyday dishes that Cristang cooks put together at a moment's notice. Combining local herbs and ingredients with inexpensive cuts of meat or offal, these dishes, more than any others, reflect the Cristang's Asian heritage.

Economical and simple to prepare, the dishes are a legacy of World War II and hard times. Fresh ingredients were at a premium and tinned meat, milk and fish were the staples immediately after the war. Cooks had to use their ingenuity to produce appetizing dishes from these bland alternatives. The Cristang found corned beef to be the most versatile of the tinned foods: it was cooked in a stew with cabbage and potatoes, fried with eggs, or used in ambiler kachang (p 46) and other meat dishes. Sometimes raw shallots and chillies were chopped up and added to the meat together with a dash of lime juice. The meat was also used as a sandwich filling, although corned beef sandwiches were considered a luxury at the time and served only on special occasions.

Invariably, it is the classic dishes such as debal, feng or semur (pp 52, 54 and 120, respectively) that receive all the attention when Cristang cuisine is discussed. The humble dishes listed in this section are now designated as peasant food by some. Be that as it may, I feel that these dishes constitute an important part of the Cristang culinary heritage. I include their recipes to preserve that heritage as completely as possible for the younger Cristang generation and to remind the older folk of those 'good old days'.

Baca assam
This piquant tamarind beef curry is typical of the simple yet delicious dishes that are still cooked in Cristang homes today.

Aberjaw
(Yellow spiced meat)

INGREDIENTS

1 kg mutton (or beef if preferred)
  bones with a little meat

2 tbsp. tamarind pulp

1½ cups water

¼ cup plus 2 tbsp. oil

blended to a fine paste
  2 stalks lemon grass (use 7 cm
    of root end)
  25 g galangal, peeled
  20 (200 g) shallots, or 2 (200 g)
    onions, peeled
  6 cloves (18 g) garlic, peeled
  10 (30 g) candlenuts, or 20
    (30 g) blanched almonds
  2 tsp. toasted shrimp paste
    (belachan)
  10 g turmeric, peeled

salt to taste

1 tbsp. salted soya beans, rinsed
  and drained (optional)

6 (½ kg) potatoes, peeled and
  quartered

sugar to taste

garnish
  5 (50 g) shallots, peeled and
    sliced
  4 cloves (12 g) garlic, peeled
    and sliced
  2 (10 g) fresh red chillies, sliced

PREPARATION: 25 MIN.

1 Soak tamarind pulp in water and
  extract juice (see p 26).

2 Heat 2 tbsp. of the oil in a pan.
  Fry each garnish ingredient until
  crisp. Remove and drain. Fry
  only a small amount of an ingredient at a time or too much
  moisture will be released and the
  ingredient will not crisp.

METHOD: 20 MIN.

1 Heat remaining oil in a tezaler
  (p 19). Add blended ingredients
  and fry until aromatic. Add salt
  and a little water, followed by
  salted soya beans and meat.

2 Add enough water to cover meat
  and bring to a boil. Put in potatoes, cover and simmer until
  meat and potatoes are cooked,
  about 20 minutes.

3 Pour in tamarind juice and add
  sugar. If necessary, allow liquid
  to boil away to keep gravy thick.
  Simmer for 5 min., stirring
  occasionally.

4 Remove from heat and let stand
  for 10 minutes before serving.
  Sprinkle fried garnish from PREP-
  ARATION, STEP 2. Serve with rice
  and sambal belachan (see p 62).

Serves 8 to 10

Cook's note Although the Cristang prefer to
use pork ribs for this dish, I have included
mutton and beef to give it a wider appeal,
as there are many who do not eat pork.

Baca assam
(Beef in tamarind gravy)

INGREDIENTS

400 g topside beef or any other
  meat marbled with some fat

2 tbsp. tamarind pulp

1 cup warm water

garnish
  1 tbsp. oil
  2 stalks lemon grass, sliced (use
    only 7 cm of root end)
  3 cloves (9 g) garlic, peeled and
    sliced
  3 (30 g) shallots, peeled and
    sliced
  ½ tsp. salt
  2 (10 g) fresh red chillies, sliced
    thickly

¼ cup oil

blended to a fine paste
  3 (6 g) dried chillies, presoaked
    in hot water
  3 (9 g) candlenuts, or 6 (9 g)
    blanched almonds
  10 (100 g) shallots, or 1 (100 g)
    onion, peeled
  5 g turmeric, peeled, or 1 tsp.
    turmeric powder
  20 g galangal, peeled

salt and sugar to taste

PREPARATION: 10 MIN.

1 Cut meat into bite-sized pieces.

2 Soak tamarind pulp in water and
  extract juice (see p 26).

3 To prepare garnish, heat oil in a
  pan and fry lemon grass, garlic
  and shallots until golden.
  Remove, drain on absorbent
  paper and dredge with salt. Fry
  chillies for 1 min. and remove.
  Set aside.

METHOD: 20 MIN.

1 Heat oil in a tezaler (p 19). Put
  in blended paste and stir-fry for
  1 min.; then add meat.

2 Stir-fry meat for 2–3 min. Add
  tamarind juice and boil for
  3 min., stirring occasionally.

3 Add salt and sugar to taste.
  Simmer till gravy thickens. Taste
  for sourness and adjust by adding
  more tamarind juice if required.
  The dish should taste fairly sour.

4 Lower heat. Simmer until meat
  is tender and most of the moisture absorbed, about 10 min.

5 Remove from heat, sprinkle
  garnish from PREPARATION,
  STEP 3 on meat and serve immediately with rice or bread.

Serves 6 to 8

Cook's note This dish must have a piquant
taste and a yellow colour. Belly pork makes
an excellent substitute for the beef.

Baca soy
(Beef in soy sauce)

INGREDIENTS

400 g topside beef or any other
   meat

marinade, mixed well
   20 peppercorns, coarsely
      ground
   ½ tsp. salt
   1 tbsp. thick soy sauce

¼ cup oil

10 g ginger, peeled and shredded

6 cloves (18 g) garlic, peeled and
   chopped

1 cup water

2 tsp. thick soy sauce

2 tsp. thin soy sauce

1 (80 g) onion, peeled and diced

1 cinnamon stick, 5-cm length

3 cloves

salt and sugar to taste

PREPARATION: 10 MIN.

1 Cut meat into bite-sized pieces.
   Rub well with marinade and set
   aside.

METHOD: 20 MIN.

1 Heat oil in a wok and stir-fry
   meat until brown all over.

2 Add ginger and garlic and fry for
   30 sec.

3 Pour in half of the water and stir.
   Add thick and thin soy sauces.

4 Simmer for 4 min. Add remaining water and bring to a boil.

5 Add onions, cinnamon and
   cloves. Continue boiling until
   meat is tender, about 5 min. Add
   salt and sugar to taste. Stir and
   remove from heat. Serve with
   steamed rice or bread.

Serves 4 to 6

Cook's note This dish was traditionally
cooked for the younger children of the
family by the Chinese maid or cook.

Carne picada
(Minced meat)

INGREDIENTS

¼ cup oil

2 (200 g) onions, peeled and diced

mixed well
   400 g minced beef or mutton
   1 tsp. stew spice powder
      (see p 28)
   1 tsp. black pepper
   1 tsp. salt
   ½ tsp. sugar
   2 tsp. Worcester sauce
   ½ tsp. thick soy sauce

2 (200 g) potatoes, peeled and
   diced

1 cup water

salt and sugar to taste

METHOD: 15 MIN.

1 Heat oil in a pan and sauté
   onions. Add meat and stir-fry for
   2 min.

2 Add potatoes and water. Cover
   and simmer for 10 min.

3 Stir and taste; season with salt
   and sugar accordingly. Lower
   heat and cook for 5 min.

4 Remove from heat and serve
   immediately with rice, bread or
   mashed potatoes.

Serves 4 to 6

Cook's note This dish can be used for
making *Mama-se frikkerdel* (p 137) or as a
filling for pang susis (p 149).

   With potatoes and carrots added to
increase its bulk, carne picada was usually
served to children when the other dishes at
the meal were too spicy for them.

Cerebo fretu
(Ox brain fritters)

INGREDIENTS

½ kg ox brain

4 cups water

batter
   1 tsp. salt
   1 (60 g) egg
   2 tbsp. plain flour
   ½ cup evaporated milk
   ½ tsp. salt
   1 tsp. freshly ground black
      pepper

2 cups oil for deep frying

PREPARATION: 20 MIN.

1 Boil ox brain in slightly salted
   water for 15 min. Remove and
   set aside to cool.

2 Remove veins on brain carefully.
   Cut into 2-cm thick slices.

METHOD: 10 MIN.

1 Heat oil over high heat. Dip
   each slice of brain in batter and
   deep fry until crisp and light
   brown.

2 Remove and serve at once with
   rice, curry and a sambal dish
   (pp 62–70).

Serves 4 to 6

Carne picada
During World War II, the thrifty Cristang cook created endless variations of this cheap yet tasty minced meat dish.

Mama-se frikkerdel
Mama's mincemeat rissoles is a great picnic dish that always brings back memories of fun times.

Mama-se frikkerdel
(Mama's minced meat rissoles)

INGREDIENTS

2 (200 g) potatoes, whole,
  unpeeled

¼ tsp. salt plus additional to taste

pepper to taste

1½ cups oil

300 g minced beef or mutton

1 (100 g) onion, peeled and
  chopped finely

2 cloves (6 g) garlic, peeled and
  chopped finely

½ tsp. stew spice powder (see p 28)

1 tsp. sugar

1 (60 g) egg, separated

6 tbsp. finely crushed cheese
  biscuits or homemade
  breadcrumbs

garnish (optional)
  2 (30 g) tomatoes, sliced
  1 (80 g) cucumber, peeled and
    sliced

PREPARATION: 30 MIN.

1 Boil potatoes in their jackets
  until soft. Peel and mash while
  still hot and season with salt and
  pepper to taste. Set aside to cool.

2 Meanwhile, heat 2 tbsp. of the
  oil in a pan. Stir-fry meat for 1
  min.; then add onion, garlic and
  stew spice powder. Stir again.

3 Add remaining ¼ tsp. of the salt
  and all the sugar. Continue
  frying until meat is tender and
  moisture is absorbed. Remove
  from heat and set aside to cool.

4 Mix egg yolk and cooled mashed
  potato well together. Combine
  cooked meat with potato
  mixture. Add 1 tbsp. of the
  crushed biscuits. Knead and
  shape into rissoles.

5 Dip each rissole in lightly beaten
  egg white and coat with remaining crushed biscuits. Repeat until
  meat and potato mixture is used
  up.

METHOD: 20 MIN.

1 Heat remaining oil in a deep pan
  over high heat. Fry 3–4 rissoles
  at a time until golden brown and
  remove with a slotted spoon.
  Drain on paper towels.

2 Serve at once, garnished with
  slices of tomato and cucumber,
  and chilli or tomato ketchup.

Makes 10 rissoles

Vinhu de arlu
(Pickled garlic meat in wine)

INGREDIENTS

1 kg beef from shoulder or leg cuts

mixed into a paste
  2 tsp. freshly ground pepper
  4 tbsp. freshly ground coriander
  2 tbsp. freshly ground cumin
  1 tbsp. freshly ground fennel
  2 tbsp. turmeric powder
  2 tbsp. vinegar
  1 tsp. salt
  1 tsp. pepper
  1 bulb (50 g) garlic, peeled and
    chopped
  50 g ginger, peeled and
    chopped

1 star anise

1 cup white wine, or ½ cup brandy

½ cup oil

PREPARATION: 20 MIN.
(COMPLETED A DAY IN ADVANCE)

1 Dry meat thoroughly. Cut into
  slices 1 cm thick and 7 cm long.

2 Coat each slice of meat with
  mixed paste. Arrange slices neatly in a glass or earthenware dish.
  Do not use metal dishes, as the
  ingredients may discolour metal.

Break off petals of star anise and
scatter on meat.

3 Pour in wine. Prick layers of
  meat with a fork to allow marinade to work into meat. Cover
  and let stand in a cool place
  overnight. The next day, turn the
  slices over. Cover until needed.

METHOD: 10 MIN.

1 Heat oil in a pan until it is very
  hot. Fry two slices of pickled
  meat at a time until crispy on
  edges.

2 Serve immediately with boiled
  rice. The meat may also be
  added to debal (p 52).

Serves 6 to 8

Cook's note This very old Portuguese dish
is also popular in Macau where leg of pork
is used instead of beef. Today not many
Cristang remember the recipe and, sadly,
even fewer attempt to cook the dish at all.
As a variation, in METHOD, STEP 1 fry 4–5
slices of the meat with some of the
marinade for 2 min. Add 1 cup meat stock
(see p 27) and cook for 5 min. Taste and
season with salt and pepper accordingly.

Pacheree
(Spiced sweet-and-sour brinjals)

INGREDIENTS

6 (300 g) brinjals, long variety

mixed well
  ½ tsp. salt
  ½ tsp. pepper
  ½ tsp. turmeric powder

2 tbsp. cumin powder

blended to a fine paste
  1 bulb (50 g) garlic, peeled
  50 g ginger, peeled
  ½ tbsp. mustard seeds
  12 (25 g) dried chillies,
    presoaked in hot water

continued on p 139

Pacheree
Its Indian origin is reflected in the amount of cumin
used in the thick and spicy gravy of this brinjal relish.

Seybah
This rich medley of meats was traditionally prepared
for festive occasions. In this picture, the dish is served
in a nineteenth century glass bowl.

from p 137, *Pacheree*

1 cup plus 3 tbsp. oil

1 cup water

3 tbsp. vinegar

sugar to taste

salt to taste.

PREPARATION: 15 MIN.

1 Cut brinjals into halves and split each half lengthwise. Score the white flesh and smear with mixture of salt, pepper and turmeric. Set aside.

2 Mix cumin powder with a little water. Add to blended paste and mix with a spoon (do not use a food processor).

METHOD: 10 MIN.

1 Heat 1 cup of the oil in a pan and fry brinjals (fry 3 or 4 pieces at a time). Remove and drain on paper towels. Discard oil.

2 Heat remaining oil in the same pan. Put in blended paste and fry until aromatic. Add water, a little at a time. Cook for 2 min.

3 Pour in vinegar and stir. Simmer for 2 min.

4 Add sugar and salt to taste. The sauce should have a sweet-and-sour flavour. If necessary, add a little more vinegar and/or sugar. Simmer for 5 min. and remove from heat.

5 Arrange brinjals on a plate. Pour the sauce over and serve immediately. Serve as an accompaniment to fish curry or fried chicken.

Serves 4 to 6

Seybah
(Braised meat medley)

INGREDIENTS

350 g mutton

350 g beef (sirloin)

300 g chicken gizzards

400 g ox tongue

1 tsp. salt

8 cups water plus additional to boil mutton and beef

2 cinnamon sticks, 5-cm lengths

2 star anise

4 cloves

25 g galangal, peeled and bruised (optional)

4 cloves (12 g) garlic, peeled and crushed

2 tbsp. thick soy sauce

1 tbsp. thin soy sauce

2 tbsp. grated palm sugar (gula Melaka), or 2 tbsp. brown sugar

chilli sauce
   3 (15 g) fresh red chillies
   5 cloves (15 g) garlic, peeled
   1 tbsp. vinegar
   2 tsp. sugar
   salt to taste

2 (120 g) hard-boiled eggs, whole, shells removed (optional)

garnish
   1 (150 g) head of leaf lettuce, chopped coarsely
   1 (100 g) cucumber, peeled and sliced thickly
   10 (120 g) bean curd puffs, sliced thickly

PREPARATION: 20 MIN.

1 Put mutton and beef in separate pots, add water to cover meats and boil until cooked. Cut into bite-sized pieces.

2 Put gizzards and tongue into a pot with salt and 5 cups of the water. Boil for 10 min. Remove gizzards and set aside. Continue boiling tongue for 10 min. more. Remove, scrape skin off tongue and rinse. Then boil tongue again for 20 min. to soften.

3 Put all the mutton, beef, gizzards and tongue into a large, clean pot. Add cinnamon sticks, star anise, cloves, galangal, crushed garlic, thick and thin soy sauces, sugar and 1 cup of the water. Stir well and let stand for 5 min.

4 To make chilli sauce, blend chillies and garlic coarsely. Add salt, vinegar and sugar and mix well. Set aside.

METHOD: 30 MIN.

1 Place pot of meats over medium heat. Cook covered for 5 min. Add remaining water. Cover and simmer on low heat until meats are tender. The gravy should be thick and black.

2 Add salt and hard-boiled eggs. Stir to coat eggs with gravy.

3 Remove pot from heat and let stand for 10 min. Cut gizzards and tongue into bite-sized pieces. Return these pieces to the pot and stir. Set aside until ready to serve.

4 To serve, place meats in a glass bowl. Top with lettuce, cucumber and bean curd puffs. Pour chilli sauce over and toss well. If not consuming all of the seybah in one serving, be sure to set aside some garnish and chilli sauce for subsequent servings.

5 Cut hard-boiled eggs into quarters and arrange them around the edge of the dish. Serve with rice or as an accompaniment to drinks.

Serves 8 to 10

Cook's note Traditionally pork was used in this classic Cristang dish, especially pig's ears, which added a crunchy texture.

Boca Doce

SWEET ENDINGS

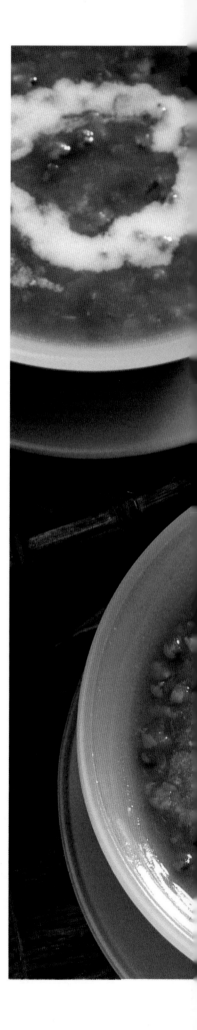

Although desserts are seldom served after a Cristang meal, Cristang cuisine includes a rich array of cakes and sweets. These delights are eaten on festive occasions, when a grand meal typically ends with a variety of light cakes, followed by coffee.

In the past, cakes and sweets were usually reserved for afternoon tea, a time-honoured ritual during which homemade sweets or treats bought from the cake-boy would be served. Rain or shine, the cake-boy used to saunter barefoot around the village, singing out the names of cakes he had for sale: '*Bi-bin-ka-dee-nyami-mengala*' or '*Pu-lo-oo-rup*'. He has been relegated to history now, but the memory of his voice lingers on and occasionally triggers a nostalgic longing for the mouth-watering treats that were nearly always served at four o'clock each afternoon in my home.

Cristang cakes are made from local staples, such as rice, tapioca flour and sago. Beans, black glutinous rice or tubers are made into various kinds of rich, sweet porridge. Thick, creamy coconut milk, palm sugar (gula Melaka) and eggs form the base for most of these sweets; dairy products are rarely used in Cristang desserts, so the cakes and sweets do not leave one feeling satiated.

Most Cristang cakes require only boiling or steaming and are easy to prepare. Baking was confined to a yearly ritual when Cristang cooks would bring out a kerosene tin contraption they called *anglor* (oven) to bake *bolu*s, *kuki*s and tarts for Christmas. Keeping the fire under the awkward oven going was a tearful experience, thanks to the thick smoke discharged by the coconut husk fuel. Yet Cristang cooks would labour late into the night, producing huge batches of cakes and sweet treats baked to perfection. Christmas simply would not be the same without traditional favourites like baje, blueda, bolu cocu, dodol sabang and sersagung (pp 143–145, 147 and 152, respectively).

Many Cristang desserts have names with roots in the Malay, Indian and Portuguese languages, reflecting the integration of cultures and indigenous tastes. *Bolu*, for example, is Portuguese for cake and *pang*, for bread. *Canje* is Tamil for porridge, and *kuih* means cake in Malay.

Canjee mungoo
Green food in green dishes, eaten by Cristang dressed in green — this mung bean sweet is always served during the Feast of St John (see Festa de San Juang, p 8), when the Cristang make sure that everything around them has a touch of green to symbolize the renewal of life.

Abor-abor
(Steamed sago pudding)

INGREDIENTS

250 g sago

3 banana leaves

200 g palm sugar (gula Melaka)

2 cups (160 g) grated coconut

1 cup warm water

½ tsp. salt

PREPARATION: 15 MIN.

1 Wash sago thoroughly and leave to drain.

2 Scald banana leaves to soften them. Cut into squares of 15 cm.

3 Cut palm sugar into small cubes and chill.

METHOD: 1 HR.

1 Put sago in a large bowl. Add grated coconut and mix thoroughly.

2 Roll banana leaf squares into cones.

3 Half fill each cone with sago mixture, followed by two cubes of palm sugar. Top with 2 tbsp. sago mixture. Bend flap of cone over mouth to close it. Secure flap with one or more toothpicks. Place cones on their sides in a steamer.

4 Steam cones for 45 min. When mixture is cooked, sago should be translucent and fluffy. Remove from heat and serve at once.

Serves 12

Cook's note This sweet used to be a speciality reserved for weddings. If banana leaf cones prove too troublesome, use this method instead: spread half the sago mixture in a dish lined with banana leaves. Dot with palm sugar cubes. Cover with another layer of sago mixture and steam. To serve, cut into diamond-shaped pieces using a wet knife. The steamed sago is sometimes formed into patties and fried. This fried sago (*goreng sago*) is served at funerals.

Agar-agar
(Golden seaweed jelly)

INGREDIENTS

30 g dry agar-agar strands (3 cups when wet)

4 cups water

2 cups rock sugar

½ cup castor sugar

2 tbsp. golden syrup

1 drop yellow colouring

2 eggshells, crushed

2 citrus leaves

PREPARATION: 10 MIN.

1 Soak agar-agar in water for 10 min. to soften; then drain.

METHOD: 3–4 DAYS

1 Put agar-agar in a deep pot with water. Bring to a slow boil.

2 When agar-agar has dissolved, add rock sugar and castor sugar. Simmer over very low heat, stirring continuously until sugar dissolves.

3 Add golden syrup and yellow colouring. Stir to blend colours.

4 On very low heat, cook for 1½ hrs., stirring occasionally.

5 Add eggshells and citrus leaves. This will bring any scum to the surface. Skim off scum; then remove egg shells and citrus leaves.

6 When mixture begins to boil again, remove from heat.

7 Strain liquid jelly through a piece of muslin placed over a mould; there should be enough liquid to fill two 15-cm fancy moulds. The jelly should have a translucent golden hue. Leave to set.

8 Cut a sheet of greaseproof paper to fit mouth of mould. Once agar-agar has set, place sheet of paper over mouth of mould. Over the next 3–4 days, leave agar-agar to dry in the sun for a few hours each day until a thin crust of sugar forms on its surface.

9 To serve agar-agar, remove from mould and cut very thin slices using a serrated knife or bread knife. To store, replace in mould and cover with paper.

Serves 20

Cook's note In the old days, agar-agar seaweed was collected by Cristang fishermen. The seaweed was dried in the sun for days to bleach it white, then packed away and stored until a few months before Christmas. The monumental task of making agar-agar the traditional way would begin at about this time: The seaweed was first boiled in water with crushed eggshells in a huge brass pan called a grengseng (p 20). When the seaweed began dissolving into a thick, cloudy liquid, it was poured into a container with holes at the sides through which the liquid was squeezed into muslin sacks. The liquid was again strained by squeezing it out of the sacks and back into the grengseng where it was brought to a boil again. This process, requiring at least two pairs of strong arms and not a little dexterity, was repeated until a clear amber liquid was obtained. Sugar was then added and the liquid was stirred until its colour turned tawny.

Agar-agar was served in paper-thin slices—anything thicker was considered unrefined!—after the guests had had a chance to admire its shape. The moulds used to make agar-agar were generally in the shape of a rabbit, a fish or a bunch of grapes. They were made from finely crafted porcelain and imported from England. Sadly, these moulds are difficult to find nowadays.

Today, making this traditional Christmas dessert is much easier as agar-agar is available in clear strands or in powdered form, both of which may be purchased from shops and require only a little boiling.

Baje (Palm-sugar rice)

INGREDIENTS

250 g white glutinous rice

3 cups (240 g) grated coconut

3 cups warm water

300 g palm sugar (gula Melaka)

200 g granulated sugar

2 screw pine leaves

1 banana leaf, cut into two pieces, 23 cm × 23 cm each

PREPARATION: 2 HRS. 30 MIN.

1 Wash rice thoroughly and soak in cool water for 2 hrs. to soften grains.

2 Soak grated coconut in 2 cups of the warm water and extract 1 cup thick coconut milk (see p 26.)

3 Boil palm sugar and granulated sugar in remaining cup of water until both kinds of sugar have dissolved. Add screw pine leaves and simmer for 5 min. Discard leaves, strain sugar water and set aside.

4 Steam rice until cooked and grainy, about 15 to 20 min. Remove and set aside.

METHOD: 1 HR.

1 Pour coconut milk into a greng-seng (p 20) or brass pan (a stainless steel pot will also do). Add sugar water from PREPARATION, STEP 3 and stir well.

continued on p 144

Agar-agar

Not many Cristang still make this golden jelly the traditional way, which requires it to be dried in the sun until a crust of sugar forms on the surface. But it is still served on festive occasions, especially Christmas.

The agar-agar is shown here with sersagung (p 152), which is also a Christmas specialty. Sersagung is usually served on a saucer and eaten with tea sprinkled on it. Children, however, are given these coconut rice granules in paper cones so that they can empty the fine, rather difficult to eat mixture into their mouths (inelegant though it is!) without making a mess.

from p 143, *Baje*

2 Cook mixture over low heat, stirring continuously until it thickens and foams. This should take about 1 hr.

3 When mixture has boiled down to ¾ of its original level (about 1½ cups), add steamed glutinous rice. Stir to coat rice thoroughly. The resulting mixture should be very thick and sticky.

4 Line a plate with a piece of banana leaf. Spoon baje onto leaf. Level surface with another piece of banana leaf or back of a spoon and leave to cool. Cut into diamond shapes before serving.

Serves 10

Cook's note This sweet was traditionally made for Christmas. However, it is not as popular these days, perhaps because of its cloying sweetness and richness. The very high sugar content helps to preserve the baje throughout the yuletide season. This sweet is also made by the descendants of the Portuguese in Macau.

Bibingka de nyami bengaler (Tapioca cake)

INGREDIENTS

4 cups (320 g) grated coconut

4 (240 g) eggs

300 g brown sugar

4 tbsp. butter, melted

½ kg young tapioca, grated

¼ tsp. salt

4 tbsp. plain flour, sifted

some butter to grease the cake tin

PREPARATION: 5 MIN.

1 Set aside 1 cup of the grated coconut. Without adding any water, squeeze ½ cup thick coconut milk from remaining coconut (see p 26; follow method

described there, but add no water). Set aside.

METHOD: 2 HRS.

1 Beat eggs and sugar until sugar has dissolved. Add thick coconut milk to mixture. Stir well.

2 Add melted butter, tapioca and salt. Mix thoroughly.

3 Heat oven to 165°C (325°F or gas mark 3) and grease a large cake tin.

4 Fold flour and the cup of grated coconut into tapioca mixture; stir gently. Using a spoon, transfer into cake tin and smooth down surface of mixture by pressing firmly with back of spoon.

5 Bake until cake shrinks from sides of tin and centre is springy, about 1½ hrs. Make sure cake is completely cool before cutting and serving.

Serves 10 to 12

Blueda (Dough cake)

INGREDIENTS

1 cup toddy (p 40)

300 g plain flour, sifted

350 g butter, softened

1 tbsp. oil or lard

12 large egg yolks

250 g castor sugar

½ cup brandy

1 tsp. stew spice powder (see p 28)

a little butter for greasing moulds

PREPARATION: 20 MIN.
PLUS 12 HRS. WAITING
(COMPLETED 2 DAYS IN ADVANCE)

1 Pour toddy into a mixing bowl. Add sifted flour gradually while stirring continuously.

2 Add softened butter and oil and fold gently to incorporate all three ingredients.

3 Cover with a clean kitchen towel and leave overnight or for at least 12 hrs. The mixture should not be refrigerated but kept in a cool place.

4 The next day, beat egg yolks with sugar until a creamy consistency is achieved. Pour into toddy mixture.

5 Stir gently to combine. Add brandy and stir once more. Cover with grease-proof paper. Leave overnight or for another 12 hrs. The mixture should rise to twice its original volume during this period.

METHOD: 1 HR. 45 MIN.

1 Heat oven to 165°C (325°F or gas mark 3). Grease brass blueda moulds (or 2 grooved 20-cm moulds) thoroughly.

2 Incorporate stew spice powder into mixture from PREPARATION, STEP 5.

3 Pour into moulds and bake until cakes are firm at the centre and the edges leave the sides of the moulds, about 1 hr.

Makes 2 cakes, serves 20

Cook's note Blueda moulds are special brass moulds that have deep grooves in them. It is important to grease the moulds well so that the dough will not stick. Any cake tin or mould of the same dimension can be substituted if blueda moulds are unavailable. Although different versions of this Dutch recipe exist, toddy is never omitted, for it is required as a rising agent.

Bolu cocu (Coconut cake)

INGREDIENTS

2 cups (160 g) grated coconut,
  toasted

12 (720 g) eggs, separated

½ kg castor sugar

sifted together
  1½ cups plain flour
  ¼ tsp. baking powder
  1 tsp. stew spice powder
    (see p 28)
  ½ tsp. cinnamon powder

3 tbsp. brandy

a little butter for greasing moulds

PREPARATION: 15 MIN.

1 Heat oven to 150°C (300°F or
  gas mark 2). Grease two brass
  blueda moulds or grooved jelly
  (jello) ring moulds.

2 Pound or, in a blender, process
  toasted coconut without any
  liquid for 1 min. until a fine
  texture is obtained. Set aside.

3 Beat egg whites until they stand
  in soft peaks.

4 In another bowl, beat egg yolks
  with sugar until a creamy
  consistency is obtained and
  mixture is fluffy. Stir blended
  coconut from STEP 2 into
  creamed mixture one spoonful at
  a time, making sure to incorporate it well.

5 Fold in sifted ingredients and
  egg whites.

6 Add brandy, stirring gently.

METHOD: 1 HR. 15 MIN.

1 Pour batter into moulds and
  bake until centre of cakes are
  firm but springy, about 1 hr.
  15 min.

2 Let cakes cool before removing
  from moulds.

Serves 6 to 8

Bolo cocu
This coconut cake was baked in the traditional brass
mould shown in the background. The mould, together
with the silver cake tray, which belonged to my mother,
represents but a small part of the Cristang legacy that
has been handed down to me.

Canje cha-cher
(Coconut milk porridge)

INGREDIENTS

50 g sago flour or starch

2½ cups boiling water

Red, blue and green food colouring

1 (100 g) red sweet potato

1 (100 g) purple yam

4 cups (320 g) grated coconut

½ cup ice water

2 (10 g) screw pine leaves

4 tbsp. sugar or to taste

½ tsp. salt or to taste

PREPARATION: 4 HRS.

1 Mix sago flour with 1 tbsp. of the boiling water (the water must be very hot or the paste will not thicken). Knead the paste into a dough.

2 Divide dough into 3 equal portions. Colour one portion red, the other blue and the last one, green. Roll each portion separately to form pencil-thick noodles and cut into 1-cm lengths. Dry sago noodles in the sun for 3–4 hrs.

3 Peel sweet potato and yam. Cut into slices 2 cm thick. Stack slices and cut into strips. Then cut strips into diamond-shaped pieces.

4 Soak grated coconut in remaining 2 cups of water and extract 1 cup thick coconut milk and 1 cup thin coconut milk (see p 26). Set aside squeezed grated coconut.

METHOD: 40 MIN.

1 Boil sago noodles in enough water to cover them. When they are soft, remove and dip into ice water to stop cooking completely. Drain and set aside.

2 Discard water and fill pot with thin coconut milk. Add sweet potato and yam pieces and screw pine leaves. Bring to a boil and cook till tubers are soft.

3 Add sago noodles, sugar and salt. There should be enough liquid to cover all of the ingredients. If not, add 2 more cups of water to the grated coconut and extract more milk. Add this to the pot and boil for 2–4 min.

4 Pour in thick coconut milk. Simmer for 2 min. before removing from heat. Serve chilled or hot.

Serves 6 to 8

Cook's note This colourful sweet is said to be made of 'precious stones' (*cha-cher*), hidden within the soft, white cotton wool that is the coconut milk. The red, blue and green sago noodles and the bits of yam and sweet potato are meant to resemble precious stones. This dessert is a favourite among Cristang ladies who love having it as they gamble at *chikee*, a card game.

Many thanks to my sister Joan for this recipe.

Canje mungoo
(Green mung bean porridge)

INGREDIENTS

2 cups green mung beans

25 g ginger, peeled and sliced thickly

3 cups (240 g) grated coconut

9 cups warm water

pinch of salt

1 cup grated palm sugar (gula Melaka), or 2 cups sugar

2–3 screw pine leaves, washed and tied together in a knot

PREPARATION: 2 HRS.

1 Soak mung beans in water for at least 2 hrs.

2 Soak grated coconut in 3 cups of the warm water and extract thick and thin coconut milk (see p 26).

METHOD: 50 MIN.

1 Fill a deep pot with remaining water. Put in beans and ginger and bring to a boil.

2 Add salt. Cover and boil until water is absorbed and beans swollen, about 30 min.

3 Lower heat. Add thin coconut milk, sugar and screw pine leaves. Simmer until beans become soft, about 20 min. or until a broth-like consistency is achieved. Taste and season with salt accordingly.

4 Serve hot or chilled in individual bowls topped with 1 tbsp. thick coconut milk.

Serves 10

Cook's note This dish is always served during the feast of St John, when three days of prayer and contemplation culminate in a mini carnival. See p 8, Festa de San Juang, for a description of this festival.

Doce de obu
(Steamed egg-and-coconut-milk custard)

INGREDIENTS

8 cups (640 g) grated coconut

1 cup warm water

1 kg castor sugar

3 (15 g) screw pine leaves, tied together in a knot

12 (720 g) eggs

PREPARATION: 10 MIN.

1 Soak grated coconut in 1 cup of the warm water and extract

about 1½ cups thick coconut milk (see p 26).

METHOD: 65 MIN.

1 Gently beat eggs using a whisk.

2 Add sugar and continue beating until all the sugar has dissolved.

3 Pour in thick coconut milk and continue beating until ingredients are thoroughly mixed.

4 Strain mixture through a piece of fine muslin into an enamel dish (1.5-litre capacity). Put in screw pine leaves.

5 Steam for 10 min. on high heat and remove screw pine leaves. Lower heat and steam for 30 min. more or until mixture sets.

6 Cool before serving.

Serves 8 to 10

Cook's note This custard, known locally as *kaya*, is soft and spreads well on warm toast. It is popular as a breakfast spread or as a topping for glutinous rice desserts.

Dodol sabang (Sticky rice flour and coconut cream fudge)

INGREDIENTS

18½ cups (1½ kg) grated coconut

8 cups warm water

3 kg rock sugar

10 (50 g) screw pine leaves, tied together in a knot

1½ kg white glutinous rice flour

300 g rice flour

200 g granulated sugar

banana leaves to line serving platters

PREPARATION: 20 MIN.

1 Soak grated coconut in 1 cup of the water and extract thick coconut milk (see p 26).

2 Using 2 more cups of the water, extract milk a second time from the same grated coconut. Do not mix this batch with the previous one. Use 3 more cups of the water and extract a third batch of coconut milk; keep all batches separate.

3 Heat remaining water in a saucepan. Add rock sugar, followed by screw pine leaves. Once all the rock sugar has dissolved, remove from heat and set aside. Remove screw pine leaves.

METHOD: I HR. 30 MIN.
(COMPLETED A DAY IN ADVANCE)

1 Mix glutinous rice flour with rice flour and dissolve in third batch of (thin) coconut milk. Strain mixture through a piece of muslin.

2 Pour thick coconut milk (first batch) into a grengseng (p 20) or brass pan. Bring to a slow boil and cook until coconut oil rises to the surface. Skim this creamy oil off into a deep bowl and leave to cool.

3 Add thin coconut milk (second batch) to thick coconut milk remaining in pan. Add rice flour mixture from STEP I and stir well.

4 Place pan over very low heat. Stir continuously for about 5 min. Add granulated sugar and sugar water from PREPARATION, STEP 3. Stir continuously for about 50 min. to ensure that mixture does not coagulate. Expect to put some extra effort into stirring as mixture thickens as it cooks.

5 When mixture is fairly thick and drops slowly when lifted with a spoon, add oily coconut cream from STEP 2, stirring continuously.

6 Test to see if mixture (dodol) is cooked by taking ½ tsp. of it and rubbing between fingers. If mixture does not stick to fingers, it is ready. Remove from heat at once.

7 Line 2 large dinner plates with banana leaves and pour mixture on them. Pat gently with the back of a spoon or with another piece of banana leaf to shape mixture. Cool and keep for at least a day before serving.

Serves 15

Cook's note Another traditional Christmas favourite, this sweet may have originated from the Malays who make a similar sweet also called *dodol*. The Malay version, however, is brown as palm sugar (gula Melaka) is used instead of white sugar.

In the Cristang language, *sabang* actually means soap, which is what dodol sabang looks like when cooked and allowed to set. One must have lots of patience and energy to make this sweet as it requires continuous stirring to achieve the right texture and consistency.

Kuih tat (Pineapple tarts)

INGREDIENTS

pineapple jam filling
    2 medium-sized half-ripe pineapples (about 1 kg each)
    1 cinnamon stick, 3-cm length
    250 g rock sugar
    5 cloves

the pastry
    500 g plain flour
    pinch of salt
    250 g butter or lard, chilled
    1 tbsp. corn oil
    1 (60 g) egg yolk
    1 tsp. vanilla essence
    2 tbsp. cold water

continued on p 149

Kuih tat
Beautiful silver cake trays such as this were used at Cristang weddings to serve the wedding cake and at Christmas to serve pineapple tarts. The chess set with leather board and the silver-plated pieces belongs to my son Julian.

from p 147, *Kuih tat*

glaze

1 (60 g) egg yolk, beaten well
a little butter for greasing
baking trays

PREPARATION 1: 40 MIN.
(COMPLETED A DAY IN ADVANCE)

1 Peel pineapple, remove eyes and
chop up flesh finely. Strain
chopped pineapple and reserve
juice.

2 To make jam, place pineapple,
cinnamon stick, rock sugar and
cloves into a grengseng (p 20)
or a deep brass pan without any
liquid. Cook over low heat for
30 min., stirring occasionally to
prevent burning.

3 If jam becomes too dry and starts
sticking to pan, add 4 tbsp. of
strained pineapple juice from
STEP 1. Simmer until jam is
sticky and light golden. Allow
jam to cool completely before
using.

PREPARATION 2: 2¼ HRS.

1 Sift flour into a mixing bowl and
add a pinch of salt. Cut chilled
butter into cubes and add to
bowl.

2 Rub butter into flour with fingers to obtain a crumbly texture.
Work quickly so that butter does
not melt too much.

3 Add corn oil and knead lightly.

4 Add egg yolk and vanilla essence.
Sprinkle with cold water and
knead to form a soft, pliable
dough. Cover and chill for 2 hrs.

5 Shape pastry dough into a ball.
Knead on floured surface until
smooth. Cover and chill for
2 hrs.

METHOD: 30 MIN.

1 Heat oven to 175°C (350°F or
gas mark 4).

2 Divide pastry from PREPARA-
TION, STEP 5 into four portions.
Roll out each portion on a
floured board to form a long
strip about ½ cm thick. Cut out
round tart shells (about 5½ cm in
diameter) from pastry using a
biscuit cutter.

3 Fill the centre of each shell with
jam to make a tart.

4 Roll out remaining pastry to
3 mm thick. Cut out thin strips
and place them round the rims of
the tarts. Flute rims with fingers
or a pair of pincers.

5 Cut small pieces of pastry to
resemble three-bladed leaves (or
any other decorative shape) and
place on the centre of the filling.
Glaze tops of tarts with egg yolk.

6 Place tarts on a greased tray and
bake for 20 min. or until pastry
turns golden. If not serving
immediately, let cool before
storing.

Makes about 25 tarts

Cook's note Malacca's oldest ethnic groups
all make pineapple tarts for their respective
festivals. The tarts may be distinguised by
their appearance. The Malays use a variety
of shapes, while the Chittys use a dot of
pastry in the centre. The Peranakan
include a lattice pattern, and the Cristang
use a three-bladed leaf as a symbol of their
belief in the Holy Trinity.

Pang susis
(Meat buns)

INGREDIENTS

1 (200 g) sweet potato

pinch of salt

dough

3 cups plain flour
1½ tsp. dry yeast
2 tbsp. sugar
100 g butter

1 (30 g) egg yolk
2 tbsp. water or milk
2 tbsp. brandy
2 tbsp. oil

3 (250 g) potatoes, peeled and
diced

1 (100 g) onion, peeled and diced

1 clove (6 g) garlic, peeled and
diced

½ tsp. stew spice powder (see p 28)

½ tsp. black pepper

300 g lean minced meat

salt to taste

sugar to taste

glaze

1 (30 g) egg yolk, beaten
mixed
½ cup milk
1 tbsp. sugar

PREPARATION: 40 MIN.

1 Peel sweet potato and boil in
slightly salted water until tender.
Drain and mash. Set aside.

2 To make dough:

i Sift flour into a mixing bowl.
Add yeast and sugar and mix
well.

ii Rub butter into flour with fingers to obtain a crumbly
texture.

iii Add egg yolk, water and
brandy to bind ingredients.
Knead well for 10 min.

iv Add mashed sweet potato from
STEP 1. Knead dough again
until it is soft and pliable.
Leave to rise for about 30 min.

METHOD: 50 MIN.

1 To make filling, heat oil in a frying pan. Put in potatoes, onions
and garlic and sauté for 1 min.

2 Add stew spice powder, black
pepper and meat. Fry for 30 sec.
Add salt and sugar to taste.

continued on p 150

Pang susis
These meat buns are also called celebration buns as they are always served during family celebrations.

from p 149, *Pang susis*

3 Remove from heat when potatoes and meat are cooked and moisture has been absorbed. Set aside to cool.

4 Heat oven to 175°C (350°F or gas mark 4).

5 Pinch off a bit of the dough from PREPARATION, STEP 2 and shape into a ball about 2½ cm in diameter. Flatten ball in palm of hand until about ½ cm thick.

6 Put 2 tsp. of filling in the centre of the dough and seal the edges to make a bun. Turn the bun over and shape into an oval. Brush the top with beaten egg yolk and place on a lightly greased baking tray. Continue making buns until all the dough has been used up.

7 Bake the tray of buns until golden, about 30 min. Remove and glaze again with the mixture of milk and sugar. Serve warm as a snack or with soup.

Makes 20 small buns

Cook's note This is my mother's special recipe. When fresh meat was expensive, she used tinned luncheon meat as a substitute.

Putugal
(Steamed tapioca-and-banana cake)

INGREDIENTS

4 cups (320 g) grated coconut

1 cup warm water

3 kg tapioca

1½ cups sugar

½ tsp. blue colouring, or juice from bunga telang

300 g ripe bananas

greased banana leaves, or greaseproof paper to line a

cake tin (about 30 cm × 15 cm and 8 cm deep)

PREPARATION: 20 MIN.

1 Steam 1 cup of the grated coconut. Set aside. Soak remaining coconut in warm water for 5 min. and extract 1 cup thick coconut milk (see p 26).

2 Peel and cut tapioca into large pieces. Grate or blend until fine. Drain off all liquid except starchy residue that appears.

3 Pour coconut milk over grated tapioca. Add 1 cup of the sugar. Mix well and divide into two equal portions.

4 Colour one portion blue evenly. Set aside.

5 Peel bananas and slice diagonally and thickly.

METHOD: 30 MIN.

1 Line a cake tin with greased banana leaves. Spoon 2 tbsp. blue coloured and 2 tbsp. uncoloured tapioca alternately into tin, spreading each layer evenly. Stop when half of both portions has been used up.

2 Arrange banana slices evenly on top of tapioca mixture. Transfer remaining blue and uncoloured tapioca onto the banana slices, alternating between the two colours. Smooth down final layer by patting firmly with a piece of banana leaf or back of a spoon.

3 Steam for 20 min. Remove from heat and let cool.

4 Add remaining sugar to steamed grated coconut from PREPARATION, STEP 1 and mix well. Sprinkle coconut over steamed tapioca and let stand for 1 hour. Cut putugal into diamond shapes and serve sprinkled with more grated coconut.

Serves 10 to 12

Putugal
This steamed tapioca-and-banana tea-time snack is, sadly, not made very often nowadays as it involves quite a lot of work—not many people appreciate that its delicate flavour is well worth all the effort.

If large, fresh banana leaves are available, wrap the tapioca mixture around whole bananas and place in the centre of a leaf; wrap neatly, secure ends with toothpicks and steam the parcels as instructed in METHOD, STEP 3.

Sersagung
(Coconut rice granules)

INGREDIENTS

750 g long grain rice, or 300 g
　ready-ground rice

1 (60 g) egg

½ tsp. salt

¼ tsp. slaked lime (optional)

3 cups (240 g) grated coconut, or 2
　cups (220 g) desiccated coconut
　if using ready-ground rice

200 g granulated sugar

2 screw pine leaves

PREPARATION: 5 HRS. 15
MIN.

1 Wash rice and soak for at least 5
　hrs., preferably overnight. (If
　using ready-ground rice, see
　Cook's note.)

2 Dry rice thoroughly, then mill or
　blend finely.

3 Beat egg. Add salt, slaked lime
　and grated coconut. Stir
　thoroughly to form a fine,
　crumbly texture.

4 Add rice a little at a time,
　making sure to lift the mixture
　bit by bit to incorporate air
　into it.

METHOD: 30 MIN.

1 Heat a grengseng (p 20) or brass
　pan and fry mixture from PREPA-
　RATION, STEP 4 together with
　screw pine leaves over very low
　heat.

2 Keep stirring continuously to
　prevent mixture from coagulat-
　ing into a lump. There should be
　granules of coconut and rice,
　which become fragrant as the
　coconut is gently toasted.

3 Remove screw pine leaves, add
　sugar and stir vigorously. Stir for
　2 min. on very low heat, making
　sure sugar does not melt.

Remove from heat when granules are a very light golden
colour. Leave to cool.

4 When completely cooled, fill dry
　glass jars with sersagung and
　store.

5 To serve, place 2–3 tbsp.
　sersagung in a deep dessert bowl
　or tea saucer and add 2 tsp. hot
　plain tea (see Cook's note).

Serves 10 to 20

Cook's note If using ready-ground rice,
begin at PREPARATION, STEP 3 but do not
include the grated coconut. Follow the
next steps until METHOD, STEP 2, then add
the desiccated coconut at this stage—stir
well to incorporate the coconut into the
rice mixture. The rest of the recipe
continues as instructed.

　Sersagung that is eaten dry tends to
splutter embarrassingly as one chews,
hence the tea.

Sugee kek (Semolina cake)

INGREDIENTS

½ kg butter

450 g semolina

15 large egg yolks

450 g sugar

3 tbsp. cream

sifted together
　　1½ cups plain flour
　　3 tsp. baking powder

115 g ground almonds

10 (30 g) pieces candied winter
　melon, chopped (optional)

1 tsp. almond essence

1 tsp. vanilla essence

1 tsp. rose essence

3 tbsp. brandy

1 tsp. stew spice powder (see p 28)

a little butter to grease a cake tin

greaseproof paper to line a cake tin

ADVANCE PREPARATION: 7
HRS.

1 Mix butter and semolina well.
　Let stand for at least 7 hrs. or
　overnight.

METHOD: 15 MIN.

1 Heat oven to 165°C (325°F or
　gas mark 3). Grease a cake tin
　(30 cm × 30 cm and 10 cm deep)
　and line with greaseproof paper.

2 Beat egg yolks with sugar until a
　creamy consistency is obtained
　and mixture is fluffy. Stir in
　semolina from PREPARATION,
　STEP 1. Add cream and stir well.

3 Fold in sifted ingredients.

4 Add almonds and candied winter
　melon and fold in gently.

5 Add almond, vanilla and rose
　essence, brandy and stew spice
　powder. Stir gently, then pour
　into cake tin.

6 Bake until a skewer inserted into
　centre of cake comes out clean,
　about 45 min. The skewer must
　come out completely clean
　otherwise the centre of the cake
　will be uncooked.

Serves 8 to 10

Cook's note Cristang tradition requires a
sugee wedding cake; anything else simply
will not do.

　Not everyone has the knack of making
the perfect sugee kek, for there are as many
taboos as there are ingredients to contend
with. Indeed, making this cake for a
wedding was not undertaken lightly, for it
was believed that a perfect cake meant a
perfect and lasting marriage. However, a
raw or uncooked centre foretold troubles,
not for the bridal couple, but for the
hapless cook!

　I dedicate this recipe to my niece
Anne-Marie Cheong, who enjoys baking
all kinds of cakes and cookies.

Sugee kek
Traditionally, the multi-tiered semolina wedding cake, decorated with marzipan and royal icing was blessed by a priest before the bridal couple cut it at the wedding reception.

Lantah Saode

JUICY DETAILS

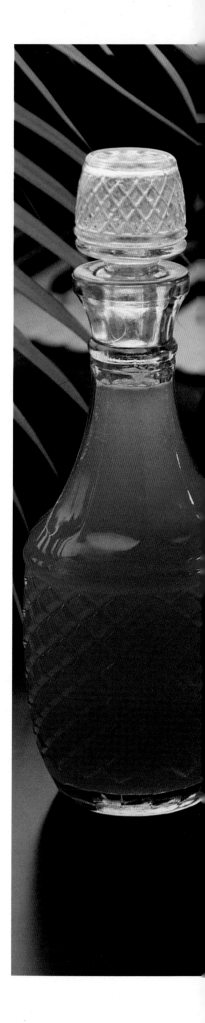

When the Portuguese first came to Malacca, they found that the wines and liquors they were accustomed to were unknown in this part of the world. The only alcoholic beverage Malaccans drank then was toddy, a potent brew obtained by fermenting the sap of the coconut flower. It was the Portuguese who introduced wine and other alcoholic drinks to the non-Muslim locals. By the beginning of the nineteenth century, alcohol had become an established part of Cristang culture. However, unlike their European forefathers, the Cristang did not serve *binhyo* (wine) with every meal; it was (and still is) coffee that took pride of place as the daily beverage drunk in copious quantities although no one is quite sure how or why this came about. Alcohol was reserved for festive occasions and for toasting auspicious events such as weddings, engagements and a baby's baptism. Wine was also served at funerals although, naturally enough, it flowed more freely at celebrations, especially during Christmas and at Intrudo (p 7).

At the turn of this century alcohol had become expensive and its appearance at a Cristang meal or a festive occasion became an indication of a person's financial status. Over the years Cristang hosts have come up with ingenious concoctions of alcohol, local fruit juices and spices. An example is *binhyu pulut pretu*, a special brew made from pulut hitam (black glutinous rice) and served at weddings. This brew and the drinks included in this section have become part of the festive fare among the Cristang today and constitute a collection of beverages that is highly unusual and unique to the Cristang culinary heritage.

Agu gingibri
This refreshing ginger drink is pictured here with an old accordion from the collection of antique musical instruments belonging to my friend Mr Don Beins, who, like many other Cristang, is a fine musician.

Agu gingibri
(Ginger syrup)

INGREDIENTS

500 g green ginger, soaked
  unskinned overnight or for at
  least 12 hours

1 kg sugar

2 cinnamon sticks, 9-cm lengths

6 cloves

rind of ½ lime or ¼ lemon

10 cups water

1 cup orange juice (from about 2
  oranges)

METHOD: 20 MIN.

1 Scrape skin off ginger and slice
  thinly.

2 Put all ingredients except orange
  juice into a saucepan and stir
  over medium heat until sugar has
  dissolved.

3 Cover and boil until ginger is
  soft and syrup is thick, about
  10 min.

4 Remove from heat and add
  orange juice.

5 Strain syrup through a piece of
  muslin into a dry container.

6 Allow syrup to cool before
  bottling.

7 To serve, mix 2 tbsp. syrup with
  iced water, beer or soda water.
  Refrigerate any leftover syrup
  (keeps for up to a month).

Serves 6 to 8, makes 1 litre

Agu sucre rosa
(Rose sugar syrup)

INGREDIENTS

500 g white sugar

5 cups water

4 tsp. rose flavouring

1 tsp. cochineal (red food
  colouring)

1 tbsp. brandy

1 empty bottle (1 litre) with cork
  or resealable cap

METHOD: 20 MIN.

1 Combine sugar and water in a
  saucepan and boil for 10 min.

2 Lower heat and simmer until a
  thick syrup is formed, about 15
  min. Skim off scum that appears.

3 Remove from heat and add rose
  flavouring and cochineal. Stir
  and strain through a piece of
  muslin or a fine meshed strainer
  into a jug. Set aside to cool.

4 When syrup has cooled, pour
  into bottle. Add brandy and cork
  or cap the bottle tightly.

*There are four ways of serving agu
sucre rosa:*

▽ Fill a glass with chilled milk
  and add 2 tbsp. of the syrup.
  Stir briskly and serve.

▽ Fill a tall glass with ice cubes.
  Add 2 tbsp. of the syrup. Top
  with soda water or ice-cream
  soda and lime slices.

▽ Fill a glass with chilled water.
  Add 2 tbsp. of the syrup. Stir
  and serve topped with a single
  rose petal. Or mix 1 tbsp. lime
  juice with 2 tbsp. of the syrup
  and add to 1 glass of chilled
  water; garnish with slices of
  lime.

▽ Fill a dessert bowl with diced
  firm jelly, canned pineapple
  (drained and diced) and boiled
  red beans. Add 1 tbsp. thick
  coconut milk on top. Do not
  stir. Cover with shaved ice.
  Drizzle chocolate sauce and 1
  tbsp. of the syrup on top. Serve
  immediately.

Cook's note A popular item with school
children of several decades ago was the ice-
ball. This firm orb of shaved ice filled with
sweet boiled red beans and dipped in rose
syrup was sold by push-cart hawkers on
the streets of Malacca and of almost every
other town in Malaysia. Unfortunately, the
health authorities have discouraged its sale,
perhaps because the hawkers used their
bare hands to shape the ice-ball.

Brande laranja
(Orange brandy)

INGREDIENTS

2 cups fresh orange juice (from
  about 8 oranges)

1 orange

3 pineapple rings

12 cloves

¾ cup water

3 tbsp. honey

1 cinnamon stick, 5-cm length

2 cups white wine

1 cup brandy

PREPARATION: 5 MIN

1 Cut 4 slices from orange, each
  ½ cm thick.

METHOD: 30 MIN.

1 Heat oven to 175°C (350°F or
  gas mark 4).

2 Stud orange slices and pineapple
  rings with cloves. Place in a
  baking dish and bake for 10 min.

3 Heat water, honey, cinnamon
  stick and orange juice in a
  saucepan, stirring over low heat
  until the honey dissolves.

4 Carefully put in orange and
  pineapple rings. Heat mixture for
  5 min. over high heat, but do not
  bring to a boil.

5 Lower heat. Remove fruit slices,
  add white wine and stir. Remove
  from heat, strain and let cool.

6 Add brandy just before serving.

Serves 4

Agu sucre rosa
Armed with glasses of this sweet rose syrup drink (two variations are shown here: mixed with milk and with soda), Cristang women would gather on the floor at each other's homes to gamble at chikee, a popular card game.

The traditional floor mat in the foreground is woven from screw pine leaves.

Char fruta mistura
This punch of tea and fruit juices is deceptively
mild—the tea disguises the alcohol, which
is the ingredient that gives the
concoction its formidable kick.

Char fruta mistura
(Mixed fruit tea)

INGREDIENTS

2½ cups strong tea

150 g sugar

1 cup fresh orange juice (from about 2 oranges)

1 cup fresh pineapple juice (from ½ a medium-sized pineapple)

1 cup fresh star fruit juice (from 6 star fruit)

1 tsp. vanilla essence

1 cinnamon stick, 5-cm length

2 tbsp. brandy

2 tbsp. rum

1 tbsp. Cointreau

2 cups soda water, or carbonated lemonade, chilled

2 slices each of orange, pineapple, lime and star fruit (optional)

METHOD: 25 MIN.

1 Pour tea into a saucepan. Add sugar and stir over low heat until all of it dissolves.

2 Add fruit juices, vanilla essence, cinnamon stick, brandy and rum. Simmer for 5 minutes; remove from heat and pour into a punch bowl.

3 Leave to cool; then chill for 2 hrs.

4 Remove cinnamon stick. Add Cointreau and top with soda and stir well.

5 Add slices of orange, pineapple, lime and star fruit before serving.

Serves 6 to 8

Codial floris sapatu
(Hibiscus cordial)

INGREDIENTS

300 g white sugar

200 g rock sugar

6 cups water

30–40 hibiscus petals, dark pink variety

5 tbsp. lime or lemon juice

50 g ginger, sliced thinly

METHOD: 15 MIN.

1 Dissolve sugar and rock sugar in water on moderate heat.

2 Add hibiscus petals and bring to a boil. When liquid turns bluish, lower heat and add lime juice until liquid turns deep red.

3 Add ginger and cook on low heat for 5 min. to release the flavour of the ginger.

4 Strain into a clean jug and leave to cool before serving. Refrigerate any leftover syrup.

There are two ways of serving codial floris sapatu:

▢ Mix 3 tbsp. of the cordial with 1 glass chilled water and garnish with slices of lime before serving.

▢ Mix 2 tbsp. of the cordial with 1 glass chilled lemonade.

Serves 10, makes 1 litre

Cook's note The Cristang and the Malays refer to *Hibiscus sabdariffa* as *asam paya* because of the sour taste of its petals when cooked. According to folk-medicine, the hibiscus plant has many curative properties. The juice of crushed hibiscus petals is believed to act as a herbal contraceptive and cure menstrual disorders; the leaves of the hibiscus plant are said to relieve eczema and the liquid derived from boiling the roots supposedly cures fevers. My grandmother referred to the hibiscus flower as *floris sapatu* (shoe flower) because the dye obtained from crushing the calyx was used as shoe polish; it was also used to tint grey hair and darken eyebrows.

Gibette (Ginger beer)

INGREDIENTS

350 g ginger, soaked unskinned overnight or for at least 12 hrs.

blended together for 30 secs.
500 g white sugar
200 g grated palm sugar (gula Melaka) (optional)
3 cups water
1 egg white and shell

7 cups water

pinch of nutmeg powder

1 cinnamon stick, 5-cm length

½ a lime or lemon

4 tbsp. lime or lemon juice

1 cup sweet toddy

2 tbsp. honey

2 dry bottles (1 litre each) with corks or caps that can be tightened or tied down (see *Cook's note*)

METHOD: 50 MIN.
(COMPLETED A WEEK IN ADVANCE)

1 Scrape skin off ginger and slice thinly.

2 In a large pot, combine blended mixture with ginger, water, nutmeg and cinnamon. Boil for 30 min. To avoid breaking up and mixing in the scum that rises to the surface, do not stir. Remove from heat.

3 Slice lime into thin circles. Add juice and sliced lime to the boiled liquid. Do not stir. Set aside to cool.

4 Strain the cooled liquid through a piece of fine muslin into a clean container.

continued on p 161

Codial floris sapatu
A refreshing thirst-quencher that is rich in vitamin C, this unusual and distinctively Cristang cordial made from the hibiscus flower is available commercially nowadays.

from p 159, *Gibette*

5 Add toddy and honey. Stir gently and strain again.

6 Pour liquid immediately into empty bottles until they are each three quarters full. Using new corks, close bottles and tie down corks securely to prevent liquid from leaking as it ferments. Keep for a week before serving chilled with ice cubes.

Makes 2 litres

Cook's note Street vendors used to sell this drink in bottles for customers to take home. When gibette was made at home, champagne bottles were traditionally used to store it because the necks of the bottles enabled corks to be tied down securely.

Leite obu bateh
(Eggnog)

INGREDIENTS

1¼ cups milk

1 (60 g) egg

1 tbsp. fine brown sugar

1 tbsp. brandy

pinch of grated nutmeg

METHOD: 10 MIN.

1 Heat milk in a small saucepan over low heat to bring to a very slow boil. Stir occasionally.

2 Meanwhile, beat egg in a small heat-resistant bowl using a whisk. Add sugar and beat until it has dissolved. Add brandy and stir.

3 When the milk begins to bubble, remove it from heat, pour into the egg mixture and whisk until frothy.

4 Pour into a cup and sprinkle with nutmeg before serving.

Serves 1

Cook's note Eggnog is believed to be an excellent pick-me-up for invalids. For those who cannot tolerate milk, use strong black coffee as a substitute. Another variation is to omit the egg and substitute with 125 g of chocolate with nuts, 1 cup hot coffee and 1 tbsp. rum. Sweeten accordingly.

Lembransa brancu
(White memories)

INGREDIENTS

250 g white sugar

3 cups water

petals from 5 fresh white carnations, plus 9 more for garnishing

15 fresh water chestnuts, peeled

5 drops anise liqueur

½ cup evaporated milk

PREPARATION: 15 MIN.

1 Mix sugar with 2 cups of the water in a pot and boil until thick and syrupy, about 15 min. Add carnation petals, reserving nine for garnishing. Stir gently once, then set aside.

2 Blend water chestnuts with the remaining cup of water in a blender. Strain and set aside.

METHOD: 10 MIN.

1 Mix liqueur with milk thoroughly in a heat resistant bowl. Add syrup from PREPARATION, STEP 1 and stir.

2 Add blended water chestnuts from PREPARATION, STEP 2 to mixture and stir. Pour into a cocktail mixer and shake well.

3 To serve, strain into cocktail glasses, add ice cubes and top with fresh carnation petals.

Serves 3

Nona rostu bremeilu
(Maiden's blush)

INGREDIENTS

½ litre sweet red wine

2 cups lemonade or ice-cream soda, well chilled

a few fresh rose petals (optional)

METHOD: 5 MIN.

1 Pour wine into a clean and dry jug. Add chilled lemonade or ice-cream soda.

2 Serve in glasses garnished with rose petals.

Serves 4

Soldadu chocolat
(Chocolate soldier)

INGREDIENTS

2 cups milk

1 bar (120 g) milk chocolate, chopped coarsely

1 cup strong black coffee

1 tsp. brown sugar

2 tsp. rum

1 tsp. almond slivers

pinch of grated nutmeg or cinnamon

PREPARATION: 5 MIN.

1 Pour milk into a saucepan, add chocolate and stir continuously over low heat until chocolate dissolves completely.

2 Pour in coffee and stir briskly. Add brown sugar and stir until it has dissolved.

3 Remove from heat, pour in rum and stir. Pour into cups and garnish with almond slivers and grated nutmeg (or cinnamon). Serve hot.

Serves 2

Soldadu chocolat
This festive drink of coffee, chocolate and rum is usually served after a heavy meal, as its slightly bitter taste refreshes the palate.

Tentasung doce
(Sweet temptation)

INGREDIENTS

50 g white sugar

½ cup water

6 cloves

1 cup orange juice (from about 2 oranges)

1 litre red wine or claret

2 cups carbonated lemonade, chilled

rind of 1 orange (in an unbroken strip)

METHOD: 30 MIN.

1 Combine sugar and water in a small saucepan. Stir continuously over low heat until sugar has dissolved; do not allow liquid to come to a boil. Set aside to cool.

2 Spike orange rind with cloves and place in a punch bowl. Pour in orange juice.

3 Add wine and cooled syrup. Chill for at least 2 hours.

4 Just before serving, add carbonated lemonade. Serve garnished with slices of orange.

Serves 6 to 8

Tentasung doce
This orange-wine cocktail with its distinctive flavour of
cloves makes for a perfect dinner aperitif.

Index

Page numbers in **boldface** refer to recipes.
Page numbers in *italics* refer to captions.
Page numbers in ***bold italics*** indicate that the recipe and caption occur on the same page.

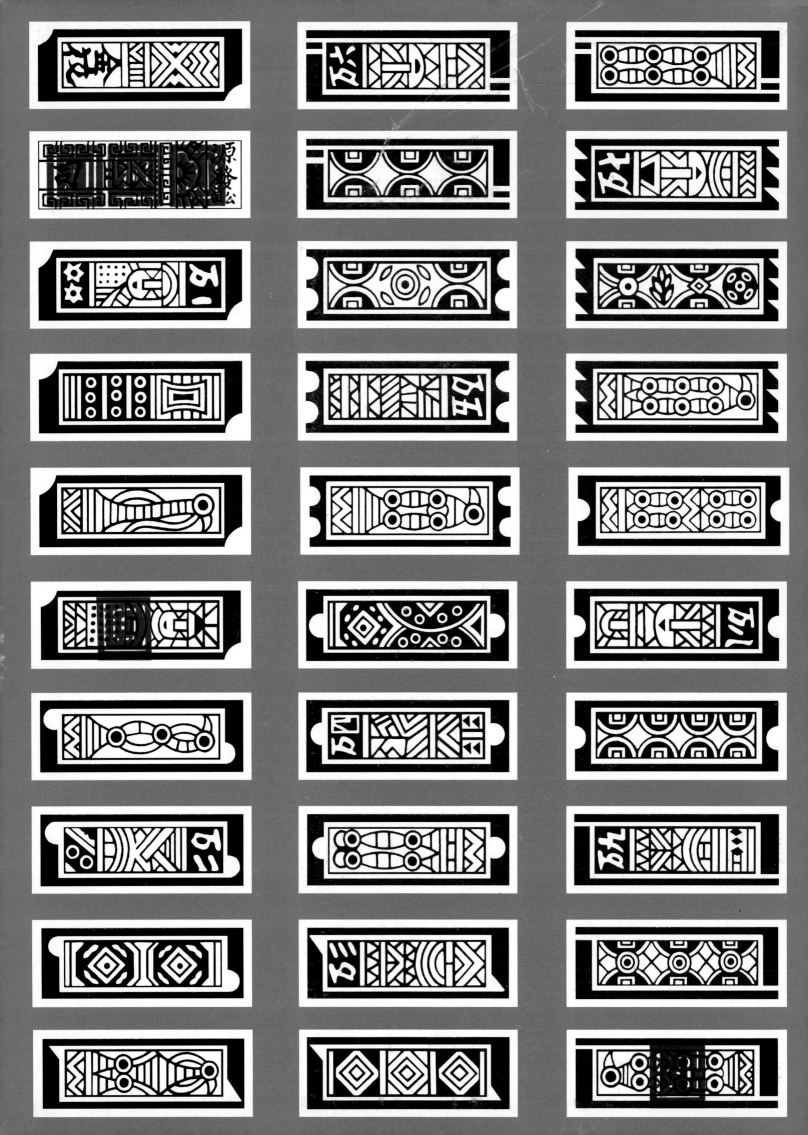